When the Husband Is the Suspect

F. LEE BAILEY
with JEAN RABE

When the Husband Is
the Suspect

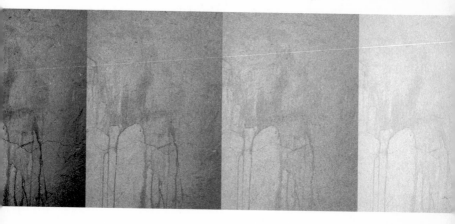

A Tom Doherty Associates Book · New York

FORGE®

WHEN THE HUSBAND IS THE SUSPECT

A Forge Book
Published by Tom Doherty Associates, LLC
175 Fifth Avenue
New York, NY 10010

www.tor-forge.com

Forge® is a registered trademark of Tom Doherty Associates, LLC.

Library of Congress Cataloging-in-Publication Data

Bailey, F. Lee (Francis Lee), 1933–
    When the husband is the suspect / F. Lee Bailey with Jean Rabe.—1st
hardcover ed.
        p.   cm.
    ISBN-13: 978-0-7653-1613-4
    ISBN-10: 0-7653-1613-7
    1. Trials (Murder)—United States.   2. Uxoricide—United States—Case studies.
I. Rabe, Jean.   II. Title.
    KF221.M8B35   2008
    345.73'02523—dc22   2007041946

First Edition: March 2008

Printed in the United States of America

0 9 8 7 6 5 4 3 2 1

Contents

Preface

BY F. LEE BAILEY

This chronicle about uxoricide—*a legal term for the murder of one spouse by the other*—*covers in dispassionate detail the investigations and trials of many of the most publicized murder cases that took place during the last fifty-plus years.*

In some of these cases, I have permission from the client to mention matters that might fall within the attorney-client privilege. Where that permission is not given, any information I have that is protected is omitted from my commentary. In no case, however, would this omitted information be considered a revelation, or likely change the reader's view of the fairness of the procedures used, or the result obtained in a given case.

That said, let me turn to the substance of the book.

The suspects in these cases, husbands all, range from innocent as the driven snow to guilty as hell to wildly insane. And although the factual matrices of the cases vary greatly, certain themes nonetheless run through them. Among these, be on the lookout for the following:

1. *When a wife is killed by what* might *be criminal means, the husband (unless he has an ironclad alibi) is the first to be scrutinized. If no other suspect appears on the horizon, police will pursue the husband relentlessly to "solve" the crime.*

2. *When a wife is in fact murdered—or in rare cases killed by accident, after which a cover-up is attempted—it is* more probable than not that the husband either committed the killing or was instrumental in causing it to occur.

3. That said, when those accused are later shown to be innocent, suspected husbands more commonly suffer this indignity than does any other classification of murderer.

With these tidbits of experience as guidelines, enjoy our twenty cases; test for yourself the old Shakespearean catchphrase that asserts that "murder will out."

·   ·   ·

Nearly one-third of the women murdered in the United States die at the hands of their husbands, ex-husbands, or boyfriends, according to statistics kept by the FBI and Bureau of Justice Statistics. More than half of those women are married, and guns are the weapons of choice.

Finances and hot tempers fuel the figures, contends Kenneth Lanning, a retired FBI agent who spent twenty years in the FBI's Behavioral Science Unit and now works as a private consultant.

"The husband is often the suspect, but why?" Lanning asked. "He's the suspect in part because of statistical probabilities. Police officers know that a good percentage of women are murdered by someone they know. In addition, something specific about the case might suggest who the murderer is."

Police look at the husbands and boyfriends, at the family, and they try to see if there were marital problems or financial problems. It can be about power, Lanning explained: The marriage is over, but it wasn't the partner's idea; he didn't give her permission to leave and so he punishes her.

"The good investigator, however, keeps an open mind and considers all the possibilities," Lanning said. "Was there forced entry or did someone lay it all out to throw off the police? Was the scene staged? Did someone make it look like there was a break-in to make it look like she was killed in the process?

"This crime, like most interpersonal crimes, can be motivated by a combination of different reasons. . . . Maybe it's financially motivated—he didn't want his wife to get the assets in a divorce settlement. Maybe a husband kills his wife out of jealousy. . . . Maybe he's abusive; he doesn't *want his wife to leave him. It goes on and on and on. Some are crimes of passion, where someone explodes in anger and rage. Other killers are more methodical, calculating, and planning."*

Lanning said that when everything falls into place, the guilty husbands and boyfriends are convicted and jailed. But every once in a while, he admitted, the guilty aren't caught, and sometimes those who end up in prison just might be innocent.

Consider the following:

A thirty-two-year-old bride-to-be was declared missing.

A $100,000 reward for information about her disappearance was offered by her family, and a mammoth search was launched.

Three days after her disappearance the search was called off as the police claimed they had no leads.

The woman's fiancé volunteered to take a lie detector test immediately . . . and did so on that same day, passing it with flying colors.

The police, however, were not impressed and wanted to test him under their own conditions. Moreover, these intrepid investigators refused to allow "their" test to be videotaped.

As a result, the fiancé did not immediately comply for their test.

All eyes of the media were upon them. The press smelled blood.

Why would an innocent man who supposedly loved his fiancé waffle on a lie-detector test?

It looked suspicious.

The following day the woman turned up, a runaway bride, highly embarrassed . . .

. . . but there was no embarrassment in the media or among the investigators who scrutinized an innocent man who not only had to cope with the dread of something having happened to the woman he loved, but also with the cold-blooded suspicion that he was now the obvious suspect. For in the current clime of twenty-four-hour media, the husband is always the prime suspect.

When the Husband Is the Suspect

Dr. Sam Sheppard

Charged with murdering his wife on July 4, 1954

Sheppard's story began more than fifty years ago and is still played out in reruns of The Fugitive *television show and the movie his case inspired. Although Sheppard was buried more than three decades ago, his son continues to work to exonerate him.*

THE MURDER

After dinner guests left for the evening, and his pregnant wife had gone to bed, Dr. Sam Sheppard told police, he watched a movie. He said he eventually fell asleep and woke very early on the morning of July 4, 1954, having heard a noise upstairs. A moment later his wife, Marilyn, screamed and called his name. This was followed by more noises. Dr. Sheppard said he immediately thought his wife might be having painful convulsions (she'd had them before during her first pregnancy).

The home was dark, but there was a light in the upstairs dressing room. Dr. Sheppard ran upstairs to the master bedroom, where he said he saw a "white form" over his wife and next to the bed.

Dr. Sheppard claimed he wrestled with the figure, not knowing if it was a man or a woman, and was struck from behind and knocked unconscious.

When he regained consciousness, he saw that his wife was lying in a pool of blood on the bed; she had been beaten.

Dr. Sheppard said he found no pulse and ran to his son's room. The son was still sound asleep, and he decided not to disturb him yet.

There were more noises coming from downstairs, and Dr. Sheppard went to investigate and said he saw a man outside the screen door. He chased him down the back steps and onto the beach. Though it was still dark, Dr. Sheppard said he could make out a "large, powerfully built man with a good-sized head and bushy hair."

Dr. Sheppard said he lunged at the man, but ended up knocked unconscious again. When he came to, his legs were in the water and his head was on the sand. He returned to the house, went back to the bedroom, and called Spencer Houk—his friend and neighbor who was also mayor of their suburb, Bay Village.

Houk and his wife came to the house shortly before 6:00 A.M., and together they called the police.

Sheppard repeated his story to the police, Houk, and later to an expert from the Scientific Investigation Unit of the Cleveland police.

The next day, local newspapers ran Sheppard's story, applauding him for trying to catch the man who killed his wife.

Their support would soon evaporate.

SAM SHEPPARD'S BACKSTORY

The youngest of three sons, Sam was born in 1924 in Cleveland, Ohio, and later attended Cleveland Heights High School, where he served as class president three years. During his senior year he was recognized for his accomplishments in football, basketball, and track, and his senior class voted him "The Man Most Likely to Succeed."

He considered becoming a professional athlete and could have chosen one of several athletic scholarships offered by small colleges, but instead he followed in the footsteps of his father and older brothers and pursued osteopathic medicine.

During World War II, Sam decided to enlist in the army but was talked out of it by his father. Instead he enrolled at Hanover College in Indiana for preosteopathic courses. (In the summer, he studied at Western Reserve University in Cleveland.)

While he was at Hanover, Sam gave Marilyn his fraternity pin, which signaled their engagement. He'd first been introduced to her in high school, when she'd dated one of his brothers. Marilyn attended Skidmore College in Saratoga Springs, New York, while Sam continued his studies, graduating from the Los Angeles Osteopathic School of Physicians. In September 1945, he asked her to move to California with him. She agreed and they were quickly married. Marilyn wanted to start a family right away. Her first pregnancy ended in a miscarriage but, in early 1947, she gave birth to Samuel Reese, who was quickly nicknamed Chip.

Sam graduated from medical school, finished his internship, and became a resident in neurosurgery at the Los Angeles County Hospital; however, at the urging of family, Sam, Marilyn, and Chip returned to Ohio in 1951, where Sam joined his father's hospital and family practices.

Their first house was a two-level Dutch Colonial in a Cleveland suburb. It was poised on a cliff above Lake Erie and close to Bay View Hospital.

While Sam worked, Marilyn stayed at home and tended the house. She taught Bible classes at the Methodist church. The Sheppards summered on the lake and co-owned an aluminum boat with neighbors J. Spencer and Esther Houk.

Sheppard reportedly had one affair during their marriage, which he said Marilyn knew about.

He said in the months before her death that their marriage had been improving.

Marilyn was four months pregnant on the night she was killed.

THE INVESTIGATION

Cleveland police and a detective from the Cuyahoga County Sheriff's Department investigated the scene, their efforts complicated by a house already filled with news reporters.

Sheppard, meanwhile, had been taken to the hospital and sedated.

As neighborhood boys helped search for evidence, the mayor's son soon found Sheppard's medical bag in the weeds near the beach.

This bag, along with other pieces of evidence, went through many different hands before the authorities tested for fingerprints.

The coroner arrived at 8:00 A.M. He estimated that Sheppard's wife had been killed between 3:00 and 4:00 A.M. The coroner determined she had nearly three dozen wounds on her head, and he noted that her watch had stopped at 3:15.

Meanwhile, investigators interviewed Sheppard at the hospital, even though he was still under the influence of the sedatives.

As police questioned Sheppard about his affair with a Bay View Hospital nurse, it was clear that they were skeptical that he had been knocked unconscious twice by a mystery man. They wondered why Sheppard's son had not woken up and if the family dog had barked during the struggle and at the noises Sheppard said he had heard. The police had found no obvious signs of a break-in in their preliminary investigation.

Though one of the investigators acknowledged that he suspected Sheppard had killed his wife, there was no arrest for a few weeks.

Sheppard posted a $10,000 reward for the capture of his wife's murderer, but it was left unclaimed.

In the media there was speculation that Sheppard was receiving special consideration from the mayor and police chief. Perhaps in response to these favoritism claims, the coroner soon announced an inquest into Marilyn Sheppard's death—more than two weeks after her body had been discovered.

Sheppard was extensively questioned during the proceedings, which his attorney was not allowed to attend, as it was not an official court action.

As questions continued to swirl around Sheppard's affair and the matter of the shakiness of his marriage, the nurse he'd had the affair with testified to sexual encounters that had gone on for years. The media reported the entire sordid story.

THE ARREST AND THE FIRST TRIAL

Twenty-five days after the murder, Sheppard was arrested.

On October 18, 1954, the trial began. It would last until just before Christmas of that year.

The prosecutor was John Mahon, assisted by Saul Danaceau and Thomas Parrino. Sheppard's attorney was William J. Corrigan, assisted by Fred Garmore, William Corrigan Jr., and Arthur Petersilge, the longtime Sheppard family lawyer.

The defense requested a change of venue. It was denied.

The names of prospective jurors had been published the month prior to the trial, and prospective jurors admitted receiving phone calls and threats, and were frequently questioned by the press. According to news reports, only one prospective juror said he had not read or heard about the case.

It took seventeen days to select the jury, and the panel was never sequestered during the trial.

The trial was a media circus from the first day. The jurors were bused to the Sheppard house to view the scene of the crime. The media had been notified ahead of time, and reporters waited at the property to take pictures and freely interview the jurors.

During the court proceedings, deputy coroner Lester Adelson described the autopsy and showed pictures of Marilyn Sheppard. He admitted to a lack of thoroughness at the autopsy, as they did not examine the contents of her stomach and did not test for rape . . . even though from the appearance of the body it certainly looked like she had been sexually assaulted.

Spencer and Esther Houk confirmed Sheppard's frantic call telling them his wife had been murdered, but Esther also cast some doubt on his story when she reported that the Sheppards had been known to argue.

Cuyahoga County coroner Sam Gerber testified to the gruesome condition of Marilyn's body, claiming: "In this bloodstain I could make out the impression of a surgical instrument." He further testified that she had been killed by blows to her head that had been made with a twin-bladed surgical instrument or something similar.

A physician who had treated Sheppard the afternoon of the murder testified that Sheppard's injuries were minor and primarily consisted of a black eye and cheekbone temple swelling, nothing serious enough to support the claim that he'd been knocked unconscious twice.

The prosecution also called Susan Hayes (the nurse with whom Sheppard had had an affair), who testified about her various rendezvous in Sheppard's car, in the clinic, and in her parents' house. She said she once received a watch from him, and said he had talked about getting a divorce so he could be with her all the time.

Defense attorneys questioned Sheppard's brother Steve, who disagreed with the physician who said Sheppard's injuries were minor. Steve also claimed that the Sheppards were happily married and did not fight. Sheppard's other brother, Richard, echoed that testimony.

Rebutting the prosecution's doctor, a Cleveland City Hospital neurologist reported that Sheppard's X-rays showed a fractured neck and a spinal cord bruise, and that the injuries might have occurred from a blow to the back of the neck. His diagnosis included a "cerebral concussion," and that Sheppard could not have faked his pain and injuries and could indeed have been knocked unconscious.

Additional defense witnesses claimed they saw a tall "bushy-haired man" lurking outside the Sheppard home the night before Marilyn was killed, and that they'd reported this to the police.

Sheppard also took the stand in his own defense, and questioning of him continued for several days. He admitted to other affairs, but was adamant that he loved his wife and that their marriage was good.

In closing, prosecutor Parrino stated: "If the burglar was in that room and took the time and trouble to strike all those vicious blows on Marilyn, I ask you why the assailant did not use that same instrument, not to hit Sam thirty-five times, but to strike one single blow against him. A burglar does not want to leave a living witness at the scene of a crime."

Parrino concluded that the notion of a "bushy-haired intruder" was fabricated.

Defense attorney Petersilge rebutted the evidence in his closing remarks. He said: "Five and one-half months after the murder of Marilyn Sheppard, the state does not know how she was killed, with what weapon she was killed, or why she was killed. Yet on the basis of this flimsy evidence, the state is asking you to send Sam Sheppard to the electric chair."

THE FIRST VERDICT

The jury had five verdicts to consider:

1. Guilty of murder in the first degree, death penalty
2. Guilty of murder in the first degree, recommending clemency, life without parole
3. Guilty of murder in the second degree—intentional, unpremeditated murder, life imprisonment
4. Guilty of manslaughter, sentencing one to twenty years
5. Not guilty

The jurors deliberated from December 17 to December 21, and though they were now sequestered, they were still allowed to make unsupervised telephone calls.

Sheppard was found guilty of murder in the second degree.

Sheppard, in a statement before sentencing (according to reports), claimed: "I'd like to say, sir, that I am not guilty. I feel there have been facts presented to this court that definitely prove that I could not have performed this crime."

The judge passed sentence. "It is the judgment of this court that you be taken to the Ohio penitentiary, there to remain for the rest of your natural life."

*In recording for my boy what I have been subjected to, it will be neces-
sary to make known American injustice perpetrated not by the laws of
our land, but by those who have sworn themselves to uphold those
laws. . . . A frightening breach of American rights has taken place,
and the important point is that the breach has happened here in
America, not who it has happened to.*

> —Dr. Sam Sheppard in his prison journal, 1955

NUMEROUS APPEALS

Shortly after Sam Sheppard's conviction, defense attorneys sought
an independent study of the murder evidence.

Criminologist Paul Kirk collected additional evidence from the
Sheppard home, including blood samples from the bedroom
walls. He presented his report in the spring of 1955 and showed
that a spot of blood in the bedroom did not match either Sheppard's or Marilyn's blood types. Further, he contended that based
on the blood and the position of the victim's body, the killer had
to have been left-handed.

Sheppard was right-handed.

Kirk also conjectured that the murder weapon was possibly a
flashlight and not a surgical instrument.

Sheppard's attorneys immediately sought a new trial based on
this evidence, but the motion was denied. This decision was appealed to the Ohio Court of Appeals, which also rejected the motion for a new trial. In January 1956, the matter was appealed to
the Ohio Supreme Court, which upheld the conviction. The minority opinion dissented and stated that Sheppard should be
granted a new trial.

Attorneys continued to appeal, this time to the U.S. Supreme
Court in August 1956.

Three months later, the court refused to hear the appeal.

A second appeal to the U.S. Supreme Court in December of
that year also failed.

A NEW APPROACH

The Sheppard family continued to press, turning to a *Chicago Tribune* crime reporter and then to attorney F. Lee Bailey.

In April 1963, Bailey filed a petition in the United States District Court for the Southern District of Ohio. Bailey contended that Sheppard's rights had been denied during his initial trial, that the jurors knew all about the case from the media, and that the motion for a change of venue should have been granted.

The judge reviewed the material and ordered Sheppard released, subject to retrial—ten years and twelve days after his initial sentencing. The court agreed that his constitutional rights had indeed been violated and that the trial had been a "mockery of justice."

Sheppard brought a civil suit against *The Cleveland Press*, its publisher, and coroner Samuel Gerber, citing a breach of his civil rights because of wrongful imprisonment.

That case was dismissed by the trial court.

THE SECOND TRIAL AND SECOND VERDICT

Sheppard was tried again in November 1966, the judge this time ruling no cameras or artists in the courtroom. There were no press tables and no radio equipment, and observers could not leave and reenter the courtroom during the sessions. The judge approved the media representatives who would be allowed to attend.

Bailey argued for a change of venue, but the motion was denied.

The jurors were sequestered at a hotel for the entire length of the trial, and a bailiff monitored all their phone calls.

Bailey told the jurors: "You will be satisfied that Sam Sheppard did not kill his wife, and you will have a pretty good idea who did." Bailey questioned the coroner, who claimed the murder weapon was a surgical instrument.

"It looked like a surgical instrument to me," the coroner stated.

Bailey persisted: "Do you have such an instrument back at your office?"

"No."

"Have you ever seen such an instrument in any hospital or medical supply catalog or anywhere else, Dr. Gerber?"

"No, not that I can remember."

"Tell the jury, Doctor, where you have searched for this instrument during the past twelve years?"

"Oh, I have looked all over the United States."

"My goodness, then, please, by all means tell us what you found."

"I didn't find one."

Bailey also questioned a man who delivered bread to the Sheppards' home. The man testified he saw Marilyn give a key to a "distinguished-looking" man who was not her husband.

Bailey said the murderer must have had "an awful hate" for Marilyn Sheppard to kill her the way he did. He concluded: "Society has given Sam Sheppard a promissory note and it is payable now."

This time the jury had three verdicts to consider:

1. Guilty of second-degree murder, parole possible after ten years
2. Guilty of first-degree manslaughter, parole possible after eleven months, sentence not to exceed twenty years
3. Not guilty

Sheppard was found not guilty.

THE AFTERMATH

Despite the acquittal, Dr. Sheppard's life spiraled downward.

While in prison, Dr. Sheppard had written to Ariane Tebbenjohanns, a German divorcée. She and Dr. Sheppard married in Chicago the day after he'd been released.

He returned to medicine, but a malpractice suit filed for the death of a patient cost him both money and his reputation. It would also contribute to the demise of his second marriage.

In 1968, Ariane filed for divorce, alleging that Sheppard stole her money, threatened her, and was under the influence of drugs and alcohol.

On his own again, Dr. Sheppard moved to Columbus for a time and worked as a pro wrestler.

In 1969, he married again, this time to twenty-year-old Colleen Strickland, the daughter of his wrestling manager.

In April 1970, Sheppard died of liver failure. (Defense attorney Bailey was one of the pallbearers.)

THE SAGA CONTINUED

A police officer reported tool marks on a basement door of the Sheppard house, even though the prosecution later contended there was no sign of a break-in. Furthermore, a trail of blood led from the upstairs bedroom to the basement and out the back porch toward the lake. The blood was not initially typed, but some of the blood that remained on a piece of wood from the house was later tested. DNA analysis suggested that the blood belonged to Richard Eberling, a man who occasionally washed windows for the Sheppards.

Other evidence also came to light after the trials.

A report found in the Cuyahoga County Coroner's Office stated that a flashlight was found on the beach several yards from the Sheppard house. It was dented and its paint had chipped off. Chips of enamel paint had been found under the Sheppard's bed, but no testing was done to see if they matched the flashlight.

Sam Reese "Chip" Sheppard and Cynthia Cooper, a writer from New York, confronted the Cuyahoga County Prosecutor's Office with the contention that Richard Eberling may have murdered Marilyn. They requested that the office reopen the criminal investigation.

The prosecutors declined.

When that failed, Sam Reese Sheppard initiated a civil lawsuit against the state for false imprisonment of his father. A family attorney tried to admit evidence suggesting Richard Eberling was involved, but unfortunately the court would not accept the evidence and nothing came of the trial.

The ruling in the spring of 2000 was that the Sheppard attorneys could not meet the "burden of proof" to show that Sam Sheppard was clearly innocent in the murder of his wife.

RICHARD EBERLING

Eberling, who was considered a suspect by some close to the case, washed windows in the 1950s, including at the Sheppard's home, where he admitted dripping blood. Eberling was born Richard Lenardic in 1929, his mother single and abandoning him at birth. (His final foster father, George Eberling, did not adopt the boy. However, Richard legally changed his name to Eberling.)

In November 1959, Eberling was arrested for burglary near Cleveland. Police discovered a ring in his possession that had belonged to Marilyn Sheppard. Eberling admitted stealing the ring when he washed windows at the Sheppard house, though he claimed he did not kill Marilyn Sheppard.

In the 1980s, Eberling lived on Lookout Mountain in Tennessee, with his companion O. B. Henderson, in a mansion filled with artwork. In 1987, police visited the mansion to question Eberling about a forged will. They'd received a tip from a woman, Patricia Bogar, who claimed that she had helped Eberling and Henderson forge a will that named Eberling the heir of the bulk of Ethel Durkin's estate, roughly $1.5 million. Eberling had worked as Durkin's caretaker. (Durkin had died early in 1984 in what was ruled an accidental fall; no autopsy was performed.)

Bogar also admitted to police that she helped Eberling stage burglaries, including one at her home, to claim insurance money. Bogar said she was snitching on Eberling because he did not give her a share of the Durkin estate.

Beverly and Dale Scheidler, witnesses to the Durkin will, confessed to their part in the scheme. (Later, Beverly Scheidler claimed Eberling killed Durkin.)

When police visited the Tennessee mansion, reports said they found antiques and other valuables, most of them stolen, including a painting from Cleveland City Hall.

Although Eberling denied killing Durkin, the coroner ruled the death a homicide after the body was exhumed and an autopsy was performed. In the summer of 1989, Eberling and Henderson were convicted of Ethel Durkin's murder and sentenced to life in prison.

Sam Reese Sheppard received a letter from Richard Eberling, who was in the Lebanon Correctional Institution in Ohio. It said: "Sam, yes I do know the whole story." In an exchange of letters, Eberling detailed incidents about the Sheppards, including a time when Marilyn asked Eberling to look after young Sam and his cousin while she went out on an errand. One of Eberling's letters included a diagram of the Sheppard house.

Eventually, Sam Reese Sheppard visited Eberling in prison. More letters followed, in one of which Eberling claimed Marilyn had been murdered by Esther Houk and that Sheppard and Spencer Houk had perpetrated a cover-up.

Eberling said that one morning while he washed windows, he heard Esther arguing with Marilyn: "If you don't leave him alone, I'll kill you." It was that very afternoon Eberling said he cut a finger and dripped blood in the house.

He made other claims: That Dr. Sheppard was bisexual, that Esther thought Marilyn and her husband were having an affair, and that Esther's husband was in reality having an affair with Dr. Sheppard.

Kathie Collins, who once worked as a nurse for Ethel Durkin, stated that Eberling told her he'd killed Marilyn. Collins said her mother told her not to believe Eberling, so she kept the story to herself; however, when she heard about the Sheppard case again in the news in 1989, she contacted a Cleveland police detective, who reportedly dismissed her information.

Eberling died in prison at the age of sixty-eight. He reportedly told fellow inmates that he was hired by Sheppard to kill Marilyn, that he raped her, and that he twice knocked out Sheppard. Eberling had been known to change his story, and another version he told inmates mirrored the one he told Sam Reese Sheppard—that Esther Houk killed Marilyn, and that Esther and her husband covered up the crime.

COMMENTARY: Dr. Sam Sheppard

The saga of Sam Sheppard is a fitting introduction into the world of accused husband-killers, because it has a little bit of everything—most of it disgraceful. On the July 4 night in 1954 when Dr. Sheppard's life was turned upside down, his wife was in her bed on the second floor, and Sam was asleep on a couch under the stairway. A man saw a light burning in the window of the second-floor hallway, which was normally left lit when Sam was called out on emergency police business; he was the official police surgeon of Bay Village, Ohio, the lakeside Cleveland suburb where he lived. At some point Marilyn Sheppard was having intercourse with that person when another person arrived, caught the lovers in pari delicto, *and proceeded to hit Marilyn in the head thirty-five times. None of these blows was fatal, indicating that the assailant was a woman or a child; Marilyn drowned in her own blood. It would be many years, long after Sam was dead, before it could be shown through DNA testing that someone other than Sam or Marilyn had left blood in the house that night. The chief of police of Bay Village told Dr. Steve Sheppard—Sam's older brother—that the police pretty much knew who had killed Marilyn, and that an arrest could be expected imminently.*

That might all have happened had it not been for two very small men—both stretching to be five feet two inches—who decided to take over and control the case.

The first was Louis B. Seltzer, publisher of the then vaunted (and since bankrupt) Cleveland Press. *Seltzer used his newspaper like a club, ordering politicians around like minions and intimidating everyone who disagreed with him. If Seltzer was roused, he would spread a personally penned editorial across eight columns of his newspaper, seeking to grind some unfortunate dissident under his heel. For some reason he took it upon himself to judge Dr. Sheppard guilty before the investigation had gotten off the ground, and demanded that he be arrested and prosecuted.*

Samuel Gerber was the coroner of Cuyahoga County, which included Cleveland and Bay Village. Like most elected officials, when Louis Seltzer gave editorial encouragement to some function within the coroner's aegis, Gerber rushed to comply like a puppy dog seeking affection from its owner. Gerber conducted a circus, which he dubbed an "inquest," in the gymnasium of the Bay Village High School and kicked Sheppard's lawyer out. Seltzer's editorial handiwork had the attending crowd so worked up that some of those present "hugged and kissed the coroner."

Dr. Sheppard was duly charged and put to trial in what could only be viewed as a venomous atmosphere. Both the trial judge and the chief prosecutor were running for judicial office, and could hardly have been unaware of what the Cleveland Press wanted from them. Louis Seltzer's continuing drumroll—read by the jurors before and during the trial—was both simple and ingenious. He repeatedly suggested—in his eight-column, banner-headed editorials that:

1. The evidence against Sheppard was admittedly somewhat "thin."
2. Because the Sheppard family consisted of rich doctors—a father and three sons—and owned a clinic they were smart and powerful.
3. Being smart and powerful, the family acted swiftly to hide the important evidence, and protect the youngest and most prodigal member of their clan.
4. It would be unjust to allow Sam Sheppard to escape conviction just because he was smart enough to hide the evidence.

That this hideous little scheme worked like a charm was all too evident when the jury convicted Sheppard, then disclosed that, when they hadn't been able to resolve the case on the prosecution's evidence, which was confusing, they had decided to test Sheppard's testimony: If they disbelieved him, they would convict. They did, and did. Louis B. Seltzer had successfully transferred the burden of proof to the defendant. To make matters worse, he boasted about causing the conviction, in a biography he wrote titled, fatuously, The Years Were Good. No publisher thought it worth an investment, so Seltzer paid to have it printed himself.

After the trial, the defense was allowed access to the Sheppard home for the first time, and a forensic expert named Paul Leland Kirk discovered evidence that would have doubtless given even this jury pause. The courts would hear none of it. The Ohio Supreme Court, in an opinion that to this day is unique, split five to two in affirming the conviction. The two dissenters, Judges Taft and Hart, opined that the state of Ohio had proven Sheppard innocent with its own evidence. It should be noted that even Louis Seltzer could not shake a stick at either of these honored old-line Ohio families, Taft and Hart. The majority, in an opinion that at least one of its authors told me he would love to withdraw, declared that "in this atmosphere of a 'Roman Holiday' for the news media, Sam Sheppard stood trial for his life." This, they ruled, was okay in Ohio.

The United States Supreme Court declined to review the case, but Justice Felix Frankfurter, who may well have voted to accept it (four votes are needed to get into the U.S. Supreme Court, five to win) cautioned that a denial of review does not in any way suggest that the court approves of the judgment it declines to consider.

Ten years short fifteen days of the day when he was clapped in jail, Sheppard was released on a federal writ of habeas corpus by a United States district judge with the courage of a lion, Carl B. Weinman, who was outraged by the record in the case. He termed the conviction a "mockery of justice," and allowed the prosecution sixty days to retry Sheppard. The case wound up in the United States Supreme Court again, this time for full review. It remains the leading case in the ever-present tension between the right of a free press to say whatever it wants whenever it wishes to do so, and the right of a criminally accused person to a fair trial. The order for a new trial was affirmed, and the duty of trial judges to protect defendants appearing before them from the often-unfortunate zeal of the press was described in specific detail. These rules still govern the conduct of trial judges some forty years later.

Prosecutor John T. Corrigan decided to retry Sheppard, and the trial, which commenced in November 1966, remained in Cleveland. It was not a level playing field. Between the forensic evidence of Dr. Kirk and Sam Gerber's making a fool of himself on the witness stand, it took the jury only a matter of hours to declare Sheppard "not guilty."

Sam Sheppard died in May 1970 from causes attributed to cancer cells placed in his armpits as part of a Sloan-Kettering experiment for which he had volunteered while in prison, as well as an excess of pills and booze. His funeral was attended by more news cameras than mourners. He never knew that DNA evidence would remove the last show of doubt from his alleged complicity in the slaying of his wife.

Dr. Carl Coppolino

Charged with murdering his wife
on August 28, 1965

It was a case that involved infidelity, jealousy, revenge, and untraceable drugs. It would span more than a decade and cross many state lines, and its details would fill newspapers and books, one of which Coppolino would write himself.

CARL AND CARMELA

Coppolino attended Brooklyn Tech, which was known for accepting academically gifted students, and he later attended Fordham University, earning a bachelor's degree in chemistry in 1954. He was torn between the notion of becoming a research scientist or going to medical school, the latter of which could prove difficult because of the cost.

During his years at Fordham, Coppolino dated Carmela Musetto, the daughter of a general practitioner from Boonton, New Jersey. Carmela was a premed student at Trinity College and had been accepted at Women's Medical College in Philadelphia.

Coppolino had the offer of a chemistry fellowship at Columbia University that carried a stipend and tuition, or a place at State University of New York in Brooklyn (which became SUNY Downstate Medical Center) with no monetary help. He opted to study in Brooklyn, borrowing money from friends and relatives to cover tuition.

Carmela transferred to State University in 1956, and she and Carl were soon married, becoming the first husband-wife students at the medical school. In November of their third year at the school, Carmela became pregnant, and gave birth the following summer. (Carmela's father claimed that he paid most of their bills during their final two years in medical school.)

Coppolino specialized in anesthesiology and became a chief resident at Methodist Hospital in June 1960. While there, he became interested in medical hypnosis and published a paper on it in the *New York State Journal of Medicine*. A year later, he accepted a position as a partner in an anesthesiologist group at Riverview Hospital in Red Bank, New Jersey.

Carmela was working for Hoffman-LaRoche, a New Jersey pharmaceutical firm, eventually becoming the assistant director for professional services. However, at the time that Coppolino switched hospitals, she was pregnant and on an extended maternity leave.

The Coppolinos moved to an upscale Middletown neighborhood in the fall of 1962 to be closer to the Red Bank hospital.

While at Riverview Hospital, Coppolino wrote a threatening letter to a nurse anesthetist who he believed was taking patients away from his anesthesiology group. The nurse anesthetist showed the letter to a hospital administrator and the FBI. Coppolino was not charged with a crime, but his contract with the hospital was not renewed. (This letter would come back to haunt him during a murder trial.)

To complicate his life, Coppolino had his first heart attack, and would learn at age thirty that he had coronary artery disease. He remained in the hospital for two weeks after the attack, and afterward took a leave of absence from the hospital. After that, he decided to suspend practicing medicine and went on disability, collecting insurance payments of about $1,800 a month.

Coppolino started writing on medical topics and hypnosis.

Among his published books were *Get Slim and Stay Slim with Hypnosis,* printed by Powers Publishing, 1966, and *The Billion Dollar Hangover,* printed by Popular Library, 1967.

THE COPPOLINOS AND THE FARBERS

The Farbers lived across the street from the Coppolinos in Middletown.

William Farber was a retired army lieutenant colonel who was working as an insurance executive in New York City. People referred to him as "the Colonel."

His wife, Marjorie (called Marge), was a housewife who, at forty-eight, was eighteen years older than Coppolino. A smoker, she sought to quit, and she turned to her neighbor in hopes that he could hypnotize her into quitting. In the late winter of 1963, Coppolino gave her a few sessions, and shortly thereafter they began an affair.

In March 1963, Marge Farber and Coppolino took a trip to Florida, and though the Colonel initially objected, Carmela insisted that she had no problem with the trip, as she thought Farber would be able to look after her husband in case he had an angina episode. (Carmela was allegedly unaware the two were having an affair.) Coppolino used the trip south as an excuse to get away from New Jersey's cold climate, which could be particularly harsh on someone with a heart condition.

Coppolino and Mrs. Farber registered for separate rooms at the Cadillac Motel in Miami Beach. They also went to San Juan, and to Sarasota, where she purchased property on Longboat Key. Coppolino bought the lot next door, intending it to be an investment since, at that time, he had no intention of moving from New Jersey.

Coppolino and Mrs. Farber continued their affair when they returned from Florida, spending time together when their spouses were at work. However, that summer, on July 30, their lives would change when the Colonel became ill and Mrs. Farber called Coppolino to treat him.

THE COLONEL'S DEATH

Marjorie Farber's version of the events of July 30, which she later told to police, was that Coppolino had given her a vial of succinylcholine chloride, and instructed her to mix it with water and then inject it in the Colonel, so that they would be rid of him.

Coppolino's explanation of that day was much different. He maintained that the Colonel was having heart problems, perhaps suffering a heart attack, and that he wanted an ambulance called and the man taken to the hospital. He contended that the Farbers declined, and so after he made sure the Colonel was resting in bed, he wrote a statement for her to sign.

The statement read:

I hereby release Carl A. Coppolino, M.D., from all responsibility for the case of my husband, William Farber. Dr. Coppolino wishes to be released because Mr. Farber refuses to be hospitalized even though he may have had a coronary. Dr. Coppolino only gave emergency care.

Signed, Marjorie C. Farber

Later that day, Mrs. Farber discovered that her husband had died. She called the Coppolinos, asking they come to help her. Carmela signed the death certificate, listing coronary thrombosis as the cause.

No autopsy was performed, and the Colonel was buried with military honors in Arlington National Cemetery.

The affair between Farber and Coppolino continued. However, in the fall of 1964, he suffered his fourth heart attack, and he and Carmela decided to move to Florida and build on the lot he had purchased. They hired contractors, sold their house in New Jersey, and moved (with their two children) in April 1965.

Farber listed her house, too, but it took longer to sell.

LIFE AND DEATH IN FLORIDA

The Coppolinos settled in Florida less than a year after the death of the Colonel. Immediately, they hit hard financial times.

Although Coppolino was still collecting disability payments, Carmela had not been able to pass the Florida physician's exam. In an effort to limit the number of physicians wanting to move to the state to retire and practice part-time, Florida's medical governing board at the time did not offer medical licensure reciprocity with other states. Coppolino was hopeful that Florida's mild climate would eventually let him return to work, but he knew that that would not happen right away. To add to their money woes, the Coppolinos had lost money on their real estate investments.

Coppolino took up duplicate bridge to keep himself occupied. His lesson partner was Mary Gibson, a thirty-eight-year-old divorcée with two children.

Farber finally sold her house and moved to Sarasota into a house next door to the Coppolinos. She had hoped to pick up her relationship with her lover, but she saw him one night with his bridge partner.

One evening shortly thereafter, Coppolino reportedly fixed drinks for himself and Carmela. It was August 28, and she had complained of chest pains earlier, he'd said, but was feeling better. They went to bed in separate bedrooms, which he said was not unusual for them, and in the morning when he checked on her, he discovered that she was dead.

Coppolino called Dr. Juliette Karow, a physician Carmela had met when she was looking at employment opportunities. Karow arrived, notified the police, and reported the death to the medical examiner of Sarasota County. Karow signed the death certificate, citing a coronary occlusion as the cause. No autopsy was ordered, and Carmela was embalmed that very afternoon at a local funeral home.

Carmela's death shocked the neighborhood and her relatives, including her physician-father. She'd had no history of heart trouble, and her father had difficulty believing that she could have died of a heart attack.

Coppolino reportedly told her father that an autopsy had been performed and that the cause of death was indeed a heart attack. Carmela was buried in her family's plot at St. Mary's Cemetery in

Boonton, New Jersey. Coppolino, however, did not attend, though he traveled to New Jersey a few days later to meet with Carmela's father. (The Coppolino children were under the care of Gibson while he was gone.)

FARBER'S SUSPICIONS

Farber immediately asked Coppolino if he had killed his wife. Coppolino maintained he had had nothing to do with it.

Less than two months later, Coppolino married Gibson in a civil service at the courthouse. They (with his two children) moved into Gibson's house, selling his house to his father-in-law.

Farber persisted in suspecting Coppolino of his wife's death, and she began telling mutual acquaintances that she believed he had killed Carmela.

That fall, Farber approached Karow, who had signed Carmela's death certificate, and told the doctor it was possible Carmela had been killed with succinylcholine chloride. Farber reportedly explained that Coppolino had given her some of the drug the previous year to use to murder her husband.

Farber hired an attorney in November, and talked to people in the Sarasota County Sheriff's Department. She insisted Carmela's death was not due to natural causes, and she fired her attorney when he warned her that she could be incriminating herself regarding her husband's death.

AUTOPSIES AND SUCCINYLCHOLINE CHLORIDE

In a sworn statement, Farber maintained that she had watched Coppolino smother her husband with a pillow. She also maintained he later killed Carmela with an injection of succinylcholine chloride, the same muscle relaxant that Coppolino had tried to get her to use to kill her husband to get him out of the way.

Based on Farber's statement, Carmela's body was exhumed from the New Jersey cemetery in December 1965 and transported to the New York City Medical Examiner's Office. There, Dr. Milton Helpern performed an autopsy. Helpern, also a professor of forensic pathology at New York University Medical Center, discovered a needle track in Carmela's buttocks, and found no evidence of heart disease or heart problems, or of poisons. Carmela's organs were given to chief chemist Dr. Charles Joseph Umberger for study and to see if he could detect traces of succinylcholine chloride.

Succinylcholine chloride is considered an anesthesiologist's drug, and rarely is used by other medical specialists. The drug, classified as a depolarization-blocking agent, is administered before surgery to make sure a patient's muscles are relaxed, particularly in abdominal surgery. In the 1960s, it was almost impossible to detect the drug in autopsies.

The drug can affect diaphragm muscles, and can therefore affect breathing. If a person is given a big enough dose, Helpern and Umberger reported, and respiration is not maintained artificially, the person can die.

Succinylcholine is made of succinic acid, or succinate, and choline, both chemicals normally found in a body. (As a result, it breaks down quickly.)

Umberger was not able to detect any succinylcholine chloride in Carmela's organs, so he attempted to compare the amount of succinic acid in them with organs from other embalmed cadavers. Umberger determined that there was succinic acid in some of Carmela's tissue, which he could not detect in the samples from other cadavers.

He also said he could not detect it in Carmela's tissue around the injection mark.

THE FLORIDA PRELIMINARY HEARING

Coppolino hired F. Lee Bailey to defend him. Already thin, Coppolino lost fifteen pounds while he waited in jail for his trials to begin, one in New Jersey, the other in Florida. In both he faced charges of first-degree murder, and both carried the death penalty as a possible outcome.

Coppolino was arraigned on murder charges on September 1, 1966, one year after Carmela's death. He had been arrested by Florida police on a New Jersey warrant stemming from the autopsy results on Carmela.

The prosecutor was Frank Schaub, and his assistant was William Strode.

In addition to Bailey, Coppolino had Florida attorneys James Russ and Red McEwan assisting in his defense.

During the preliminary hearing, Dr. Edmund Webb testified that he had supplied Coppolino with succinylcholine chloride.

Webb had worked as Coppolino's chief resident and had helped Carmela get a job with Hoffman-LaRoche. Webb asserted that Coppolino had told him that he wanted the drug to euthanize Farber's dog. Webb added that later, when Coppolino was in Florida, he asked for more of the drug, saying he was working on a research project involving detection of the drug. Webb said he supplied it, but was a little puzzled, since Coppolino was not employed.

Helpern testified about the autopsy performed on Carmela in New York, and Bailey vigorously cross-examined him.

Bailey asked if succinic acid was present in everyone, and Helpern replied yes.

"It is a natural body chemical?" asked Bailey.

"Well, yes."

"And choline is present in the human body at the time of death in the average case, is it not?"

"It may be present, yes."

Bailey read from a report chief chemist Umberger gave to Helpern: "Liver and brain tissue showed chemical findings of choline and succinic acid. Controlled cases examined by the same procedure failed to show the substances. The positive findings indicated quantities in excess of medical levels. It is possible that the choline and succinic acid were derived from the drug succinylcholine, which is rapidly broken down following absorption by the tissues."

He asked Helpern, "Can you point to one single word in the medical literature where it is authoritatively stated that the presence of succinylcholine can be detected from the succinic acid and choline?"

"No."

At the end of two days, the evidence was ruled substantial enough to bring Coppolino to trial for the first-degree murder of Carmela. Bail was set at $15,000, which he was able to post. Some people involved in the case believe the bail was kept low so Coppolino would post bond and could be whisked away to New Jersey for the first murder trial.

Florida governor Hayden Burns ordered Coppolino's immediate extradition to New Jersey. Four days prior to the preliminary hearing in Florida, Coppolino had been indicted in New Jersey for first-degree murder of the Colonel. After that trial, he would be brought back to Florida for another one.

COPPOLINO'S NEW JERSEY TRIAL

The trial was held in Freehold in Monmouth County, and the first day of testimony was December 5, 1966.

The prosecutor was Vincent Keuper, who began by quoting the Ten Commandments. "Though shalt not covet thy neighbor's wife," he said, adding that thou shalt not kill thy neighbor, either.

Keuper contended that Coppolino murdered the Colonel so it would be easier for him to continue his affair with the Colonel's wife. Then, after the Coppolinos moved to Florida, he met Mary Gibson, with whom he fell in love and for whom he spurned both Carmela and Farber. Prosecutors believed Carmela would not agree to a divorce, based on her Catholic background, and so Coppolino killed her so he could wed Gibson and collect Carmela's life insurance money.

Farber had received immunity for her part in the Colonel's death, in exchange for her testimony at the trial. She told the jurors that through the hypnosis sessions, she had fallen under Coppolino's sexual power. She claimed that he had hypnotically suggested that she inject her husband with the succinylcholine chloride, and although she tried, and actually started to use the needle, she couldn't go through with it.

Farber testified that she had played a part in her husband's murder, holding the Colonel's arm while Coppolino injected him with the succinylcholine chloride, and that she watched Coppolino smother him when the drug did not immediately work.

Farber said that after the Colonel was dead, she helped Coppolino turn the body over, and then she wrote a note: "Daddy is sleeping. Don't disturb him." She said Coppolino left her house around 1:00 P.M. and told her to call Carmela around dinner, when she would have returned from work.

She testified that Coppolino then got his wife to sign the death certificate, listing a heart attack as the cause. Coppolino did not sign the death certificate himself, she said, as he had retired from practice for health reasons.

Farber also maintained that she was certain Coppolino later used the same drug on his wife, whose death was also listed as a heart attack.

Bailey asked Farber why she didn't try to save her husband, and she replied that she had no free will in the matter because Coppolino had hypnotized her earlier, though she could not remember the date that Coppolino allegedly put her in a trance and planted the suggestion that she kill her husband.

Bailey asserted that Farber came forward with the story of her husband being murdered because Coppolino had passed her over in favor of Mary Gibson.

Farber retorted that she came forward after Carmela's death because she was worried that Coppolino might try to kill Gibson, too.

Helpern Testifies Again

The Colonel's body had also been exhumed for autopsy, and Helpern testified that the remains showed that the cricoid cartilage had been cracked. The cartilage nests near the Adam's apple in the larynx and can crack easily, he explained.

The prosecution asserted that the cartilage had been cracked when Coppolino smothered the Colonel with a pillow.

Helpern said he found no evidence of coronary artery disease in the Colonel's heart, and no evidence that he'd suffered a heart attack. Helpern said he believed the Colonel died because of the fractured cricoid cartilage.

Bailey asked Helpern if the cracks in the cartilage could have occurred after death, such as during the exhumation.

Helpern replied that he noted no bruises on the neck, or shovel marks. However, he admitted that except for the fracture there was no indication of cause of death.

The Defense's Turn

Dr. Joseph Spelman, Philadelphia medical examiner, and Dr. Richard Ford, Boston medical examiner, testified for the defense that there was a substantial amount of atherosclerotic disease present in the Colonel's body to support the theory of a heart attack. Furthermore, they said cartilage fractures probably occurred after death, since the surrounding tissues showed no signs of hemorrhaging.

Hypnosis experts testified that Farber's claims of a continuing hypnotic trance were impossible. Trances could not last days or weeks, they said, and someone could not be compelled to commit murder because of one.

The funeral director involved with the Colonel's exhumation testified that the body had been flipped over. He said shovels were used, but he did not see one striking the body's head or neck. The scalp was missing, which resulted from rough handling of the body, he said.

Coppolino's Testimony

Coppolino admitted he had the drug succinylcholine chloride, and that he'd acquired it to euthanize Farber's old dog . . . however, he said she'd changed her mind about the dog, and so he never used the drug. He added that he'd never given her any of it—for the dog or for the Colonel.

Coppolino described the events of the day the Colonel died. He said that Farber called him about three thirty that morning and asked him to come over and check on her husband. The Colonel was in the bathroom, weak and having trouble breathing.

Coppolino said it appeared to be heart problems, and he gave the Colonel Demerol to help with the pain, a barbiturate for anxiety, and the drug Pronestyl to ease heart irritability.

Next, Coppolino said he tried to get the Colonel to go to the hospital, but the Colonel refused. Later, Coppolino gave the Colonel a tranquilizer, Sparine, and again tried to get him to go to the hospital. Farber supported her husband's decision to stay home, he said.

Coppolino testified that he went back to the Farber house about 10:30 A.M. to check on the Colonel again, and found that he had low blood pressure and an irregular heartbeat.

The Colonel still refused hospitalization.

Coppolino said Farber went across the street to his house and signed the release he requested, and testified that Farber called Carmela around 6:30 P.M. to tell him the Colonel was dead.

Carmela signed the death certificate, with the time of death at about 4:00 P.M., adding according to Coppolino, that she claimed she had attended the Colonel from 3:30 A.M. to 6:00 A.M. and last saw him alive at 1:30 P.M. Coppolino said Carmela did not want him to risk trouble for treating someone while he was not officially practicing medicine.

Bailey concluded the defense's part of the trial by attacking Farber's hypnosis claims and her belief that she was acting under a trance.

Bailey said: "Her convenience of slipping in and out of hypnosis is exceeded only by the convenience of her forgetful memory. Her story is an agony of contradiction."

THE NEW JERSEY VERDICT

The jurors deliberated a little more than four hours before finding Coppolino not guilty in the Colonel's death.

Farber's testimony and claims of hypnosis had been successfully discredited, and the scientific evidence revealed in the Colonel's autopsy was not conclusive.

THE FLORIDA MURDER TRIAL

Bailey requested a change of venue, citing too much pretrial publicity that might hamper Coppolino getting a fair trial. (He hoped for Miami, where the greater population would provide a mixed pool for the jury.) Instead, Judge Lynn Silvertooth, who had presided over the preliminary hearing, moved the trial from Sarasota to Naples.

Succinylcholine would play a more major role in this trial. Helpern had turned to Dr. Bert LaDu, pharmacology chairman at New York University Medical Center. LaDu found material with similar properties to succinylcholine in a tissue sample from Carmela's body.

Dr. Frank Cleveland, a medical examiner from Ohio, testified that he supported Helpern's stance that Carmela's death was due to asphyxiation caused by an injection of succinylcholine chloride.

The defense countered with Dr. Francis Foldes, an anesthesiologist, and Dr. John Smith, a research biochemist, both from Montefiore Hospital in New York. Their findings opposed those of LaDu and Helpern.

Farber was prevented from testifying about her husband's death. Instead, she testified about her affair with Coppolino, their vacations to Florida, San Juan, and Atlantic City. She told the jurors she'd spotted Coppolino and Gibson in a car on the night of their bridge session, and that she'd called Carmela and told her about the bridge partner.

Farber claimed that Coppolino told her he stayed in a motel for three days contemplating his marriage, and after that told Carmela he no longer loved her. Farber admitted she'd attempted to prevent Coppolino from getting a license to practice medicine in Florida.

Despite Bailey's advice, Coppolino elected not to testify. His testimony would have been the only avenue to introduce information that Carmela injected herself with vitamin B_{12}, which could have explained the needle mark found in the autopsy.

Carmela's father testified for the prosecution, telling the jurors that he became suspicious when he learned that Coppolino had lied to him when he said there had been an autopsy.

Closing Statements

Bailey pointed to the lack of evidence regarding cause of death, stating there was no proof Coppolino had killed his wife with an injection of succinylcholine chloride. Too, he cast off Farber's allegations as those of a jealous woman who did not get the man she wanted.

Prosecutors argued that the scientific evidence presented was valid and proved homicide. They contended that Coppolino had murdered his wife for insurance money and because he'd fallen in love with Gibson.

The Verdict

The jury deliberated from shortly after 5:00 P.M. until ten thirty the night of April 27, 1967, then resumed the next morning. One-half hour after reconvening, they found Coppolino guilty of second-degree murder, which carried a penalty of twenty years to life. Analysts were surprised at the verdict, as first-degree means a murder was premeditated, planned in advance, and that if Coppolino had killed his wife with an injection of the drug, it would have had to have been planned out.

LIFE IN PRISON AND AFTER

Coppolino spent twelve years in Florida State Prison, in Raiford and Avon Park, prior to being paroled.

He appealed his case to the Second District Court, but it was rejected in 1968. Later, the Florida Supreme Court supported the lower courts' decisions. Other attorneys and physicians worked for Coppolino's release, citing the medical care in the prisons was not adequate for his heart condition.

Dr. Franco Fiorese, a former student of Umbergers, conducted independent studies of Carmela's brain and released his findings.

Fiorese, an expert on succinic acid, could not support his teacher's rulings on the presence of succinic acid.

Gibson, who had remained married to Coppolino, turned to Dr. Arnett Girardeau, a Florida state representative and retired dentist. Girardeau was chairman of the legislative committee that oversaw paroles and probation.

The news stories about the succinylcholine reports, coupled with Girardeau's help, resulted in Coppolino's being paroled for good behavior on September 26, 1979.

COMMENTARY: Dr. Carl Coppolino

The twin murder cases of Dr. Carl Coppolino were strange at least, and probably in combination, unique. As set forth, the husband of his lover passed away in Freehold, New Jersey, and two years later, his rather young wife died in Sarasota, Florida. Both were initially signed off as having resulted from "natural causes." But later, largely because of the dogged determination of "a woman scorned," Marjorie Farber, prosecutors in both states would charge that the "causes" were induced by a diabolical Dr. Coppolino through injections of succinyl dicholine chloride, a synthetic chemical that emulates the characteristics of the deadly drug curare, used by native tribes in South America to coat the tips of their arrows. Although not a poison in the ordinary sense of the word, curare paralyzes smooth muscle tissue, including those muscles that enable one to inhale and exhale. In other words, it causes death by suffocation while the victim remains conscious, and induces a most unpleasant way to pass from this life.

Succinyl dicholine chloride has the same characteristics. It is used by surgeons to prevent a patient from "bucking"—that is jerking about involuntarily—while surgery (especially that of the upper torso) is in progress. When administered by an anaesthesiologist, as Coppolino had done countless times during his active and successful career in that specialty, the patient's inability to breathe is covered by a respirator. Without that mechanical apparatus—or at least some sort of first aid in the form of artificial respiration—the victim will not survive, unless . . .

Unless the injection is given intramuscularly (which may take twenty-odd minutes to take effect, and then must last long enough for suffocation to be complete) rather than intravenously, where the effect is immediate. It was the theory in both homicides that an intramuscular injection was given to the victim by Coppolino, and that this was the cause of death. But there was a serious hitch in all this; once it enters the body, succinyldicholine chloride breaks down into two substances already found in every healthy person: succinic acid and choline. Since the bodies of both victims had been embalmed and interred for some time before the authorities exhumed them, there was no known way to show a prior injection of succinylcholine.

Prosecutor Frank Schaub, in Sarasota, Florida, indicted Coppolino first, relying in large part on Marge Farber's assurances that she was certain that Coppolino had killed Carmela. Sarasota Circuit Judge Lynn Silvertooth ordered Coppolino freed on the posting of $15,000 bail. Meanwhile, Prosecutor Vincent Keuper in Freehold, New Jersey, had indicted Coppolino for the murder of William Farber, charging that—in Marjorie Farber's presence—Coppolino had injected William Farber with succinylcholine, but strangled and suffocated him with a pillow as well.

In a most unusual move, Florida allowed Coppolino to be transferred to New Jersey; rather obviously, Florida had a very weak case that was scientifically unprecedented, whereas New Jersey had an on-the-scene eyewitness to murder, and did not have to rely on the alleged injection of succinylcholine. Strangulation, even to an unsophisticated layman, was nothing new.

Once saddled with a conviction in New Jersey, Coppolino would be an easy target in Florida. No matter where the case was tried nor who was picked to be on the jury, every juror would know that Coppolino was being charged with "doing it again."

In December 1966, Monmouth County Superior Court Judge Elvin Simmill began the task of jury selection. The process went surprisingly well, given that every prospective juror knew that the accused had another murder charge waiting for him. With less ado than I had expected, we had twelve jurors and four alternates seated and sworn. One prospective juror, however, who struggled mightily to be accepted, was the former chief of police from a small town nearby. He was adamant that he would afford Coppolino the presumption of innocence, would require the prosecution to carry a strict burden of proof, and generally be very, very fair.

After listening to these assurances, and even though I could simply have excused the chief with a peremptory challenge, I could not resist:

> "Chief, you've known Mr. Keuper here for more than thirty years, isn't that true?"
>
> "It is."
>
> "And during that entire period you have known him to be a man of honesty, integrity, and truth, have you not?"
>
> "That's true," said the chief.
>
> "Now, Chief, do you really think that Vincent Keuper would bring an innocent man in here and ask a jury to execute him?"
>
> The chief was undone. "I could never believe that," he muttered softly. Judge Simmill, with a kindly smile, excused him from further service.

The document set out on manuscript page thirty-three was as powerful a stick of dynamite as has ever been dropped in a courtroom, simply because Marge Farber had either (1) forgotten about it, or (2) remembered it but withheld it from Vincent Keuper for fear that he might not prosecute the case once he read it. To make matters even rosier, she was the state's first witness, and I had her on cross-examination a little before four o'clock on Friday afternoon, a wonderful time to score points with a jury and let them think about it for two days.

The document was handwritten. Coppolino had kept the original, and it may well be that Marge Farber had never had a copy. I showed her the document, and asked her to identify that signature as hers. She did, and suddenly looked a little wild-eyed. I then asked her to explain the words on the document; she said that she had never seen it before in her life, and had no idea how her signature got on it. She did so in a very guilty voice. From looking at the jury as she mumbled on, I thought that the case was over, right then and there. Keuper did bring Dr. Milton Helpern to the stand, who said he thought he saw evidence of manual strangulation in the cricoid cartilage of the corpse of William Farber. He was promptly impeached by a book he had authored—a leading text in pathology to be sure—which demonstrated that the injury he was describing (the cartilage was in a glass jar, for all to see) was necessarily postmortem, and thus could not be the cause of death.

For good measure, two other distinguished pathologists, from Boston and Philadelphia, demolished what was left of Dr. Helpern's testimony.

When the Florida trial rolled round in May, it had been transferred to Naples, rather than to Miami as the defense had requested. Naples was then and continues to be a well-to-do community of older people, many of whom were retired. I did not like that venue for a trial of Carl Coppolino, an admitted philanderer whose accuser was an older woman herself. During jury selection every candidate promised solemnly that he or she could "put out of mind" anything that had been in the press about a trial in New Jersey. The way that these jurors looked at Coppolino, however, did not bode well.

Like the chief in New Jersey, we had one candidate who was bound and determined to be on the jury. She announced herself as "Mrs. Waples from Naples" and went on to recount that her recently deceased husband, a lawyer, had relied heavily on her advice throughout his years of legal practice. She opined that she could be an excellent juror. The courtroom was all a-chuckle as she carried on. When it came my turn to examine her—I had already decided to use a peremptory challenge to eliminate her—I could not resist a little fun:

> "Are you truly Mrs. Waples from Naples?" I asked almost reverently.
> "I am." She beamed.
> "Well," I said sweetly, "this gentleman is Coppolino from Portofino, and you are excused."
> Most everyone laughed. Mrs. Waples did not.

But things did not go well for the defense. First, Frank Schaub nearly convinced Judge Silvertooth to let in evidence of the accusations in New Jersey, even though Coppolino had been acquitted there. Second, Dr. Helpern's chief toxicologist, Dr. Charles Joseph Umberger, testified that based on tests he had conducted he had found an excess of succinic acid in

Carmela's corpse. While he would not say that this proved an injection of succinylcholine, Dr. Helpern—still smarting from being ridiculed by the press in New Jersey, was more than willing to make the quantum leap. Umberger's tests, he said, together with a needle track in Carmela's buttock that he claimed to have found, were sufficient to satisfy him that she had been injected with succinylcholine.

Thereafter, several of Umberger's assistants came forward, timorously and putting their jobs in peril, to say that Umberger's "tests" were not scientific at all but merely an effort to appease Dr. Helpern, who was a tyrant. The beaker jars used, they reported, were not even clean.

When Umberger was threatened with impeachment by his own witnesses, he agreed to return to the stand as a defense witness and declare that his tests revealed only a "possibility" of an excess of succinic acid, and no more. I moved—unsuccessfully—to strike Helpern's testimony, since if it rested only on a "possible" toxicological finding in a field where he admittedly had no competence himself, he had no right to bootstrap that "possibility" into a "reasonable medical certainty," which was the proper criterion for the admissibility of expert medical opinion. Had the testimony been struck, Judge Silvertooth would have been forced to throw the case out.

The jury returned a verdict of murder in the second degree, which under Florida law (and the law of practically every other state) was a legal impossibility. Second-degree murder involves an intentional and deliberate killing, but without premeditation. To kill with succinylcholine, one must inject the victim and stand by and watch him or her suffocate. If the culprit is a doctor, then he or she would know that artificial respiration could probably save the day, and thus the premeditation must be ongoing and continuous. In the case of an intramuscular (as opposed to intravenous) injection, the culprit would have to hang out for twenty minutes, waiting for the drug to take hold. Coppolino's conviction remains today as the only case of "second-degree poisoning" on record. Had he not decided to drop his appeals in the hope of an early release (he served twelve years), an appellate court might have ruled—as the U.S. Supreme Court once had in a second-degree arson-murder conviction—that since the killing could have been only first degree, the jury had in fact acquitted the defendant by finding him not guilty of that charge.

Dr. Jeffrey MacDonald

Charged with murdering his wife and children on February 17, 1970

THE MURDERS

In the early hours of February 17, 1970, a Fayetteville, North Carolina, telephone operator received an urgent call from Captain Jeffrey MacDonald. He begged her to contact the military police and send an ambulance to his residence at 544 Castle Drive. He said there had been a stabbing.

The operator put the call through to Fort Bragg's military police headquarters. An ambulance was not sent until MPs reached MacDonald's home and declared that an ambulance was indeed required.

On the way to the residence, a few blocks from the MacDonald house, one of the MPs reportedly spotted a woman in a raincoat and a floppy-brimmed hat. He considered it unusual, as it was shortly before 4:00 A.M., and would have investigated were he not on an urgent call.

At the MacDonald house, the MPs went through the back door, as the front was locked and the place was dark. Inside, they discovered Colette MacDonald in the master bedroom, lying on her back and covered in blood. Next to her was Captain MacDonald, unconscious. The MPs revived him with mouth-to-mouth resuscitation.

MacDonald told the MPs that three men and a woman were responsible. He reportedly said one of the men wore a field jacket with sergeant's stripes, and the woman was wearing a floppy hat.

In another bedroom, they discovered Kimberley, age five. Her head had been smashed in, and stab wounds were evident on her neck. Across the hall, Kristen, age two, was dead from stab wounds to her chest and neck.

An ambulance arrived, and MacDonald was taken to the hospital, where he was treated for his wounds and a collapsed lung.

Later that day, agents from the FBI and the army's Criminal Investigation Division (CID) questioned the captain about the family's activities of the previous evening. MacDonald reported that he and his wife had had a drink, and then she went to bed while he stayed up longer to watch television. He said he gave Kristen a bottle when he heard her cry, then returned to his television program and fell asleep on the couch.

MacDonald claimed he woke up when he heard Colette scream, and that he was immediately attacked by a man with a baseball bat. He said he saw two other men and a woman (who was wearing a floppy hat) holding something glowing that might have been a candle, and talking about acid, and that the man with the bat hit him until he lost consciousness.

When he came to, he said he tried to revive his wife, then tried to help the children.

Then he called the operator.

One of the CID investigators looked at the crime scene and reportedly fixated on MacDonald as the culprit, believing he had made up the story.

Army investigators began to focus almost exclusively on MacDonald.

JEFFREY MACDONALD

MacDonald had been the quarterback of his high school football team and served as president of the student council. During his undergraduate years at Princeton, he married Colette Stevenson, whom he had dated in high school. He attended the Northwestern

University Medical School, interned at New York's Columbia-Presbyterian Medical Center, and then joined the army. He was accepted into the Green Berets, and the young family was stationed at Fort Bragg in North Carolina.

THE MACDONALD FAMILY

A native of Patchogue, New York, Colette had known MacDonald since grade school. She attended Skidmore College for two years before marrying MacDonald, and continued to take college classes after that, intending to get a degree in English literature. Daughter Kimberley was born in April 1964 and Kristen in May 1967.

Colette was pregnant with her third child when she was murdered.

THE WOMAN IN THE FLOPPY HAT

Investigators at the scene initially seemed uninterested in the earlier sighting of a woman in a big floppy hat, though a tip eventually led to her identification. An informant for the local police, she was identified as Helena Stoeckley, the daughter of a retired army officer.

Stoeckley allegedly practiced witchcraft and was into drugs. She was known to often dress in black, and reportedly she had hung funeral wreaths outside her apartment on the day of Colette and the children's funerals.

THE ARTICLE 32 HEARING

In April, MacDonald was informed he was the prime suspect in the murder investigation. Colonel Warren Rock headed up the Article 32 inquiry (which is required to determine if charges are warranted or if any further action should be taken). The hearing began July 6, 1970.

During the hearing, Bernie Segal, MacDonald's attorney, questioned Lieutenant Joseph Paulk, who was heavily involved in the murder investigation. Paulk admitted he was unaware of just how many MPs were in the house and had never gotten a list of their names. Further, he admitted that no roadblocks were set up when MacDonald described that there had been four assailants in the house, even though others investigating the scene had suggested it.

Paulk also testified that he was unaware of whether the scene had been contaminated by men going into and out of the house.

The Article 32 hearing was closed to the media, and some authorities believe that was to prevent embarrassment to the army regarding the handling of the scene.

Segal also questioned the CID investigation of Helena Stoeckley, the so-called woman in the floppy hat, and learned that the officer who interviewed Stoeckley did not take written notes, which went against common practice. Furthermore, one of the military police who spotted the woman in the floppy hat in the early morning hours of the murder was ordered not to mention the incident during the Article 32 hearing.

Segal pointed out there was no evidence of drugs in MacDonald's system when he was taken to the hospital, and tests revealed only a low level of alcohol.

Witnesses affirmed that MacDonald was a good husband, father, and doctor.

CRIME SCENE INVESTIGATION AND CONTAMINATION

One of the main issues regarding the murder was the disruption of the crime scene. MacDonald's attorney, Segal, contended that an ambulance driver had moved things around, which might have contributed to a CID investigator thinking that MacDonald had staged the scene. Segal claimed there were insufficient samples of fingerprints and hair, and that prints had been wiped off the telephone and other surfaces. A hair sample taken from MacDonald's coat turned out to be from a pony he'd bought for his daughters. Segal maintained that fiber evidence was disturbed by an army doctor examining Colette.

In addition, an ambulance driver allegedly stole MacDonald's wallet.

Psychiatrists who had examined MacDonald termed him "warm and personable" and found no signs of mental illness or indication he was lying about the events surrounding the murders.

Segal questioned many people who knew MacDonald, his wife, and children. MacDonald's father-in-law firmly emphasized that he believed MacDonald was innocent and said the army never made an effort to look for the real killers.

The hearing did bring out one mark against MacDonald's character: admitted flings on business trips, which his wife had not been aware of.

The Article 32 hearing lasted six weeks, and at the end of it Colonel Rock recommended the army dismiss the murder charges. Furthermore, he suggested Stoeckley be investigated by local law enforcement officers. Stoeckley reportedly told Nashville police officers she'd witnessed the MacDonald murders and sought immunity from prosecution. However, she was denied the immunity, and her fingerprints did not match prints taken from the scene, and so the CID did not consider her a suspect.

Eventually, the charges against MacDonald were dropped for "insufficient evidence," wording that would allow the army to reopen the case later.

AFTER THE ARTICLE 32

Captain MacDonald applied for and was granted a discharge from the army. He embraced the publicity, and freely discussed with the media what he believed was army incompetence in the investigation of the murders, appearing on television with Walter Cronkite as well as on various talk shows. MacDonald complained about CID's mishandling of the investigation, and seemed upset that the army took no action against the CID investigators.

MacDonald's mother had sold her house to help pay for his legal bills, so he needed to get a job and repay her. He moved to Long Beach, California, in the summer of 1971, where he worked in the emergency department of St. Mary Medical Center. While there, he was made an honorary member of the Long Beach Police Department for saving officers' lives.

During the early 1970s, the army CID gave the case's evidence to the FBI.

In early 1972, a CID lawyer attempted to bring civilian charges against MacDonald.

In September of that year, attorney Warren Coolidge informed the Justice Department that he would not prosecute MacDonald. The CID continued its investigation, and in the following year Assistant Attorney General Henry Peterson wrote that the case was too weak to prosecute.

However, in 1974, a citizen's complaint was filed against MacDonald, requesting a grand jury. The jury was convened and presented the evidence. MacDonald was indicted for the murders of his wife and two children. His friends put their homes up as collateral to make the $100,000 bail.

MacDonald was arraigned in May 1975, pleading not guilty. And in January 1976, the Fourth Circuit Court of Appeals dismissed the charges, citing that MacDonald had been denied a speedy trial.

However, nearly two years later, the Supreme Court reversed the ruling, and MacDonald's trial was set for July 1979.

MACDONALD'S TRIAL

Judge Franklin Dupree Jr. requested the case. The lead prosecutor was James Blackburn, who would later become the U.S. attorney of the Eastern District of North Carolina. (Years after the MacDonald trial, Blackburn admitted stealing more than $200,000 from his law firm; he was disbarred and served a little more than three months in prison for charges of embezzlement, obstruction of justice, and corruption on a matter not related to the MacDonald trial.)

Bernie Segal again defended MacDonald during the criminal trial. Segal hired John Thornton, a forensic scientist, to examine the evidence the FBI had tested, though Thornton was not given the evidence until only a few weeks before the trial.

The defense disputed some of the evidence, such as the fact that a long blond fiber that had been taken from Colette's hand was the type used in wigs, the defense claimed, pointing out that Stoeckley admitted to wearing a blond wig that she'd disposed of after the murders.

Army CID investigators had claimed there was no evidence of intruders in the MacDonald's home on the night of the murders, but the defense contended that the fiber and hairs, and wax drippings that had not come from the candles in the MacDonald's home, constituted such evidence, as did a burnt match found in one of the girl's rooms. In addition, a bloody syringe had been found, but the syringe was lost in the CID lab.

Segal said he did not know during the trial that Stoeckley told an FBI agent in 1978 that she had played a part in the murders. At the trial, she testified that she was with Greg Mitchell, her boyfriend, and they were taking drugs with other soldiers from Fort Bragg. She told Segal she did not remember what she was doing around the time of the murders, nor did she remember telling six individuals that she was in the MacDonald home.

Judge Dupree ruled that those six individuals could testify during the trial, but not about any statements Stoeckley made to them regarding the murders. He ruled that Stoeckley's statements were not trustworthy because of her admitted drug use. (After the trial, the defense learned that she had allegedly confessed regarding the murders to one of the prosecutors.)

The prosecution claimed that MacDonald and his wife had a fight, which also explained most of the wounds to MacDonald. They contended that he inflicted at least one on himself to support his story. (MacDonald's injuries had been recorded by doctors at Womack Army Hospital, and included bruises on his head, left shoulder, and upper arm; there was a knife wound on his left bicep and cuts on his left hand and fingers; in addition, there were punch marks on his stomach and cuts on his chest.) At

MacDonald's trial in 1979, doctors had testified the wounds were not self-inflicted.

Evidence showed three weapons were used on Colette: an ice pick, a knife, and a blunt object. A knife and a blunt object were used on Kimberley, and a knife and an ice pick were used on Kristen.

MacDonald was found guilty of the murders and sentenced to life in prison.

FREE AGAIN—TEMPORARILY

MacDonald was released after serving a year in prison, as an appeals court had ruled that he had been denied a speedy trial.

MacDonald returned to working at St. Mary Medical Center. However, in March 1982, that ruling was overturned and he was once again sent back to prison. MacDonald's attorneys appealed the decision, stating errors were committed during the trial. That appeal was denied. Other appeals followed and were also denied during the next few years, in one case the judge stated that no evidence tied an outside group to the murders.

THE SAGA OF HELENA STOECKLEY AND GREG MITCHELL

MP Kenneth Mica was first on the scene in 1970, and he had reported seeing a woman with a floppy hat standing in the rain a few blocks away. Mica said if he had not been responding to an emergency call, he would have stopped to check on the woman because of the early hour. Mica further suggested someone investigate her, but no one did, and he was ordered by a superior not to mention the woman. However, Mica reported her anyway.

CID agent William Ivory said the woman was a "red herring," a drug addict, and a snitch. Records showed that she'd provided information to local police that helped lead to arrests in more than one hundred drug-related crimes. In addition, records released in 1983 revealed that Stoekley had been used by the Nashville Police Department for Internal Affairs investigations.

Stoeckley had said that a man named Greg Mitchell, her

boyfriend at the time, had killed Colette, and that she knew the other two male assailants. Too, she signed confessions that she was involved in the murders, and admitted she'd been using drugs the night of the murders.

Mitchell had been a soldier at Fort Bragg and was an admitted drug user. Sometime before his death in 1982, he reportedly confessed his part in the murders to several people, including his boss. Some of these people signed statements to that effect. Mitchell was left-handed, and some forensic experts contend that Colette was murdered by a left-handed person. Further, Mitchell had brown hair, and brown hair was found under Colette's fingernails.

MacDonald was right-handed and blond.

Mitchell was found dead of cirrhosis of the liver several months after Stoeckley's death, which was also attributed to cirrhosis of the liver.

MORE APPEALS

In 1990, MacDonald's attorneys continued their struggle, this time claiming evidence relating to Stoeckley and her associates had been suppressed during the initial trial, including the fibers from Stoeckley's wig. The judge denied the appeal, and in 1992 an appeals court upheld the judge's ruling.

Though MacDonald became eligible for parole in 1991, he did not seek it, as that would have required him to express remorse for the murders. He continued to proclaim his innocence.

Then in 1997, MacDonald's attorneys filed a motion to reopen the case, seeking to use new DNA testing to prove the presence of intruders in the MacDonald home. In the fall of that year, the Fourth Circuit Court of Appeals granted the use of the DNA testing.

MacDonald was imprisoned in Oregon, California, then in the spring of 2003 transferred to Maryland, closer to his home. He remarried in the summer of 2002 to longtime friend Kathryn Kurich, the operator of a drama school for children.

In November 2004, he applied for parole, still maintaining his innocence. In May 2005, he went before the parole board, and parole was denied.

The parole board's ruling was upheld on appeal that summer.

As of January 2006, the DNA tests requested in 1997 had not been finished. Also that month, attorneys' request for a hearing involving new evidence was granted, this based on James Britt's statement that he had witnessed a prosecutor from the original trial threaten Stoeckley so she would alter her testimony.

In December 2005, MacDonald's attorneys filed papers claiming that prosecutors in the murder trial were guilty of misconduct.

Stoeckley, who had been mentioned in connection with the murders several times before, was one of the keys to their claims. According to the attorneys, Britt, a U.S. marshal, drove Stoeckley to MacDonald's trial, where she would testify on behalf of the defense in 1979. During the trip, Stoeckley reportedly admitted being in the home around the time of the murders. She described details of the home and said she and other people were at Mac-Donald's looking for drugs, thinking there would be some because MacDonald was a doctor. When prosecutors threatened Stoeckley with murder charges, she claimed amnesia during the trial and was no help to MacDonald's case.

Britt had come forward, reportedly to clear his guilty conscious about the Stoeckley incident.

MacDonald's attorneys maintained that they had been blocked from conducting an independent investigation of the evidence collected at the scene of the murders, and was only allowed to see that evidence several days before the trial. Furthermore, the attorneys said evidence had been lost, including human skin that had been found under Colette's fingernail.

A club, a knife, and an ice pick that were found in the yard were not handled properly, and there were discrepancies of when and precisely where those objects were found, they maintained. In addition, a bloody footprint that had been discovered on a section of hardwood floor was lost; investigators said it fell apart when the wood was sawed out.

Other claims of mishandled evidence included that photographs were not taken of hair and thread samples before separating and washing them. A bloody palm print that was found on the bed and did not match any of the MacDonalds, and was never identified. Brown hairs taken at the scene of the murders did not match MacDonald's hair.

MACDONALD'S CIVIL SUIT

MacDonald was the subject of the bestselling novel *Fatal Vision*, by Joe McGinniss. In 1979, MacDonald offered McGinniss the opportunity to cover the case from the defense's point of view. McGinniss accepted, and an agreement was made to share a portion of the book revenue, which MacDonald intended to use for legal expenses.

According to reports, MacDonald and McGinniss became friends, and McGinniss sometimes stayed with MacDonald and was invited to defense team meetings.

But when the book came out in 1983, it portrayed MacDonald as the murderer. It became a huge best-seller and a subsequent TV movie. In August 1984, MacDonald sued McGinniss for fraud and breach of contract, and sought $15 million in damages.

Gary Bostwick served as MacDonald's lawyer in the civil suit and claimed McGinnis wrongly edited passages from tapes MacDonald had made regarding the murder case. McGinniss offered to settle the case out of court for $200,000, but MacDonald declined.

The jurors could not agree on a verdict, and so the judge declared a mistrial. That left open the possibility of another trial.

McGinniss made another offer to settle, this time for $325,000.

MacDonald eventually agreed to a settlement, though the amount was increased.

COMMENTARY: Dr. Jeffrey MacDonald

The conviction of Dr. Jeffrey MacDonald is one of the most unsettling cases described in this book. The slaughter of his wife and two children was horrendous, to be sure. And while the U.S. Army did not think there was a case to be made against MacDonald, the office of the United States attorney general pressed on relentlessly.

Disturbing is the fact that MacDonald had no motive at all to kill his family; equally disturbing is the fact that there were and are some holes in his story about the "hippie" intruders who broke into his home and killed his wife and young daughters while sparing him, although he did suffer some significant injuries.

In any case, there can be little question but what the investigation conducted by the army was botched in many ways. In an effort to convince skeptics that MacDonald was blameless, his lawyer, Bernie Segal, submitted him to a polygraph test by a well-established examiner. MacDonald reportedly did not pass. Contrary to popular misconception, this did not mean that he was implicated in the murders; it did mean that he was withholding information from the examiner. If, for instance, while the murders were in progress MacDonald somehow become more interested in saving himself than in facing almost certain death by resisting or attacking the culprits, his concealing that degrading fact could have caused the reaction on the polygraph test, thought to indicate deception.

MacDonald is still serving his sentence and has never relented in his claim of innocence. Sadly, if law enforcement should discover that others, and not he, had committed the crimes, there are some within its ranks that would strongly oppose ever letting this injustice—if it was one— become public.

Claus von Bülow

Charged with attempting to murder his wife on December 21, 1980

Four days before Christmas 1980, millionairess Sunny von Bülow slipped into an irreversible coma. Speculation ranged from her medicating herself during a bout of depression, to her husband's administering drugs to kill her so he could inherit her fortune and marry his mistress. It wasn't the first time she had lapsed into a coma, and it wasn't the first time suspicion had fallen upon Claus.

SUNNY'S COMA

Sunny and her husband, Claus von Bülow, along with their children Alexander and Cosima, dined at their Newport, Rhode Island, home, Clarendon Court on the evening of December 21. The family recalled that Sunny had insisted on partaking of an ice-cream sundae with caramel, even though she'd been told to limit sweets. The family then went to the movies to watch Dolly Parton in *9 to 5*.

Upon their return home, von Bülow went to his study, and Sunny, Alexander, and Cosima stayed up to visit. Later in the evening, Sunny seemed to have trouble talking, and her son carried her into the bedroom. He then left to meet some friends at a nearby bar.

The next day, the family found Sunny unconscious in her bathroom. She was rushed to Newport Hospital, where doctors said her body temperature was more than ten degrees below normal. Sunny went into cardiac arrest, was resuscitated, and was soon transferred to a hospital in Boston. There, CAT scans revealed that she was in an irreversible coma.

CLAUS VON BÜLOW

Claus Cecil Borberg von Bülow was born in Copenhagen in 1926 and raised by his divorced mother, Jonna Bülow, and his grandfather, Frits Bülow. Claus's father was the playwright Svend Borberg, who headed the Danish-German Literary Society.

Claus von Bülow's family was tied to the German von Bülows, known for their patronage of German composer Richard Wagner. (Wagner had carried on a long-term affair with Cosima von Bülow, the wife of an orchestra conductor; von Bülow's daughter with Sunny would be named Cosima.)

Von Bülow attended Swiss schools at Saint Moritz, graduated from Trinity College in Cambridge, England, in 1946, and then moved to London, where he worked as a barrister through the 1950s. He met J. Paul Getty, who hired him in 1959 as a personal assistant.

Von Bülow married Sunny in 1966, and two years later quit working for Getty. He had an allowance of $120,000 a year in interest income from a trust Sunny had established for him.

After thirteen years of marriage, the von Bülows often talked about divorcing. He openly courted Alexandra Isles, an actress. Von Bülow maintained he had Sunny's permission to seek affairs as, after the birth of Cosima, she'd lost interest in sex.

MARTHA "SUNNY" CRAWFORD

Sunny was born in 1931 and raised by her mother and grandmother. Her father had died when she was four. They lived in a suite of apartments in New York City, where Sunny attended the prestigious Chapin School. The family spent their summers at the Tamerlane estate in Greenwich, Connecticut. She was known for being timid and friendly, as well as attractive and rich, as she had inherited a fortune of $75 million.

She opted not to attend college, though she took the entrance tests to prove she was smart enough to be accepted. She traveled instead, at one juncture going with her mother to Europe. One of the places they visted was the Schloss Mittersill resort in the Austrian Alps, where she met Alfie, Prince von Auersperg.

In July 1957, Sunny and Alfie married, and she gained the title Princess von Auersperg. They had two children, Alexander and Annie, called Ala. The marriage ended when Sunny grew too homesick for New York and tired of Alfie's affairs. During the separation, Sunny met the next man she would marry.

She married von Bülow, and they had one daughter, Cosima. She became active with volunteer work and charity fund-raisers but, despite her wealth and her family, she was unhappy, often suffering bouts of depression.

The family was happy, however, in December 1979. They came together to celebrate the holidays at Clarendon Court.

Until the day after Christmas, when the family was shattered.

THE "OTHER" WOMAN, ALEXANDRA MOLTKE ISLES

From 1966 to 1968, the actress Alexandra Moltke Isles appeared in more than three hundred episodes of *Dark Shadows*, a soap opera that became a cult classic. She refused to voluntarily take the stand in von Bülow's 1982 attempted murder trial, and so was subpoenaed.

Isles testified to the details of her affair with von Bülow, admitting that she had asked him to leave his wife. (She also testified in von Bülow's second trial.)

GROWING SUSPICIONS

While von Bülow attempted to have Sunny taken off life support, a neurologist told Alexander and Ala that he believed their mother's coma was induced by injected insulin. Von Bülow called Alexander and Ala daily, asking that they agree to have Sunny taken off life support. Reports say he appealed to them emotionally and financially. His arguments, however, soon became futile when Sunny was taken off the respirator and began breathing on her own.

Alexander and Ala hired a criminal lawyer—Richard Kuh—to investigate Sunny's coma and possibly bring charges against von Bülow. Kuh, a former New York district attorney, went to the Rhode Island State Police for help.

State Police Sergeant John Reise interviewed Sunny's family, friends, employees, and doctors before talking to von Bülow. Von Bülow told them that Alexander and Ala had been collecting evidence against him. He also gave the police conflicting images of Sunny's use of drugs and alcohol.

Alexander and Ala talked at length with Kuh about their suspicions involving Sunny's coma. They told him about a black bag, drugs, and syringes they'd seen, and that they were certain their mother's coma was attempted murder.

Kuh, with a locksmith and a former police detective in tow, went to Clarendon Court, searching for the infamous black bag. They found it and opened it, noting pills, a vial of blue liquid, a syringe, and hypodermic needles, one of which they thought had been used. The items were sent to a private laboratory, which determined the blue liquid was a mix of Valium and amobarbital, and that the used needle held traces of insulin.

Circumstantial evidence against von Bülow grew as the investigation continued and, in July 1981, there was enough to present to a Rhode Island grand jury, which indicted Bülow for attempted murder.

He was set free on $100,000 bail.

VON BÜLOW'S FIRST TRIAL

The trial was a media circus, even luring reporters and cameramen from other countries. Von Bülow's attorneys were John Sheehan and Herald Fahringer. Sheehan and Fahringer attempted to exclude the black bag from evidence, claiming it had been illegally obtained without a search warrant. However, it was ruled that a warrant had not been required to obtain the bag, as the men who recovered it were not working for the police.

The defense also tried to have Sunny's medical history excluded, but the judge ruled it was germane to the case.

It took eight days to select a jury, as many prospective jurors said either they did not consider themselves peers of someone rich and powerful like von Bülow, or they were prejudiced against him because of his lifestyle.

The jurors were taken to Clarendon Court and shown the bathroom where Sunny had been found unconscious as well as the closet where the black bag had been discovered. They were lectured to by an expert about hypoglycemia, blood sugar, and insulin.

Among the Witnesses

Alexander, Sunny's son, testified about finding his mother ill when she lapsed into her first coma. It was a story he would repeat at von Bülow's civil trial. He admitted his mother was considering divorce. (That particular conversation between Alexander and his mother had been at the end of November 1980, one month before she had slipped into her final coma.) Alexander told the jurors he hadn't seen his mother abuse pills, and the only time she'd appeared disoriented was on the two times she had slipped into comas.

Maria Schrallhammer, Sunny's housekeeper, spent twelve hours on the stand. She was adamant that Sunny did not have a drug or alcohol problem. She talked about seeing von Bülow's black case.

Medical personnel also testified. Technicians who had tested Sunny's blood and discovered a raised insulin level said the first samples might have been mixed with later samples. Some technicians asserted that they thought Sunny had a drug overdose, based on the high insulin levels.

Harris Funkenstein, a Boston neurologist, told the jurors that when Sunny was brought to him when she went into her second coma, he eliminated aspirin overdose and other drugs, and settled on injected insulin.

Alexandra Isles was called to support the prosecution's contention that one of the reasons von Bülow had attempted to kill his wife was to marry her. She admitted that she asked von Bülow to leave his wife. When von Bülow was indicted, she broke off her relationship with him at the suggestion of her attorneys. Isles testified that she didn't know if she still loved him.

Prosecutors concluded that von Bülow had killed Sonny for the inheritance. Her fortune was valued at about $75 million, $45 million of which was held in trusts. The rest was a combination of real estate, cash, and art. Von Bülow would inherit $14 million of the liquid assets. Prosecutors contended the money was obviously a significant motive.

DETAILS OF THE COURT STORIES

Von Bülow's version of the night that Sonny initially became ill left him blameless. He said after Alexander had put Sonny to bed, he joined her, and she began arguing about his work. (At the time, he was working for Artemis International Art Advisors, and traveled extensively to visit clients.) He also said she was upset that Ala was leaving for Austria to be with her fiancé. He testified that she was depressed, and that they talked about a trial separation.

The housekeeper, Schrallhammer, testified that when she walked by the bedroom door, she heard someone moaning, as if ill. She entered and found Sonny unconscious. Von Bülow lay in another bed nearby, reading. Schrallhammer said she had tried futilely to wake Sonny up, and insisted on calling a doctor. Von Bülow, however, maintained that that would not be necessary, and the housekeeper backed down.

Von Bülow testified that the events were not as severe as Schrallhammer claimed. He said the housekeeper was concerned about Sonny's cough. He admitted that the woman wanted to call a doctor, but he said Sonny merely had a sore throat.

Alexander, twenty at the time, testified that when he came back from playing tennis and was told Sonny was sick, he went to the bedroom and saw von Bülow standing at the foot of the bed. Alexander said he could not wake up his mother, and she was breathing hoarsely. Finally, he said, von Bülow looked concerned and asked him what should be done.

Alexander told the jurors he replied, "Call a doctor!" He added that von Bülow did just that, asking a local physician to make a house call.

Dr. Janis Gailitis arrived fifteen minutes later and promptly called for an ambulance. Sunny stopped breathing, and Dr. Gailitis performed CPR, and said she started breathing again, though she did not regain consciousness. Gailitis, a general practitioner, had treated Sunny before for minor problems.

Doctors at the hospital discovered that Sunny had an above-normal level of insulin. They did not suspect foul play and worked to stabilize her blood sugar level. She regained consciousness and underwent a variety of tests in an attempt to discover the insulin problem and what might have put her in a coma. She told doctors that she did not inject herself with insulin and that she did not have a drinking or drug problem.

In the end, the doctors diagnosed her as being hypoglycemic, and warned her not to overindulge in sweets or to go too long without eating.

The housekeeper, Schrallhammer, testified that in the weeks after Sunny returned home, she began to suspect that von Bülow had made Sunny sick. Schrallhammer said she found a suitcase in a closet she was cleaning, and inside that was a black leather case. Schrallhammer said she wasn't sure why she opened it, but she did, and inside she saw pills and a vial of liquid. Schrallhammer said she called Ala, and took the case to her apartment to show her.

Ala said she made notes of the case's contents, and of the label on the bottle of pills; it was a prescription made out to someone named Leslie Baxter. She took samples of the liquid and some powder, and turned these over to a family physician, who said the substances were a barbituate (called secobarbital) and Valium, both of which the doctor had prescribed for Sunny before. The physician, Dr. Richard Stock, said those drugs were not available by prescription in the forms they were in, and they would not have come from a typical pharmacy.

Schrallhammer testified that, in April 1980, Sunny appeared weak again, and once more had become disoriented. The housekeeper said she called Dr. Stock, who admitted her employer to a New York hospital for a series of tests. Again, Sunny was diagnosed with hypoglycemia, and told to avoid alcohol and limit sugar.

Schrallhammer told the jurors that Sunny had improved and attended the festivities of her daughter Ala's marriage. That fall, the housekeeper said she found the black bag again in the closet, opened it, and found syringes and a vial labeled "insulin." She said she told Alexander about her discovery.

After Thanksgiving, Sunny was hospitalized for a week, suffering from aspirin poisoning, from taking too many for a sinus infection. Again, she got well and life went back to normal, Schrallhammer testified. However, she added that things changed at Christmas.

When the family went to Clarendon Court for the holidays, Schrallhammer stayed in New York. She testified that she had seen the black bag in von Bülow's luggage, but had said nothing to Sunny or von Bülow, an act she regretted, as she never saw Sunny conscious again.

THE DEFENSE'S CASE

Defense witness Joy O'Neill claimed she spent five years as Sunny's personal trainer. She testified that Sunny had discussed injecting insulin to lose weight. O'Neill said she sometimes exercised with Sunny five days a week, and that she'd become as close as a sister to her. However, a rebuttal witness argued that the studio's records showed O'Neill had not worked with Sunny during any of her two hundred visits in 1978 and 1979.

The defense called eleven other witnesses, two of them testifying that Sunny was stressed and depressed around the time of the onset of her second coma.

In closing arguments, the defense said it was likely that Sunny injected herself with insulin. After recovering from the first coma, she didn't express much curiosity about the episode because she knew why it had happened, they said: Sunny had the time and opportunity on each occasion to inject herself, as she had retired to her bedroom or bathroom and had spent some time alone there.

Perhaps Sunny had indeed induced the hypoglycemia episodes, the defense suggested, or had tried to lose weight with insulin, or perhaps even take her own life.

THE VERDICT

The jury asked to hear some of the testimony again during its twelve hours of deliberations. Before noon on March 16, 1982, the jury returned guilty verdicts on both counts of attempted murder. Von Bülow was allowed to remain free on the $100,000 bail, pending the hearing on a motion for a new trial.

DEFENSE ATTORNEYS SEEK A NEW TRIAL

Fahringer, one of von Bülow's attorneys, engineered publicity for his client, appearing on news programs. Von Bülow was interviewed by Barbara Walters. The publicity did not help win a new trial, however, as the court denied that request in April 1982. Bail was raised to $500,000, which von Bülow quickly met.

Von Bülow was sentenced to ten years for the first count of attempted murder, since Sunny had recovered from that episode. For the second count, he received twenty years. Bail was raised again, this time to $1 million, allowing von Bülow to be free pending his appeal.

Von Bülow added another lawyer to his defense team: Alan Dershowitz, a Harvard Law School professor. Fahringer later withdrew from the case.

To gain a new trial, the defense would have to bring in new evidence or prove mistakes were made in the first trial. Dershowitz contended that the contents of the black bag should not have been introduced.

Author Truman Capote came forward to help provide the needed new evidence. Capote, in a sworn affidavit, said that Sunny taught him thirty years earlier how to inject himself with stimulants. Capote said Sunny had used various intravenous drugs. Joanne Carson supported Capote's claims.

Unfortunately, Capote died before von Bülow's appeal was heard. His affidavit could not be used because he had not been cross-examined about it.

The black bag became the crucial element, and the defense showed discrepancies involving the people who handled it. There were enough differences that Dershowitz was able to claim that it was an unreliable piece of evidence. The defense had experts test the items in the black bag, and those experts claimed the supposedly used needle had no traces of human tissue or blood on it. Valium had been found on the needle, but there was no hint of Valium in Sunny's body.

Von Bülow filed an appeal.

THE APPEAL

Dershowitz's brief for the appeal was massive and began, "Claus von Bülow is facing thirty years in prison for a crime he did not commit."

Dershowitz described von Bülow's wife as depressed and self-destructive. He said her chauffeur made frequent stops at pharmacies for her.

Rhode Island prosecutors answered with a 101-page brief as to why justice had been served in the case, and the defense answered with its rebuttal. In most cases, the appeal-response-rebuttal routine would be the end, giving the defense the last word, but in this case the Rhode Island Supreme Court allowed the prosecution to give a response to Dershowitz's rebuttal.

As a result of Dershowitz's work, the court reversed von Bülow's conviction and ordered a new trial, and the contents of the infamous black bag would not be a part of it.

THE SECOND TRIAL

Von Bülow went on trial again in April 1985, almost three years after the first trial ended in a conviction. Dershowitz served as a consultant to von Bülow, who hired Thomas Puccio to head his legal team. (Puccio was known for prosecuting congressmen caught in the Abscam bribery sting.)

The prosecution again relied on housekeeper Maria Schrall-hammer and Sunny's son, Alexander, to testify. The medical experts they called were strenuously cross-examined, and Puccio got one to admit that there was a chance the second, irreversible coma could have been the result of something other than injected insulin.

Alexandra Isles again testified, reluctantly. She had fled the country to avoid the case, but was required to return. She told the jurors that von Bülow said he'd seen his wife take sleeping pills and drink spiced eggnog, then fall unconscious.

Puccio called nine experts who said Sunny's comas were not consistent with an insulin overdose.

Closing arguments were made on June 5, 1985, von Bülow and Sunny's nineteenth wedding anniversary. Four days later, the jury found von Bülow not guilty.

COMMENTARY: Claus Von Bülow

The conviction, then acquittal at retrial after an appellate reversal, in von Bülow's case, raises serious questions about the thoroughness of his defense in the first instance. If von Bülow was able to successfully challenge the cause of his wife's coma, why didn't all of that happen during the first trial? Why did Alan Dershowitz and his team demonstrate that a coma such as the one suffered by Sunny von Bülow was not consistent with an insulin overdose, when the first jury had been invited to believe—and apparently did believe—just the opposite? The best answer from this distance can only be that defense counsel may have thought they had turned over every rock in the preparation of their case, but indeed had not.

Dr. Robert Bierenbaum

Charged with murdering his wife on July 7, 1985

A prominent cosmetic surgeon fell under intense police scrutiny when his wife disappeared. Police believe he dropped her body in the ocean. After more than fifteen years, and although the body was never recovered, Bierenbaum was charged with murder and successfully prosecuted.

GAIL KATZ-BIERENBAUM

The product of a middle-class Long Island Jewish family, Gail Katz led a troubled life. She dropped out of college and reportedly suffered bouts of depression, took drugs, drank heavily, and once attempted suicide after she broke up with a boyfriend. She never stayed in a romantic relationship long until she met Robert Bierenbaum in 1979, when she was twenty-three. He was working at Mount Sinai Hospital in New York City. She was attracted to him—he was Jewish, had a father who was a doctor, played the guitar, and flew airplanes. They quickly became engaged.

Before the wedding, Gail reportedly told friends that Bierenbaum confessed to accidentally killing his former fiancée's cat, and that she later believed he tried to kill her own cat, which she subsequently took to an animal shelter to keep it safe. She told them Bierenbaum had fits of anger that made her nervous, and they suggested she call off the wedding.

Despite their pleas and warnings, she married Bierenbaum. Friends and relatives said they fought often and loudly. On one occasion, she phoned police and reported that he had tried to strangle her, but she did not press charges.

During the next few years she returned to college, graduated, and started having affairs. She told friends she was going to reveal those affairs to Bierenbaum, and supposedly did so on July 7, 1985.

A MISSING WIFE

On July 8, 1985, Dr. Robert Bierenbaum, forty-four, a cosmetic surgeon from Grand Forks, reported that his wife, Gail Katz-Bierenbaum, twenty-nine, was missing from their Upper East Side apartment.

He informed the police that they'd had an argument the previous day, that she had left, and that she had not yet returned. The police investigated and immediately suspected that Bierenbaum had murdered her, but did not have enough evidence to charge him.

A woman living in the apartment below the Bierenbaums had heard a fight that Sunday morning, and reported that it was followed by a door slamming, hinting that one of the Bierenbaums had stormed out.

Not long after the fight, one of Gail's friends called the apartment, and Bierenbaum answered and said Gail had left.

Later that afternoon, Bierenbaum rented a Cessna at New Jersey's Caldwell Airport for a two-hour flight. When he returned, he went to a birthday party for a nephew, and then went to a friend's house. He reportedly called his apartment a few times, trying to find Gail at home.

Bierenbaum had also contacted several of Gail's friends and relatives on that same day, asking if they'd seen her. He told them about the argument, and that Gail had left the previous day.

The police were forced to treat it as a missing person's case, as there was no body and the woman in the apartment below told them she heard the door slam, as if someone was leaving. Bierenbaum said it was possible that Gail had run to one of the men she'd had an affair with or was trying to find someone to sell her drugs. (He had also told police Gail was still using drugs from time to time, despite his insistence that she quit.)

During the next several years, Bierenbaum would travel, moving from New York to Las Vegas in 1990, then moving to North Dakota before finally returning to New York in 2000, when prosecutors charged him with second-degree murder.

PEOPLE V. DR. ROBERT BIERENBAUM

Twelve years after Bierenbaum had initially filed the missing person report on his wife, district attorneys reopened the case. Investigator Andy Rosenzweig, in the Manhattan District Attorney's Office, wanted to close a few old cases before retiring, and the Bierenbaum case was one of those.

His investigation had revealed that Bierenbaum provided conflicting explanations for his wife's absence. Detectives delved into the case again, taking a closer look at the physical evidence that had been culled from the apartment, and interviewing more than fifty people in ten states, including North Dakota, California, and Nevada. Detectives also talked to psychiatrists who had treated Bierenbaum and his wife, as well as police officers who had been assigned the case.

Following several months of work, the detectives found flight logs that Bierenbaum had reportedly altered. On the day he said his wife was missing, he had flown his rented Cessna for two hours over the Atlantic Ocean. Prosecutors believed he had killed Gail in their New York apartment, wrapped her body and taken it to New Jersey, and dropped it in the Atlantic from the Cessna.

There still was no body, but now there was enough evidence to charge Bierenbaum for murder.

His trial was slated to begin in September 2000.

Although it was conceivable that Gail met a tragic end at the hand of someone else or killed herself, as she'd attempted suicide before, Bierenbaum was targeted. Trying to alter the flight log when he rented the Cessna directed suspicion at him.

THE TRIAL

Prosecutors had to make their case without a corpse.

They stated in their opening argument that they had "no body, no forensics, no murder weapon, no bloody clothes, no finger-prints, no brain matter, no body parts."

Attorneys relied on the testimony of several witnesses and ex-perts and based their case on considerable circumstantial evidence. For example, they showed the jurors a video of police dumping a bag of sand from a plane to illustrate how easily Bierenbaum could have disposed of his wife's body the day he flew the Cessna over the Atlantic Ocean.

On October 25, 2000, the jury convicted Bierenbaum of second-degree murder, and he was sentenced to serve twenty years to life in a New York State prison.

PSYCHIATRISTS' RECORDS ARE KEPT SEALED

The New York statute governing psychotherapist-patient privi-lege allows a court to overrule the privilege in rare circum-stances. However, the "rare circumstances" did not necessarily include cases such as a murder trial, and so prosecutors went to court to get at Bierenbaum's records. Prosecutors were attempt-ing to use the records to bolster their case against him.

The confidentiality matters in the Bierenbaum trial dated back two years prior to his wife's disappearance and included the rec-ords of three psychiatrists who had treated him. In therapy ses-sions, Bierenbaum discussed what he considered serious marital problems. One of the psychiatrists was concerned about violent threats Bierenbaum had made against his wife. The psychiatrist exercised his "Tarasoff duty," which meant he alerted Gail Katz-Bierenbaum that she could be in danger. According to the rec-ords, Bierenbaum had approved of this notification.

Prosecutors had targeted the psychiatrist's 1983 "Tarasoff duty" warning to argue successfully that Bierenbaum and the psychiatrist had waived the doctor-patient confidentiality privilege: because Bierenbaum had consented to have his wife warned, the privilege had been broken.

Prosecutors pushed for the three psychiatrists to turn over all of Bierenbaum's medical records, which could then be admitted into evidence during the murder trial. They further argued that Bierenbaum told others he was in therapy and having marital troubles, conversations that aided in waiving his therapy privilege.

The New York State Psychiatric Association and the American Psychoanalytic Association disagreed with prosecutors, stating that the psychiatrists who treated Bierenbaum could not waive doctor-patient privilege; only the patient—Bierenbaum—could do that. The organizations further stated there was no cause to believe Bierenbaum had waived the privilege.

On September 12, a judge ruled that the points made by the New York State Psychiatric Association and the American Psychoanalytic Association were stronger, and so kept the records out of the hands of prosecutors.

Despite the absence of the psychiatric records, prosecutors got their conviction.

COMMENTARY: Dr. Robert Bierenbaum

Female victims of uxoricide such as the one here—Gail Katz—are often given solid clues that the boyfriends they are planning to marry have a screw loose, often an ominous screw. Dr. Bierenbaum apparently told his betrothed that he "accidentally" killed his former fiancée's cat; Ms. Katz was sufficiently unnerved by this to take her own cat to an animal shelter, in the belief that the good doctor had tried to kill it as well. She insisted on marrying him despite these clear signals of hostile mental fragility, and predictably entered a tumultuous and abusive relationship.

It is truly remarkable that Dr. Bierenbaum's strange proclivities did not manifest themselves in the workplace to the point where his career was in trouble; however, it is generally thought that cosmetic (or "plastic") surgeons are more like artists than people of medical science, and perhaps his own specialty supported a tolerance for unusual behavior.

Gail Katz's decision to have affairs with other men is understandable, if one conjures up an image of what home life with Dr. Bierenbaum must have entailed; her decision either to assuage her own guilt, or to taunt him for being such a bummer of a husband (we will never know) was, to pun a bit, fatally flawed. Confessing infidelity to a spouse sometimes proves to be the correct course of action, but more frequently does not. To make admissions of this sort to a violent person such as Dr. Bierenbaum is foolhardy at best.

Police are always faced with a difficult chore when it comes to proving a murder when there is no corpse to establish the fact of death, and in most cases the cause of death. Nonetheless, convictions when no body has been found are sufficiently numerous to show that victim disappearance is anything but an airtight defense.

Dumping victims at sea most often occurs through the use of a boat of some kind. Throwing them out of airplanes in flight, while a little more risky in the sense that the falling corpse might be seen by someone in a boat (or another airplane, for that matter), can work as well. Assuming that this is what happened to Mrs. Katz-Bierenbaum in 1985, it is unlikely that the feat could be repeated today, thanks to heightened scrutiny of the skies in the vicinity of New York because of 9/11.

Reconstructing as best we can what Bierenbaum did with his wife's body, let's assume that he went to Caldwell-Wright in New Jersey and rented a Cessna airplane, which we know to be the case. Assume further that it was a single-engine Cessna; its likely cruise speed in 1985 was no more than 150 miles per hour. If it headed straight for the Atlantic Shore, staying clear of the Newark International Airport control area, it could have been over water within twenty minutes of taking off, despite the slower speed associated with climbing.

However, not far east of the shoreline is an imaginary line which marks the western edge of the Air Defense Identification Zone (ADIZ), and aircraft which cross that line are apt to be (even in 1985) very closely scrutinized. Indeed, when I carelessly drifted into the ADIZ off the coast of

Florida in my Lear Jet in the seventies, an air traffic controller warned me to get back where I belonged or I might be blasted out of the sky by a Sidewinder surface-to-air missile as a threat to the United States.

If he needed to get rid of a corpse and wanted to be far enough offshore to avoid being observed by the many sportfishing boats that venture eighty and ninety miles out in the summertime to fish the "canyons" off New Jersey, he would have needed to stay low (to avoid radar detection by air traffic control and the many military installations that watch the skies over the northeastern shore) and go long—perhaps a hundred miles out. This was well within the capability of the aircraft, allowing him to return it to the airport within the two hours for which it appears to have been rented.

Something must have been amiss if Bierenbaum saw fit to alter his flight logs for the day of his wife's disappearance, as prosecutors proved he did. It is probable that after five or ten years, he thought the risk of prosecution was behind him, and that he had nothing to fear from law enforcement. Murderers too often forget that there is no statute of limitations for murder, or that some very "cold" cases have been reopened, revived, and successfully prosecuted.

Steven Sherer

Charged with murdering his wife on September 30, 1990

Twenty-six-year-old Jami Sherer disappeared September 30, 1990, from her Redmond, Washington, home. The mother of a two-year-old boy and a Microsoft secretary who was well liked by her co-workers, she was declared dead in 1997. Her body has never been found.

On and off for a decade, Redmond police detectives investigated Jami's disappearance, interviewing hundreds of people and searching futilely for her body. Sherer remained their chief suspect, but they lacked enough circumstantial evidence to charge him until January 2000.

JAMI AND STEVEN SHERER

The couple met in 1986. At the time, Sherer had a criminal record for abusing previous girlfriends and causing the hospitalization of one. He was known to threaten and harass the women he dated, and a restraining order was in place from one of them. Despite this record, Jami became romantically involved with him.

She was small, five foot one, and weighed a little less than one hundred pounds. Per his request, she had dyed her hair blond and received breast implants.

Although Jami's friends discouraged her from marrying

Sherer, she went ahead with the plans and they were wed in 1987. A son was born the following year.

Sherer was convicted of assaulting a police officer in 1987 while drunk. He started treatment for alcoholism but continued to have problems with the law. He had been convicted for a series of traffic violations and thefts, and was labeled a habitual offender.

Reportedly, he also pushed Jami into group sexual gatherings. She started seeing one of his friends who'd also been involved in those gatherings, shortly before she disappeared.

On September 29, the day before she vanished, she drove to her parents' house with her son, Chris, and told them she was going to leave Sherer the following day. She planned to move back into her parents' house until she could figure out her next step.

SEPTEMBER 30, 1990

Judy Hagel told police that her daughter had agreed to meet Sherer that morning. He had called his wife at the Hagel house the previous night and begged to meet with her one last time. Jami left Chris with her parents and drove to the meeting spot, where Sherer grabbed her purse and fled.

Jami called her mother at 8:30 A.M. and said Sherer was probably heading to the house, that she would go there to get her purse back. She called her parents again shortly before noon, saying she was with Sherer and that she would be coming back to their house after she gathered up a few things and stopped for lunch at Taco Time, one of her favorite fast-food restaurants.

Jami was not seen or heard from after that call.

Sherer called the Hagels twice in the early afternoon, looking for Jami, and then again at 6:00 P.M. Police reported that around this time Sherer started telling his relatives that Jami was missing.

Sherer went to the Hagel house and picked up his son. He returned later, saying he was too upset to stay at his house, and the Hagels invited him to spend that night and other nights on and off during the following week.

THE POLICE INVESTIGATION

Sherer was the suspect from the beginning, but he repeatedly denied any involvement in his wife's disappearance.

Police found Jami's car, a 1980 Mazda, in a church parking lot in Shoreline, Washington. A suitcase containing some clothes, but no underwear, was in the car. The seat had been pushed far back, as if a tall person had been driving it. Jami, at shorter than average height, would not have been able to reach the pedals.

In the weeks following her disappearance, Sherer cashed out Jami's Microsoft assets.

Jami's friends reported to police that Sherer started acting strangely. He started going to bars and tied her undergarments around his arm because he claimed they made him feel closer to Jami.

Police looked into several allegations.

Sherer's sister told police there was a red spot on the carpet in the house. Police discovered that the carpet had been professionally cleaned and a new piece of carpet had been installed.

One friend of the couple's said he spotted a shovel in Sherer's truck the day after Jami disappeared. He said he'd not seen a shovel in the truck before.

There was no evidence that Jami was alive. Friends and relatives said she lived for her son, and police were certain she would have contacted him.

She hadn't made any effort to access her finances, either.

SHERER'S TRIAL BEGINS

Prosecutors painted Sherer as an abusive husband who regularly threatened his wife. He was documented as seeing other women after his wife had been missing only two weeks. Prosecutors pointed out that he was quick to cash in her Microsoft stock options and took money for her accrued vacation time.

Sherer was thirty-eight at the time of this trial, and was ten years older than when he first reported Jami missing.

Marilyn Brenneman, senior deputy prosecutor on the case, admitted at the beginning of the murder trial that the evidence against Sherer was entirely circumstantial. The body of his wife was never found. No murder weapon was found. And there were no witnesses to a crime.

In her opening statement, Brenneman said: "She vanished without a trace. She left behind a loving family. She left behind her friends. She left behind all her worldly possessions. And she left behind her most precious possession of all, her two-year-old son."

Prosecutors presented to the jurors a Halloween card that Sherer had sent to his son. The boy was living with Jami's mother. In the card, Sherer wrote: "Hope you will understand. Be strong. You have your mother inside you, and that is a lot. Fight the bad urges my blood brings you! Fight hard—I am watching and will help if at all possible. Never be violent. Don't ever hurt anyone."

Peter Mair, Sherer's attorney, told the jury that prosecutors indeed had little hard evidence, and that witnesses had inconsistent memories—their tales had changed several times during the past decade.

Mair conceded that the Sherers had a sometimes-fiery marriage, and that his client had once pulled out a clump of his wife's hair during an argument. But an argument like that is a big jump to proving murder, he pointed out.

There is no concrete evidence that Jami is dead, although that is likely the case, Mair said. He told the jurors, "At the end of this case, we'll be where we were in 1990—with an unsolved mystery, as unpleasant as it is."

Sherer's criminal record included convictions for attacking a police officer, making threatening calls to an investigator looking into Jami's disappearance, and second-degree assault for attacking a former girlfriend.

In addition, police records showed nine domestic violence complaints against Sherer regarding Jami and previous girlfriends.

JAMI'S MOTHER TESTIFIES

Judy Hagel testified that she had repeatedly urged her daughter to leave Sherer. Hagel said she was certain that Sherer physically abused her daughter and that he was aggressively possessive.

Sherer would call Jami frequently at work, sometimes every fifteen minutes, Hagel said, adding he would call Jami at relatives' homes to check on her. She told the jurors: "We couldn't even go out shopping without him calling."

Hagel reported that on the day that Jami disappeared, she had planned to leave her husband. Her daughter had allegedly told Sherer she wanted a divorce.

Sherer's behavior was stranger than usual after Jami disappeared, Hagel continued. He seemed calm, which didn't make sense given that his wife was missing, and he did not participate in posting missing persons fliers. Hagel said that she wasn't aware that he went out with any of the groups searching for Jami.

Hagel recalled that, during the marriage, there were often bruises on Jami's face and arms. Her daughter claimed that she fell or banged into things; however, Hagel said she thought Sherer beat her. When Mair cross-examined her, she admitted that Jami had never mentioned a beating.

OTHER WITNESSES FOR THE PROSECUTION

Jami's friend Shannon Baker told the jury that Sherer was a violent man, and that Jami had told her about his past relationships in which he was also abusive. She said her friend wasn't thinking right to stay with Sherer, adding that she knew Jami was unhappy and felt trapped in the marriage.

MAKING THE CASE AGAINST SHERER

Court documents and testimony from the trial detailed the Sherers' relationship, and included reports that friends and relatives noticed a change in Jami after the marriage in 1987. Jami's mother said her daughter had lost weight because Sherer wanted her to be overly thin, and he did not let her eat M&Ms, her favorite candy, because he was afraid she would gain weight.

Friends reported that Sherer had forced Jami into three-way sexual encounters, that he often struck her, and that on several occasions bruises were visible on her face. Once, he pushed Jami in front of a friend and threatened to kill her. The witness called the police, and Sherer stabbed himself in the stomach and fled. Jami said she was going to work things out with her husband, declined to press charges, and then declined help in leaving him.

During a later fight, Sherer hit Jami over the head with a vase and pulled out a piece of her scalp when he grabbed her hair. He reportedly dragged her across the floor by her hair, and pulled the phone cord out of the wall when she tried to call police. Later she did call police, and an officer saw the piece of scalp attached to a clump of hair. Jami spent that night at her parents' house, but she later returned to Sherer after he sent her flowers.

Jami often had trouble with Sherer. One day, he allegedly smashed all of the picture frames filled with photographs from their wedding.

Sherer would call Jami often, and would call people she had been with wanting to know what they did together. He appeared at Microsoft one day, following her. On another occasion at the company, he screamed at her and was escorted out by security. He sent her flowers on more than one occasion to apologize, witnesses said.

DRUGS AND SEX

The couple used cocaine, sometimes with one of Sherer's friends, Toby Parker. Sherer reportedly pressed Jami into having sex with Parker while he watched. Jami was believed to have spent the night before her disappearance in a hotel with Parker.

THE ISSUE OF DOMESTIC VIOLENCE

Karil Klingbeil, an expert on domestic violence, testified that it was not unusual for someone like Jami to stay in an abusive relationship so long. Klingbeil testified that victims of domestic violence tend not to see a way out of their abusive relationship. They are ruled by fear and terror, and sometimes they believe they can work out the relationship. Some victims do not realize how serious and dangerous a situation they are in, he said.

JAMI'S LAST DAYS

Investigators pieced together the last three days Jami was seen alive.

SEPTEMBER 28. Jami told a friend it was time she left Sherer, and that she was going to tell him during the upcoming weekend.

SEPTEMBER 29. Sherer reported that he could not find Jami. He had said he knew that she was with Parker. Friends said that Sherer had threatened to kill Jami if he caught her cheating on him.

SEPTEMBER 30. Jami admitted to Sherer early in the morning that she spent the night at the Crest Motel, but she did not admit to being with Parker. After an argument, Jami went to her parents' house and said she wanted to leave Sherer and move in with them. She admitted to her mother that she spent the previous night with Parker.

Jami reportedly called Sherer and told him that she wanted a divorce, and he talked her into meeting with him at a nearby club. There, he grabbed Jami's purse and fled with it. She went to their house to get the purse and to pack clothes for herself and Chris. Sherer wasn't there, but he arrived later and they argued again.

Shortly before noon, Jami called her mother and said she was on her way, but would first stop to get some lunch. She never arrived and, at 12:15 P.M. Sherer called the Hagel house, looking for Jami. He called again fifteen minutes later, and did not call again until 6:00 P.M. Jami's mother told police she thought her daughter was with Sherer, since he had stopped calling and since Jami had not arrived.

At 2:00 P.M. that day Sherer drove to his mother's in Mill Creek. She and her husband were out of the country, and Sherer later told police he was there to get some sleep. None of the neighbors reported seeing Sherer's car.

Phone records show that at 6:20 P.M., Sherer called his sister and announced that Jami had disappeared. Then he called the Hagels again and asked for Jami. Shortly thereafter, Sherer came to pick up Chris. He called again after 9:00 P.M. and asked if he could come back, as he couldn't stay at the house; it upset him too much. Sherer and Chris spent the night with the Hagels, and stayed with them off and on the rest of the week.

THE SEARCH FOR JAMI

On October 1, Sherer returned home, telling the Hagels that Jami might be there. Jami's mother called Parker and Microsoft, and, still unable to find Jami, she called the police and reported her daughter missing. She went with Sherer to the police department to file a missing persons report.

Police searched the Sherer's house and noted clothes and suitcases on the bed. Sherer told police that Jami had taken a toothbrush and a duffel bag with some clothes in it. Relatives and friends organized search parties, and Microsoft employees printed hundreds of missing person fliers. Sherer was given fliers to post, but was seen handing out only one. Nearly a year later, police found fliers folded in the glove box of Sherer's Blazer.

LOOKING CLOSELY AT SHERER

Sherer avoided talking to police and did not return their phone calls; however, on October 8, he allowed police to walk through his house. They did not move anything.

One day later, Sherer had his carpets professionally cleaned.

On October 10, he told police that he was going to miss Jami; however at a bar later that day, patrons reported that he was happy, and one of them claimed Sherer said: "The bitch is gone."

Less than a month after Jami's disappearance, Sherer started dating. He allegedly told one woman that his wife had died in a car accident. He told another that Jami was his ex-wife and that another man had stolen her away.

Friends reported that Sherer said the police were idiots and that they could not prove he was involved in Jami's disappearance. He repeatedly said he did not miss Jami and that he knew she was going to leave him anyway.

In 1993, Sherer moved to Arizona and stayed at his mother's

condominium. He told his employer there that his wife had been killed in a car accident. He told the landlord that he was divorced.

He moved back to Washington in 1998 and surrendered to police on several warrants for drunk driving. He was sentenced to eight months in the King County Jail.

JAMI DECLARED DEAD

On May 13, 1997, Jami was officially declared dead. "Probably violence of unknown origin," was listed as the cause.

Police had used cadaver dogs and radar, and had searched for her remains in several locations, including around the Sherer house, and around the house belonging to Sherer's mother.

THE INVESTIGATION CONTINUED

Eight years after her disappearance, in 1998, police again searched the Sherer house, removing the carpet and finding no evidence of blood. Records showed that Sherer had purchased a piece of carpet a few months after Jami vanished. This piece of carpet, police determined, had been installed by an amateur, and the concrete under it had been painted with primer, suggesting the primer was covering something up. That revelation led to Sherer's arrest.

THE DEFENSE'S APPROACH

During the trial, the defense tried to shatter the prosecution's theory that Sherer murdered Jami because he was going to lose her and therefore lose control of her. The defense suggested that Sherer did not abuse her, as she did not report the abuse and refused to testify against him. Too, Sherer had alleged that Parker, his former friend who was involved with Jami, had killed her.

Christopher Moon was one of the defense's witnesses, called because he was certain he'd seen Jami in a card room three days after she had reportedly disappeared. Moon said it looked like Jami was waiting for someone.

The defense also called a businessman who said Sherer asked

if he could put posters in his window about his missing wife, proof that Sherer had helped in efforts to find Jami.

Defense attorney Peter Mair read a suicide note Sherer had written to show further proof that his client was despondent over his missing wife. Prosecutors argued that Sherer had only staged a suicide by carbon monoxide poisoning, and had not intended to go through with it.

The suicide note read:

I am sorry everyone, but Jami is my life. She made me a better person and kept me under control. But I kept hurting her with games I would play.

I can't live without her. I really need her and I have lost her one way or another. Maybe now, she won't be afraid to come home. I have been a real bad person in the past and she has changed me. But I had ruined what we had!

Jami honey, just remember I really do love you and Chris, and Chris when you can read and understand this, please understand that I need your Mom real bad and if she won't come back, I won't be able to handle that, much less your life."

The note ended with instructions that Sherer's father's ring should go to Chris when he is married.

SHERER'S SENTENCING

Sherer was convicted of first-degree murder, one of the few times in the state's history when a conviction was won without a body.

The jury deliberated five days before finding him guilty. After the verdict was announced, Sherer turned to Jami's family and told them that, when his wife resurfaces, "You can all rot in hell."

He was sentenced to sixty years in prison and sent to the state penitentiary at Walla Walla.

Factors that played into Sherer's lengthy sentence included his prior convictions, his history of domestic violence, and his apparent lack of remorse.

SHERER'S FAILED APPEAL

Sherer filed an appeal after his conviction, contending that the evidence presented against him was insufficient to support the claim of premeditated first-degree murder.

The Court of Appeals ruled that there was overwhelming evidence that Sherer had caused his wife's death. Witnesses testified that Sherer controlled Jami and had threatened to kill her if she cheated on him. He had assaulted her in the past, including pulling out a piece of her scalp.

Sherer had his Blazer professionally cleaned, as well as the carpets in his house. He purchased carpeting to replace a section—both attempts at covering up evidence of a crime.

The court cited that he was uncooperative with police, and reports surfaced that he alternately told other women that his wife had been killed in a car accident or had divorced him. Before she was officially declared dead, he gave away her clothes. The court noted that bloodhounds traced Sherer's scent leading away from Jami's car that had been found abandoned in a church parking lot.

Sherer also claimed that the jury should not have heard witness testimony about statements he made that were self-incriminating, and it should not have heard reports of his history of violence against Jami. He had tried to exclude statements he made to others after Jami's disappearance, but the trial court had denied that motion. The appeals court ruled that the trial court had properly admitted Sherer's statements to others.

Sherer said the court allowed witnesses to testify that they saw him assault Jami, and that this evidence should have been excluded. He cited a 1995 case, *State v. Powell*, which said: "Evidence of other crimes, wrongs, or acts is presumptively inadmissible to prove character and show action in conformity therewith."

However, such evidence could be used to prove motive, which the court decided those witnesses did. The court believed that Sherer's assaults against his wife demonstrated hostility.

The court turned down Sherer's appeal.

SHERER CHARGED IN ARSON PLOT

In the spring of 2003, Sherer allegedly asked a cellmate to set fire to a house in Bellevue, Washington, where Jami's mother lived. Sherer reportedly offered $17,000 in jewelry for the arson. Sherer was still in jail at the time, in Walla Walla's Washington State Penitentiary serving his sixty-year sentence for murdering his wife. The motive in the fire was apparently revenge for Hagel's testimony at his murder trial.

Police said they received a tip about Sherer's arson plans, and would not disclose their source; however, police said it was credible enough to warrant their listening in on Sherer's telephone calls from jail and putting a listening device in his cell.

In the penitentiary, Sherer's cellmate was a young man who had nearly completed his sentence for an attempted kidnapping charge. Sherer reportedly told his cellmate that he wanted the people in the house killed; however, he did not tell the cellmate who those individuals were.

When Sherer's cellmate was released in February 2002 and went to a bus station in Walla Walla, police showed up and searched him, finding a small book with Judy Hagel's address in it, along with driving instructions. The cellmate admitted that he had agreed to burn down the house in exchange for jewelry. He cooperated with police rather than returning to jail, and disclosed the entire plan, saying that he had to show printed proof that he'd burned down the house.

The cellmate also revealed that Sherer wanted him to kill Marilyn Brenneman, the King County senior deputy prosecutor, and her four children. He said a previous cellmate had been offered the job but did not follow through.

The Bellevue Fire Department staged a fire, generating smoke to make it look like the Hagel house was burning. The fire department enlisted the help of the sheriff's department and a local newspaper, the *Eastside Journal*, which reported that the house "might have been targeted."

The controversial *Journal* article was mailed to Sherer. In return, Sherer mailed directions to his mother's old house to the cellmate, and wrote that he would find $17,000 worth of jewelry buried in a crawl space. Police searched the property but found no jewelry or cash.

During the arson trial, prosecutors played recordings of phone conversations between Sherer and his former cellmate. In one of the conversations, Sherer described where the jewelry was hidden that would be payment for burning the house.

The jury deliberated less than two hours before finding Sherer guilty of solicitation to commit arson. He had waived his right to be present for the reading of the verdict. It was Sherer's third conviction under Washington's persistent offender law, the other two convictions being for the murder of his wife and a felony assault charge in 1987. As a result, Sherer will spend the rest of his life in prison.

Inmates at the penitentiary had reported that Sherer repeatedly told them he strangled his wife because she was going to leave him, and that he hid her remains.

COMMENTARY: Steven Sherer

The Sherer case presents echoes of that of the case of its predecessor, Dr. Bierenbaum. Once again, there is no corpse. And once again, ten years pass from the date of the victim's disappearance until the date the defendant is charged. However, in this case there was no airplane used to explain the missing body. After ten years, what tripped Steven Sherer up? With his past record of violence and abuse toward women, he was an excellent candidate as a murder suspect.

Sherer was also sexually adventuresome. He induced his wife to engage in threesome sexual adventures and, like so many others, she wound up pairing off secretly with one of the players. The fact that her husband was a brute greatly heightened the likelihood that she would take up with one of her group-sex lovers.

When a wife or a female lover suddenly disappears, police usually study very carefully the conduct of the husband or boyfriend for evidence that he knows that the missing person will not return. Sherer quickly provided such evidence by cashing in his wife's Microsoft-related assets, including the vacation time she had accumulated. He certainly didn't much help the case against himself by wearing her undergarments tied to his arm. Then, too, a sincerely grieving or perplexed husband is unlikely to start frolicking with other women within two weeks of his wife's alleged disappearance. Carrying a shovel in the back of his truck for others to see—when he normally did not use one—was pretty stupid as well.

At the jury trial, his past record for attacking a policeman and a former girlfriend, and for threatening an investigator who was looking for his missing wife, no doubt were given great weight. Corpse or not, there was more than ample evidence to convict.

But this was not just someone dangerous principally to women who got close to him. Steven Sherer was (and presumably is) an extremely dangerous creature who is consumed by the urge to seek revenge against any and all he perceives to be "against him." His efforts to burn down the home of his mother-in-law for testifying for the state at his trial and trying to have the prosecutor murdered for convicting him disclose a personality infused with mayhem.

It is a sad fact that from time to time we get specimens like Steven Sherer in our custody and control, and yet almost never try to find out what made or makes them tick. If Sherer's victims and intended victims were the subject of an aircraft disaster, our government would spend whatever it took to reconstruct and explain the accident, and try to learn how to avoid similar accidents in the future.

Here is a relatively young man who was a walking time bomb—doubtless from his adolescence, and perhaps before. Our lack of interest in studying the Sherers of this world—once we have identified and apprehended them—denies us the criteria that might enable us to cause them to be civilly restrained or committed before they destroy other innocent human beings. This state of determined ignorance on our part seems to be, as of this writing, unrelenting.

O. J. Simpson

Charged with murdering his ex-wife on July 12, 1994

Called the "Trial of the Century," more than a decade later it continues to evoke recollections of a white Bronco fleeing on a Los Angeles freeway, the "Dream Team" of defense attorneys, a racial clash, and an ill-fitting bloody glove.

The coverage evolved into a cross between a reality show and a legal soap opera, where tales of sex, drugs, celebrity, and violence played out in the courtroom and on televisions across the country. All the while, the media spotlight shown brightly on football legend O. J. Simpson, accused of brutally murdering his ex-wife, Nicole Brown Simpson, and her friend Ronald Goldman.

The case was tried in downtown L.A., not in Santa Monica, the affluent neighborhood where the murders occurred. Prosecutors cited an earthquake-damaged building as one of the reasons for the change in location.

THE MURDERS

The saga began when the bodies of Ronald Goldman and Nicole Brown Simpson were found outside her residence by a neighbor walking his dog. The dog pulled him to the scene, the neighbor would later tell the jury.

He testified: "I saw a lady lying down, full of blood. I could see the person was blond, I could see her arm. There was a lot of blood."

Nicole's neck was so badly slashed, she was nearly decapitated. Blood spots led to the condominium's master bedroom.

When police went to O. J. Simpson's home to notify him of the deaths, they discovered more blood there.

THE TIME LINE

JUNE 12. Ronald Goldman and Nicole Brown Simpson were murdered. Shortly before midnight, O. J. Simpson flew to Chicago for a promotional engagement.

JUNE 13. The bodies were discovered shortly after midnight. O. J. checked into a hotel near Chicago's O'Hare airport about four hours later. He checked out shortly after that when L.A. police contacted him about the deaths. Simpson arrived at his home before noon, and he was questioned for three hours by police.

JUNE 15. Police confirmed a match of the bloodstains found at the crime scene and at Simpson's home. His Bronco was broken into while in police custody.

JUNE 16. Simpson attended the funeral for his ex-wife.

JUNE 17. Simpson was charged with two counts of murder with special circumstances. In the span of a few days, O. J. Simpson's image as a movie star, gridiron superstar, and sports announcer tarnished into that of an accused killer.

THE FAMOUS SLOW-SPEED PURSUIT

His attorneys convinced the L.A. Police Department that Simpson would turn himself in at 11:00 A.M. on June 17. More than a thousand reporters waited for Simpson to arrive; he was expected to give a statement after his booking. But when he didn't appear by 2:00 P.M., police issued an all-points bulletin. A friend of Simpson's, Robert Kardashian, read a letter to the media. The letter, written by Simpson, said: "First everyone understand I had nothing to do with Nicole's murder. . . . Don't feel sorry for me. I've had a great life."

At 6:45 P.M., a sheriff's patrol car spotted Simpson's Bronco traveling north on Interstate 405. When the deputy approached, the driver—Al Cowlings—called out that Simpson had a gun to his head. The deputy backed off and the famous slow-speed chase began. People crowded overpasses along the freeway, some displaying signs that encouraged Simpson to keep running. A KCBS news helicopter had exclusive coverage of the chase for some time, but it was eventually joined by nearly a dozen more helicopters from news agencies around the country. Estimates claimed that more than 90 million people watched at least some of the chase. Radio stations provided live reports, and one station coaxed USC football coach John McKay to go on the air. McKay complied and urged Simpson to turn himself in.

In the end, at 8:00 P.M., Cowlings drove back to Simpson's house, 360 North Rockingham Avenue. Simpson did not leave the Bronco until forty-five minutes later, sparking fears of a suicide or a shoot-out. When Simpson finally surrendered, police confiscated from the Bronco $8,000 in cash, a change of clothes, a loaded .357 Magnum, a passport, family pictures, and a fake goatee and mustache.

ORENTHAL JAMES "O. J." SIMPSON
His Career

O. J. Simpson was born in San Francisco on July 9, 1947. Nicknamed "the Juice" during his football years, he was named to the Football Hall of Fame in Canton, Ohio, in 1985. Simpson played for the Galileo Lions at Galileo High School in San Francisco. He continued to play football during junior college at the City College of San Francisco, but transferred to the University of Southern California. There, he won the Maxwell Award and the Heisman trophy.

Simpson, considered to be one of the best running backs to have ever played the game, racked up so many yards in his years at the University of Southern California that he was the first player selected in the 1969 draft by the Buffalo Bills. He played for the Bills from 1969 to 1977, and then for the San Francisco 49ers in 1978 and 1979. He appeared in six Pro Bowls—1969, 1972, 1973, 1974, 1975, and 1976.

In 1973, he became the first player to pass the 2,000-yard running mark and was named the league's MVP. He totaled more than 11,000 yards and ran for 200 yards in a half-dozen games. He earned All-Pro honors five times.

Simpson enjoyed a successful television and film career after he retired from football. He appeared in the television mini-series *Roots* and once hosted an episode of *Saturday Night Live*. His movies included *The Klansman* and *The Towering Inferno* in 1974; *The Cassandra Crossing* in 1976; *Capricorn One* in 1978; and the Naked Gun trilogy—*From the Files of the Police Squad!* in 1988, *The Smell* of *Fear* in 1991, and *The Final Insult* in 1994. He was also known for his television commercials for the Hertz car rental company. In addition, Simpson worked as a sports commentator for *Monday Night Football*.

Family

Simpson's first marriage, to Marguerite Whitley, resulted in three children: Arnelle, born in December 1968; Jason, born in April 1970; and Aaren, born in September 1977. Aaren died nearly a month before her second birthday, in the family's swimming pool. That year, O. J. and Marguerite divorced.

His second marriage, to Nicole Brown, was in February 1985. Sydney Brooke was born in October of that year, and Justin Ryan was born in August 1988. Nicole and O. J. divorced in 1992.

NICOLE BROWN SIMPSON

Nicole was born in 1959 in West Germany. Shortly thereafter, she and her family—with her younger sisters, Dominique and Tanya, and her older sister, Denise—moved to Dana Point, California. She was elected the Dana Point High School homecoming queen. She worked as a waitress in the Daisy, a Beverly Hills nightclub, where she met Simpson. She was eighteen and he was thirty, and they began living together a year later. When she divorced him in 1992, she won a cash settlement of $433,000 and $10,000 a month in child support.

There was speculation during the trial that her relationship with Ronald Goldman was more than simply friends. They exercised and attended dance clubs together, and often met for coffee and meals.

RONALD LYLE GOLDMAN

Born in 1968, Ronald Goldman grew up in the Chicago suburbs before his family moved to the L.A. area in the late 1980s. He was a part-time model and an aspiring actor who worked as a waiter at Mezzaluna, a restaurant in L.A. The day of the murders, Nicole, who had been at the restaurant, called him and said she had left her mother's glasses at one of the tables. The glasses were found outside, and Goldman said he would bring them over after work. Police believe Goldman arrived close to the time Nicole was murdered and might have tried to protect her.

THE TRIAL OF THE CENTURY

Simpson pleaded not guilty to the murders at his arraignment on June 20. A grand jury that had been called to determine whether to indict on the charges was dismissed because of excessive media coverage. Then, following a weeklong hearing, a superior court judge determined there was ample evidence to try Simpson for the double murder.

On July 22, at Simpson's second court appearance, he pleaded "absolutely, one hundred percent not guilty."

The trial convened January 29, 1995, and lasted eight months. There were 133 days of televised testimony, and 150 witnesses. The initial makeup of the jury was eight blacks, one white, one Hispanic, and two people of mixed race; eight women, four men.

THE DISTRICT ATTORNEYS

Deputy District Attorney Christopher Darden spoke first for the prosecution. He called Simpson a jealous batterer, a murderer, and "an extremely controlling and possessive man." He told the jury in opening statements: "He killed her out of jealousy. He killed her because he couldn't have her." Then he discussed seven years of physical and emotional abuse Nicole suffered before being murdered.

Deputy District Attorney Marcia Clark discussed the evidence, including the blood leading from Nicole's condominium to Simpson's home. "That trail of blood . . . is devastating proof of his guilt," she told the jury. Clark argued that Simpson, in a fit of jealousy, killed Nicole and her friend Ronald Goldman. Clark played a 911 call Nicole made in 1989, fearing that Simpson was going to hurt her.

In the trial's second week, Darden told the jury that Nicole feared for her life and left evidence of that in a safe-deposit box. Those items included her will, letters from Simpson, and Polaroid pictures of her bruised and battered face from the 1989 incident.

The prosecution showcased dozens of experts who testified on DNA evidence, fingerprinting, and shoe-print analysis that they contended placed Simpson at the scene of the crime.

Prosecutors were confident that they had presented a solid case and expected to gain a conviction. In polls, the majority of whites agreed with them. However, in those same polls many African Americans believed that Simpson had not committed the murders. The split was indicative of the racial tensions that grew across the country throughout the proceedings.

THE DREAM TEAM

Simpson spent $4 million on high-profile attorneys, including Robert Shapiro, Johnnie Cochran, and F. Lee Bailey. Cochran's opening remarks to the jury centered on the prosecution's "rush to judgment." "This case is about a rush to judgment, an obsession to win at any costs."

He maintained that the police ignored at least two witnesses who could clear Simpson, one of them a woman who said she saw four men walking near Nicole's home on the night of the murder. The other claimed to have spotted Simpson's Bronco at his home that night.

In the second week of the trial, Cochran resumed his opening statement, telling the jury that the prosecution's evidence was "contaminated, compromised, and ultimately corrupted." He told the jurors that Simpson was working on his golf swing about the same time prosecutors claim the murders took place. Cochran proposed a time line that made it impossible for Simpson to have committed the killings. And he countered that the trail of blood prosecutors claimed implicated his client was the result of police mishandling a vial of Simpson's blood.

The defense team further argued that their client was the victim of police fraud and contaminated DNA evidence. They contended that LAPD detective Mark Fuhrman planted evidence at the crime scene. (In the second month of the trial, Fuhrman denied on the stand that he was a racist and said he had never used "nigger" to describe black people, but the defense later presented tapes of him using the word, and these infamous tapes served as a cornerstone in the case to discredit Fuhrman and to help acquit Simpson.)

In June 1995, Darden asked Simpson to put on a leather glove. The notorious bloody glove was found at the murder scene, but it was too tight for Simpson's hand.

This caused Johnnie Cochran to speak the famous line: "If it doesn't fit, you must acquit."

Prosecutors tried to explain that the glove shrank when the blood dried, but the damage to their case had been done.

HIGHLIGHTS FROM EARLY IN THE TRIAL

FEBRUARY 3. Nicole's sister Denise Brown told the jurors that once when Simpson was drunk in a crowded bar he grabbed Nicole's crotch and said, "This belongs to me." She said that, on another day, Simspon threw Nicole against a wall.

FEBRUARY 7. Prosecutors worked to establish the time of the murders, estimating it at 10:15 P.M., based on when Ronald Goldman would arrive after work and when a dog was heard barking. The defense maintained that given the time frame, Simpson could not have committed the murders, disposed of evidence, and returned home to catch a limousine at 11:00 P.M. for his ride to the airport.

FEBRUARY 9. The first police officer arriving at the scene described the bloody shoe prints, a knit cap, a glove, an envelope, and other evidence near the bodies. He reported seeing Nicole's body first and that the door was open. He said he entered the house to look for other victims or a suspect. He found the children sleeping, a tub filled with water, and candles burning.

FEBRUARY 12. The jury toured the murder scene and Simpson's mansion two miles away.

FEBRUARY 15. Prosecutors revealed that Simpson's blood was discovered on a gate near the bodies. Police testified that Simpson was not initially a suspect.

FEBRUARY 16. Police testified that Simpson was "very upset" when notified of his ex-wife's death.

FEBRUARY 21. Detectives testified they believed Nicole was killed first, as there was no blood on the bottoms of her bare feet, and so she didn't walk through blood. The prosecution believed Nicole was the target and Ronald Goldman was murdered when he came upon the scene.

FEBRUARY 27. Rosa Lopez, a maid who lived at the estate next to Simpson's home, told the jury she saw Simpson's Bronco parked outside his home at the time prosecutors contended the murders took place.

MARCH 2 AND 3. Prosecutors cross-examined Lopez and pointed out inconsistencies in her previous testimony.

MARCH 6. A detective testified that the police *never* considered anyone other than Simpson as a suspect in the murders. One detective stated they only "superficially" looked at a drug angle as cause for the double murders.

MARCH 10. Prosecutors introduced a shovel, a towel, and a large, heavy-duty plastic bag that were found in Simpson's Bronco.

MARCH 13. Defense attorney F. Lee Bailey portrayed Fuhrman as a racist cop who planted a bloody glove on Simpson's property to advance his career. Bailey told Judge Lance Ito during a hearing: Fuhrman "is very definitely a suspect" in such misconduct.

"And that's what we intend to show with circumstantial evidence far stronger than the people will ever offer against O. J. Simpson for the murders."

MARCH 14. Judge Ito ruled that the defense could introduce new allegations that Fuhrman once called a black marine a "nigger."

MARCH 16. Fuhrman ended his fifth day on the witness stand. Other police officers told the jury that Fuhrman never had an opportunity to take a glove from the murder scene and plant it behind Simpson's home.

MARCH 17. Detective Philip Vannatter described eight blood drops at Simpson's home between the Bronco and the main entrance. Vannatter said he also found two more drops in the foyer.

LATER HIGHLIGHTS

JUNE 6. The jury saw the autopsy photographs and heard detailed testimony about the murders. L.A. County Medical Examiner Dr. Lakshmanan Sathyavagiswaran testified that the photos helped prove the theory that Nicole Simpson was bleeding to death while the killer pulled back her head by the hair and slit her throat. He said there were more than two dozen stab wounds on the victims. Sathyavagiswaran later admitted that the doctor who performed the autopsies made as many as thirty errors.

JULY 27. Defense attorneys supported their theory that police officers tried to frame Simpson for the murders. A blood spatter expert testified that stains on socks found in Simpson's bedroom looked like they were applied to the fabric, and that some of the blood had seeped through. He said this could not have happened if Simpson were wearing the socks at the time.

AUGUST 31. Judge Ito ruled that the jury could hear only two of more than forty tape recordings in which Fuhrman referred to blacks as "niggers."

SEPTEMBER 26. District Attorney Clark began her closing arguments. She admitted to the jury that Fuhrman was a racist and a liar. She said: "It would be a tragedy if, with such overwhelming evidence, you find the defendant not guilty because of the racist attitudes of one officer." Her argument lasted five hours. Darden argued for only a little more than an hour and concentrated on Simpson's history of abusing his wife to prove motive.

SEPTEMBER 27. "If it doesn't fit, you must acquit," Cochran repeated in his closing arguments. He attacked the prosecution's time line and the police investigators' probe. Cochran's main targets were detectives Fuhrman and Vannatter, as he contended that they had tried to frame Simpson.

SEPTEMBER 28. The defense made its final arguments. Cochran told the jury that if Simpson went free, the jurors would be making themselves custodians of the Constitution and saviors of the Los Angeles Police Department.

SEPTEMBER 29. The case went to the jury after prosecutors concluded their final remarks emphasizing the brutal nature of the murders. Clark played a tape of one of Nicole's 911 calls, from 1993, in which she pleaded for police help: "He's back. He's O. J. Simpson. I think you know his record." Pictures of Nicole were flashed before the jury, including one with her face battered, one with a swollen arm, and the one of her murder. Clark told the jury: "I don't have to say anything else. Ladies and gentlemen, on behalf of the people of the state of California, because we have proven beyond a reasonable doubt, far beyond a reasonable doubt, that the defendant committed these murders, we ask you to find the defendant guilty of murder in the first degree of Ronald Goldman and Nicole Brown."

OCTOBER 2. After less than four hours of deliberations, the jurors announced that they had reached a verdict. Legal analysts had predicted it would take from two days to two months. During their deliberations, the jury asked to hear again the testimony of the limo driver who took Simpson to the airport shortly after the murders occurred. The driver was one of the more important witnesses regarding the time line of events.

OCTOBER 3. The not-guilty verdict was announced at 10:00 A.M.

THE VERDICT

Prosecutors said they were shocked by the verdict. Some news commentators said the verdict revealed the impact of money on the judicial system. In post-trial interviews, a few jurors said they thought Simpson likely committed the murders, but the prosecutors fumbled the case.

Vincent Bugliosi, a former prosecutor who had handled the Charles Manson trial, echoed that view in his book called *Outrage: The Five Reasons O. J. Simpson Got Away with Murder.* Bugliosi pointed out gross errors Darden and Clark made. He contended that prosecutors should have introduced the "suicide" note Simpson wrote and that hinted at guilt, and that they should have shown the jury the contents of the Bronco: the cash, passport, disguise, and change of clothing. Bugliosi also claimed Clark and Darden did not go into enough detail about past complaints of Simpson abusing his wife.

ALTERNATE THEORIES ON THE MURDERS

Simpson had suggested a hitman killed Nicole and Ronald, part of a string of connected murders. (Casimir Sucharski, a friend of Simpson's, was murdered two weeks after Nicole and Ronald. In March 1995, another friend, Charles Minor, was murdered. And eleven months prior to Nicole and Ronald's deaths, Brett Cantor—a friend of Ronald's—was killed. Cantor owned the Dragonfly, a Hollywood nightclub. He was murdered in a similar method to Ronald and Nicole: stabbed repeatedly on the chest and arms, and his throat slit. Nicole Simpson and Ronald Goldman had frequented the club.)

Another Mezzaluna waiter had barely survived a car bombing. Finally, Michael Nigg, a waiter at the Mezzaluna, where Ronald also worked, was shot in the head and killed. Reports suggested that several employees of the Mezzaluna were connected to the drug trade or to the Mafia.

Barry Hoestler, a private investigator hired by the defense, reported that Nicole was considering opening a restaurant with

Ronald and paying for it with cocaine money. Furthermore, the news displayed photographs of Nicole with known drug figures, lounging in a hot tub. Simpson stated that he was upset his children were so close to the drug scene. The defense claimed that Nicole and Ronald might have been killed by drug dealers.

Another theory is detailed in William Dear's book *O.J. Is Guilty, But Not of Murder*. In it, Dear postulates that Simpson's son, Jason, committed the murders. He claims Jason was enamored with Nicole, was angry at her lifestyle, and that he had no alibi for the night of the murders.

THE CIVIL TRIAL AND BEYOND

Though Simpson was acquitted of murder, on February 4, 1997, a civil jury in Santa Monica found him liable for the wrongful death of Ronald Goldman, battery against Ronald Goldman, and battery against Nicole. Simpson was ordered to pay millions of dollars in damages. The jury consisted of nine whites, one black, one Hispanic, and one individual of mixed Asian and African descent.

In November of the civil trial, which lasted more than forty days and in which more than one hundred people were called as witnesses, Simpson testified before a jury for the first time. He vehemently denied murdering his ex-wife and her friend.

The February 1998 issue of *Esquire* magazine quoted Simpson as saying: "Let's say I committed this crime. . . . Even if I did this, it would have to have been because I loved her very much, right?"

In 2000, Simpson won custody of his children in high-profile cases against Nicole's parents. He moved with his children to Florida.

In November 2004, a memorabilia collector was ordered to turn over Simpson's press credentials from the 1984 Olympics. It was part of the process of meeting the $33.5 million award. At that time, Goldman's parents had collected only about $500,000.

To this day, the judgment remains largely unpaid.

In 2005, Simpson appeared at a horror convention in L.A., an event that was touted as his first public appearance in the area since the double-murder acquittal. He signed autographs, from $5 for a photograph to $195 for a football helmet.

COMMENTARY: O. J. Simpson

While as one of his defense counsel it would be tempting to use this space to argue the case for O. J. "Juice" Simpson, a proper delineation of what would need to be said would subsume this entire book. Such an effort is best left for another day.

However, in a culture where a major segment of the white community remains enraged because some sloppy news reporting was thought by many to have all but guaranteed a conviction, and a major segment of the black community remains convinced that Simpson was wrongfully prosecuted because of embedded racist proclivities within the Los Angeles Police Department, as exemplified by the admitted conduct of convicted perjurer LAPD detective Mark Fuhrman, little of the conflict has been attenuated. One might have thought that, in ten years, hostilities would ease.

In a way, the Simpson case is a replay of the tidal wave that initially engulfed Dr. Sam Sheppard. The similarities as to the manner in which the cases steamrollered forward are striking, but there is one large and important difference: the circumstances which led to the internationally famous "low-speed chase," which in truth was nothing more than an escort to a designated surrender point.

This event probably caused more people to assume that Simpson was guilty than did any other single circumstance in the case. He had agreed to surrender at 11:00 on the morning of June 17, 1994, to be charged with two counts of murder. Instead, he told his longtime friend Robert Kardashian that he was going to kill himself, that he was unable to handle the dual apocalypse of losing his friend Nicole and then being falsely accused of her murder. Kardashian said, "If you're going to do that, don't do it here at my home." Simpson promptly got in his Bronco with a friend and disappeared. He did not say where he was going.

His threats to kill himself with a pistol he was holding in the back of his Ford Bronco, driven by his longtime friend Al Cowlings, certainly exacerbated the notion that he must have done something terrible. Adding to this situation were the comments to the media of then–chief counsel Robert Shapiro and Kardashian that strongly intimated that Simpson had committed suicide, which they believed to be true at the time. The multitudes asked: "Who but the perpetrator, having suffered the outrage of knowing that the mother of his children had been coldly butchered, would pursue suicide as an end? Certainly this is not the conduct of an innocent man!"

A further factor leading to a strong anti-Simpson bias was the change over the seventies and eighties in the reporting by the media, which is for most of the public their only access to what was going on in the case. With one exception, long gone was the cadre of newspaper reporters whose accounts of case and trial development were crisp and dependably accurate. Dorothy Kilgallen, Theo Wilson, Art Everett, Doc Quigg, Wallace Turner, Helen Dudar—these were reporters who could be trusted to grasp and write up the wheat, casting the chaff aside. The remaining giant in this field, Linda Deutsch for the Associated Press, covered the entire proceeding; when at the end, after the verdict, she wrote that in her view the result was justified, her bosses called her in to explain why she had taken such a wildly unpopular stance. She then wrote a short follow-up piece explaining her reasons, and so far as I know she was thereafter left alone. Within a short time, she retired.

Television, sadly, has become the main source of information for the American public. Unfortunately, that medium rarely gives more than snapshots, often tainted by commentary from lawyers, many of whom are called upon to analyze cases too complex for them to handle themselves. Johnnie Cochran and I labeled them "the Pundits," and had many a laugh over how far off the mark they would venture in their analyses, smiling confidently as if they had unearthed revealed wisdom.

When the cops announced that they had "a mountain of evidence" tying Simpson to the murder of his wife and Ron Goldman, most reporters echoed the cops' statements, and viewed the "mountain" with awe and belief rather than digging into it to see what was really there. This publicity, coupled with the "low-speed chase," led many to believe that the trial was just an exercise to see if Simpson and his pricey "Dream Team" (it was not) could "beat the rap." When the defense spoke, many reporters didn't listen, and those that did didn't report what was being described. It is little wonder that the verdict caught them flabbergasted, almost gibbering in shock.

Those who think the verdict was correct will have no quarrel with what is said below, although they may find that even they missed some important points. But as to those resolute naysayers who would readily bet the farm on the notion that Simpson is in fact guilty, I offer a suggestion, most respectfully:

.   .   .

Write down a list of the five most compelling facts favoring conviction, facts that would have caused you to vote "guilty" had you been on the jury. Then try to figure some rational answers to the following questions:

a. What about the TIME LINE? A time line is a compound alibi, where no one witness can prove that the suspect wasn't at the scene of the crime, but a combination of witnesses and circumstances can preclude the possibility that the suspect had an opportunity to commit the crime. According to several witnesses, supported by barking dogs, these murders occurred within a minute or two of 10:25 P.M. on June 12, 1994. The killer, covered with blood, left the scene and then returned, apparently to retrieve something (undoubtedly the knife), in the considered opinion of renowned FBI footprint expert William Bozniak. According to timed runs by the LAPD, it was a fifteen-minute drive from Nicole's home to Simpson's house. If O. J. was the killer, he had to take some time to stash the bloody clothes and the murder weapon (and stash them so well that to this day they have never been found, despite an intense and wide-ranging search by law enforcement), then go home and shower, then be in the waiting limo at 10:55. How did he do that?

b. The DEMEANOR: O. J. Simpson was a heroic running back in the National Football League, a fair sideline announcer for NBC (which then broadcast the AFL games), a fun character running through airports for Hertz, and a mediocre actor (The Towering Inferno, etc.). One must question whether Sir Laurence Olivier or Sir Anthony Hopkins—two of the finest actors of the past hundred years—could have killed two people in cold blood, then minutes later appear in various public groups acting casual, relaxed, and happy. Simpson, however, arrived at the Los Angeles International Airport to board an American [Airlines] "red-eye" flight to Chicago to play in a Hertz-sponsored golf match, late as usual. He paused at the curb to give a friendly autograph to two delivery truck drivers, then scrambled onto the plane and into his first-class seat just as the door was closing, smiling and joking with all.

He met a friend on the flight (who had to come up from coach to chat with him), a famous photographer, and acted relaxed and carefree. The captain of the flight came back and chatted with Simpson for fifteen or twenty minutes, and got him to sign his log book.

Simpson's demeanor was anything but nervous or tense; he was, once again, relaxed and happy. The limo driver who picked him up at Chicago's O'Hare and took him to his hotel had a similar impression; good ol' affable O. J. "Juice" Simpson.

All of this changed abruptly when Simpson got to his room and, a few minutes after entering but before he could catch forty winks, got a call from Detective Ron Phillips of the LAPD. Nicole Brown Simpson, reported Phillips, had been murdered. The detective gave little detail. Simpson's first reaction was to crush a drinking glass he was holding, cutting his finger rather severely. At the same time, he told Phillips he would return to Los Angeles on the first flight available. That turned out to be an American flight also, but there was no room in first class. Simpson was assigned to the aisle seat in the first row of coach, on the right side of the airplane.

When Simpson appeared at the hotel's front desk to check out, he was given a cloth by the desk clerk to stem the flow of blood from his finger. The clerk noticed that Simpson was a nervous wreck. The same limo driver who had collected him at O'Hare an hour or so earlier was assigned to take him back to American's terminal. According to his testimony, he saw a changed man: distraught, fidgeting, eyes darting about, Simpson was obviously very upset about something.

On the flight back to Los Angeles, Simpson had the good fortune (although he did not know it at the time) to be sitting next to a Harvard-educated patent lawyer from a Chicago firm, traveling to Los

Angeles for a client. This seatmate watched and listened as Simpson monopolized the SkyPhone, calling many different people to try to find out what had happened. Realizing that this was a matter of some significance, Mark (the lawyer) made detailed notes of what he heard. When he returned to Chicago, he sent copies of those notes to both the LAPD and to defense counsel. He was an extremely effective witness.

Was this the most extraordinary piece of acting in history, deserving of far more than an Oscar, or in truth the natural conduct of one who was in the catbird seat and suddenly tumbled into hell?

c. When Simpson got back to Los Angeles, he went to his home to see what was going on, and what had happened. He was immediately handcuffed. His attorney, Howard Weitzman, appeared shortly thereafter, and asked that the handcuffs be removed unless Simpson was charged with a crime. They were. After a bit of conversation, lead detectives Tom Lange and Philip Vannatter asked Simpson if they could talk to him down at Parker Center, police headquarters. He said sure. When they arrived, Weitzman was informed that he could not sit in. He was furious, and said there would be no interview, but Simpson overruled him, saying that he had a duty to help the police find the killer, and would assist in any way he could.

For the next three hours, Simpson was grilled by the two most experienced detectives in the LAPD's Robbery-Homicide Division, the elite of the elite. It is doubtful that a guilty layman—or even an experienced criminal—could have made it through that ordeal of interrogation with one or more significant slip-ups. Simpson never made a one. More than a dozen times the defense tried to introduce a transcript of the interview (it had been taped) into evidence, and each time the prosecution successfully persuaded Judge Ito to prevent the jury from hearing it, just as he blocked the jury from hearing the vile taped comments by Mark Fuhrman. If Simpson committed two cold-blooded murders, how was he able to hold up to such skilled questioning?

d. The trial started with twenty-four jurors in the box: twelve regular jurors and twelve alternates. By the time the defense got its case into *gear, ten of the alternates had been removed; of the two remaining, one was seventy-six and one was complaining of chest pains. Because this was not a capital case, it would have been possible to proceed with as few as six jurors if both sides consented.*

Since there was a genuine fear in the defense camp that we could lose three more jurors before the case was given to the jury, we made a formal motion before Judge Ito asking that the trial proceed with as few as six. One would have thought we had touched a hot poker to the rectal area of both prosecutors, who were emphatic: NO WAY! If we got down to eleven jurors, they would insist on a mistrial, and more than a year of litigation would go down the drain. One ought to wonder: Unless the prosecutors knew that an acquittal was in the wind, why wouldn't they want to finish the case?

As a result of this posture, the defense had no choice but to sharply curtail the evidence it had at hand, some of it very significant. We could not run the risk that three more jurors would go. Someday a list of those witnesses (including Simpson himself) and that evidence, when described in detail, will make it even more apparent why the jury (who had been shielded from all of the nonsense in the press) voted as they did, with little hesitation.

Rabbi Fred Neulander

Charged with murdering his wife on November 2, 1994

Newspapers were filled with articles about the wife of a Cherry Hill, New Jersey, rabbi who was beaten to death on a chilly Tuesday night. The fifty-two-year-old local businesswoman was found in her living room shortly after 9:00 P.M., lying face down in a pool of blood.

THE MURDER

Fred Neulander came home from Congregation M'kor Shalom in Cherry Hill, New Jersey, where he was the senior rabbi.

Investigators said it did not appear that anyone made a forced entry into the home, though robbery was a possibility. They said there were signs of a struggle, and it was clear that Carol Neulander had been struck on the head many times. But police did not find a murder weapon. Investigators spent hours at the scene, searching the wooded lot the Neulander home sat on, digging through the recycling bin, and looking on the roof.

Carol allegedly had brought home the day's receipts from the Classic Cake Company. The bakery had been robbed the previous month, and she'd been taking home the receipts as a precaution. The receipts and any personal money she had in her purse were missing from the house. The jewelry she was wearing was not taken.

Police believed she was killed sometime between 7:00 and 9:00 P.M. (An employee at the bakery told investigators that Carol was still at the store at 5:00 P.M.; neighbors said Carol had not come home at 6:00 P.M., when Rabbi Neulander and his son were home; the rabbi left around 7:00 P.M. to go to the synagogue, and the son, Matthew, an EMT, left to go to his job at the Ashland Ambulance Squad.)

Neulander returned home at about 9:20 P.M., discovered his wife's body, and called the police. Cherry Hill officers arrived at 9:22 P.M. and were soon followed by an ambulance. The Neulanders' daughter, Rebecca, told police that she had been talking on the phone to her mother when her mother said someone—the bathroom man—was at the door. Carol hung up the phone to answer the door. Investigators believed "the bathroom man" originally appeared at the Neulander house two weeks prior to the murder, disguised as a plumber so he could case the house. During the visit, he had asked to use the bathroom, then left.

The rabbi did not have a drop of blood on him, they noted; they believed he should have if he had tried to tend to his wife.

The murder, which shook the neighborhood and the entire community, would be followed by eight years of police investigations, two trials, and eventually a murder conviction. Police initially had few leads to follow and did not originally suspect the rabbi. However, rumors surfaced of an affair the rabbi was having, and police began to believe that the rabbi had his wife killed to avoid the embarrassment of a divorce.

FRED AND CAROL NEULANDER

Carol and Fred had married in 1965. In 1974, the Neulanders started the reform synagogue Congregation M'kor Shalom. The synagogue grew to become one of the largest in New Jersey. The couple had lived at the Cherry Hill home since 1975. Their son Matthew lived with them. Their son Benjamin lived on campus at the University of Michigan, and their daughter, Rebecca, lived in Philadelphia.

Carol managed the Classic Cake Company, a business she had once owned but then sold several years earlier. She volunteered on the Camden County Child Placement Review Board and was active in M'kor Shalom.

In February 1995, Neulander resigned from the M'kor Shalom Synagogue. Rumors had swirled about his being involved in Carol's murder. Shortly after his resignation, he admitted to having affairs, one with Elaine Soncini. In response, the Central Conference of American Rabbis suspended him.

ELAINE SONCINI

In August 1995, Neulander's lover, a Philadelphia morning radio host, contacted the police.

Socini claimed she went to Neulander for counseling when her husband died. She told police what started innocently, lunches and counseling sessions, turned into a two-year affair. She admitted that she eventually told Neulander she would end the affair if he didn't leave his wife.

THE ARREST

Four years after the murder, police arrested Neulander. Prosecutors asserted that Neulander hired two hit men to kill his wife on November 1, 1994, so that he could continue an extramarital relationship with Soncini and avoid the notoriety of a divorce. One of two alleged hit men, Len Jenoff, confessed to his part in the slaying. Jenoff, who was a friend of Neulander's and a former member of the congregation, said the rabbi paid him to kill Carol.

Len Jenoff confessed to police that he and another friend, Paul Daniels, murdered Carol by beating her to death with a metal pole. They attempted to make it look like a robbery by taking money from her purse. Jenoff and Daniels pleaded guilty to robbery and aggravated manslaughter, and Jenoff agreed to testify against Neulander. Jenoff and Daniels were sentenced to twenty-three years in prison. The men said Neulander paid them $18,000 for the murder.

Despite Jenoff's claims, Neulander said he was innocent.

THE FIRST TRIAL

Because of the hit men's confessions, a Camden County grand jury was called, and they indicted the rabbi on charges of conspiracy to commit murder, felony murder, and capital murder. The community reacted in shock and anger, and some feared it would draw unwanted and unfortunate publicity to the Jewish sector.

Neulander was indicted for murder late in 1998 on circumstantial evidence. That evidence included a statement from Myron Levin, a former friend and racquetball partner of Neulander's, who claimed the rabbi had asked him if he knew anyone who could kill Carol.

Though Jenoff and Daniels admitted to killing Carol at Neulander's request, their character and credibility were questioned. Jenoff had been known to tell people he was a former CIA operative, a claim he said bolstered his low self-esteem. Daniels was known to abuse drugs. In addition, Levin once told police the rabbi had confided that he wished his wife was "gone." Levin had also served time for fraud.

Key witnesses for the prosecution told the jurors the rabbi's behavior seemed unusual after the murder:

Margaret Miele, Carol's sister, said Neulander called her the day after the murder and said there was a break-in at the house, that things had gotten out of hand, and that Carol was killed. She said Neulander seemed calm and told her they probably wouldn't find the person who did it.

Robin Gross testified that she'd had an affair with Neulander from 1993 through 1994, and that the rabbi told her he was not happily married but that he could not divorce Carol because of his position in the synagogue.

Rabbi Gary Mazo, Neulander's assistant, told the jurors about Neulander's affair with Soncini. Further, Mazo said it was odd that Neulander was at the synagogue the night of the murder, as it was a Tuesday, and Neulander was rarely there on Tuesdays.

Anita Hochman, a cantor of M'kor Shalom, said she also thought it odd that Neulander was at the synagogue on a Tuesday night. He rarely visited choir rehearsal, she said.

Matthew Neulander, now a physician, told the jurors that he'd witnessed a fight between his parents two days before the murder. Matthew said his mother told him that his father was leaving. Matthew said he believed that his father had arranged to have his mother killed.

Dr. Robert Segal, the Camden County medical examiner, said the autopsy he performed revealed that Carol died from having vomit in her lungs, which was a result of the attack. There were seven head wounds and other defensive wounds. The murder weapon was likely something like a tire iron, he said.

Soncini told the jurors that Neulander asked her to lie to the police about their affair. In addition, she said Neulander promised her that they would be together as a couple by the end of 1994.

Also, investigators said there was jewelry on Carol's body, making a robbery unlikely. There was no evidence of a struggle, and Neulander did not have a spot of blood on him, which meant he did not go close to his wife's body. One officer said Neulander looked disgusted by his wife's body, rather than upset.

Witnesses for the defense were called to discredit the two alleged hit men. Neulander took the stand in his first trial. He would not in the second.

• At one point Neulander told the jurors that he and his wife shared an "open marriage," and they could seek other partners. Furthermore, he admitted that he lied to Soncini when he told her they would be together as a couple; he had no intention of leaving his wife. During questioning, Neulander admitted he loved Soncini. However, he later said he merely wanted to stay in a physical relationship with her. Under pressure, he agreed that he was more concerned about hiding his affair with Soncini than in solving his wife's murder.

- FBI agent George Stukenbroeker painted Jenoff as a liar. He told the jurors that Jenoff claimed he'd been with the CIA for twenty-one years. Jenoff's other claims included that he once served as vice president of the Playboy Club and that he'd been recruited by the Mossad.
- James Keeny, who belonged to Jenof's AA group in prison, said that Jenoff told him the rabbi had nothing to do with Carol's murder. In addition, he said Jenoff claimed he only wanted to rob Carol, not kill her.
- Jenoff's former cellmate, David Beardsley, also told the jurors that Jenoff confessed to the murder and said the rabbi was not involved.
- Fred Stahl disagreed with statements made by others that the rabbi rarely came to the synagogue on Tuesdays. Stahl, who worked security at M'kor Shalom, testified it wasn't odd at all to see Neulander at the synagogue on days off or late at night.
- Cherry Hill Police chief Brian Malloy told the jurors that at one point Soncini was under 24-hour surveillance and was considered a potential suspect in the murder.

THE DEADLOCK

After deliberating for five days, the jurors sent a note to the judge, stating they were having trouble coming to a unanimous decision. The jurors were deadlocked on all three counts—conspiracy, felony murder, and capital murder. Previously, after only two hours of deliberation, the jurors had sent a note to the judge hinting at their deadlock and asking what would happen if they could not agree on the charges against Neulander.

The defense asked for a mistrial after the jury notice, and initially the judge refused. In a statement to the defense and prosecution, she said she was asking the jury to continue deliberating. The jury complied, promptly asking for readbacks of testimony from various witnesses.

However, after seven days of failed deliberations, the judge declared a mistrial. Judge Linda Baxter was quoted as telling the jurors: "The jury I find is at a complete standstill, you are dead-locked, and no further amount of time could be productive."

Neulander's attorneys quickly asked for a bail hearing. The attorneys said their client had been held for more than a year and a half in jail and deserved to be released. Further, they contended that since the jurors were split on the charges, it was uncertain if Neulander would ever be convicted.

Prosecutors made it clear they would pursue another trial, as they were certain of Neulander's guilt. The judge denied bail while he waited for the second trial.

THE SECOND TRIAL

Judge Baxter agreed to move the rabbi's second trial out of the county because of the publicity the case had received. The defense had argued it would be difficult to get an impartial jury because of the news reports, talk shows, and other publicity. The trial was held in Freehold, in Monmouth County, New Jersey, roughly fifty miles from Neulander's house.

Prosecutor James Lynch told the jurors in his opening statement that Neulander lied to the police about his affair with Soncini. He said Neulander was clearly guilty. "He planned it. He plotted it."

Attorney Jeffrey Zucker defended Neulander. Zucker told the jury there were too many gaps in the case, and that, though Neulander was guilty of having an affair, he was not guilty of having his wife murdered. Zucker questioned the police's investigation at the murder scene—finding a knife hidden under a cushion three days after the murder, and not initially realizing money had been taken from Carol.

THIRTY TO LIFE

Although the jurors unanimously convicted Neulander of soliciting his wife's murder, they could not come to a unanimous decision on whether he should get the death penalty.

Earlier, he'd begged the jury to spare his life, saying he would atone for his acts and spend his days teaching illiterate prisoners how to read, and would counsel them. After deliberating an hour and a half, the five men and seven women said they could not reach a unanimous decision on the death penalty. As a result, Neulander would receive a minimum sentence of thirty years. The judge sentenced him to life in prison. He would be in his mideighties before having the opportunity to apply for parole.

Neulander had tried to avoid attending the sentencing hearing, but was denied the request. At the hearing, his dead wife's siblings called him cold and selfish. Two of his own children read letters calling him evil and saying they wanted nothing else to do with him.

Neulander made a twenty-minute statement in which he quoted from Scripture and said he was betrayed by his former friend Jenoff. He said he loved his wife, and that he missed her.

COMMENTARY: Rabbi Fred Neulander

The ingredients of the Neulander Case exemplify the utter stupidity characteristic of amateur murder-plotters like the rabbi. He left a trail a mile wide, and baited it as if to attract the attention of any sleuths who were missing the clues.

First, as a married person having an affair, he had waved a big red flag at the police at the outset of their investigation. It did not take them long to discover Elaine Soncini and her sordid-looking affair with the rabbi.

Indeed, they at one point suspected that she may have coveted the rabbi to the extent that she murdered his wife so as to have him for herself.

Since Neulander had arranged for himself a respectable and convenient alibi, the police were quite naturally led to look for a "hit man," one with no nexus to the victim. If a capable, professional assassin is hired to carry out a killing, both the perpetrator and his principal are unlikely to get caught. Professional killers are careful to look and live like middle-level bank employees, and have trained themselves (or were trained by the military in wartime) to make murder look like death by accident, or from natural causes. They charge big fees, and if caught in some other crime seldom "rat out" undetected principals in order to "cut a deal" with the prosecution.

But people from the rabbi's walk of life do not have access to professionals, even though there might be one or two within their church membership. Instead, they wind up trusting low-life men like the culprits in this case, who are bound to get apprehended for something eventually, and will very quickly respond to an invitation to benefit by accusing someone else of an unsolved crime—sometimes falsely. It is clear that the jury in the first case simply could not rely on Jenhoff "beyond a reasonable doubt." They may also have been impressed by the rabbi's testimony in his own defense.

But the prosecution's case at the second trial was nothing short of overwhelming. Had the rabbi not been a man of the cloth, he would likely have been sentenced to die. Homicide by assassin(s) is necessarily premeditated murder in the first degree, with no lesser degrees to choose from.

Mark Winger

Charged with murdering his wife on August 29, 1995

Mark Winger was initially hailed as a hero for shooting the man who'd broken into his house and killed his wife, but as the months passed and the investigation continued, he became the suspect in a double murder.

THE MURDER

It was a late summer afternoon when police and paramedics were called to a Springfield, Illinois, home on Westview Drive. In the dining room, Donnah Winger, thirty-one, lay on her stomach. She'd been beaten on the back of her head, and a pool of blood spread under her. Spatter marks were thick on furniture and a nearby wall, and reached up to the ceiling. A few feet away lay Roger Harrington, twenty-seven.

Mark Winger had called the police, frantically telling them that he had been in the basement, working out on exercise equipment, when he heard "strange noises" coming from upstairs. He said he went upstairs to investigate, grabbed his gun, and saw Donnah on her knees and a man he'd never seen before was standing over her, striking her with a hammer.

Winger said the man looked toward him, and he shot him in the head because it looked like the man was going to hit his wife again. Winger told police the man fell away from Donnah.

Ambulances took Harrington and Donnah to the hospital. Harrington died soon after arrival, and Donnah died a few minutes later.

Winger told police that the hammer was his, and that Donnah had left it sitting out to remind him to hang a hat rack. During the interview, he asked police whom the man was he'd killed, and a police officer answered, "Roger Harrington."

Winger acted surprised, then quickly explained that Harrington was the man who'd driven Donnah and their daughter, Bailey, back from the St. Louis airport, that he'd complained about Harrington, and that subsequently Harrington had been making harassing phone calls.

Harrington had been treated by a psychiatrist, and was said to have had delusions. One of the officers had run into him before, when he'd broke up a fight between Harrington and his wife.

Winger said he expected to be taken into custody, since he'd just killed a man. But the police declined, calling him a victim rather than a killer. One of the officers considered Winger a hero.

A veteran police officer at the Winger house said it was one of the most severe and bloody crime scenes he'd ever worked.

The following day, the Sangamon County District Attorney's Office announced that no charges would be filed against Winger and that he had acted in self-defense.

Initially, Donnah's family was supportive of Winger and believed that the wild ride Donnah and Bailey had taken from the St. Louis airport had led to the murder.

Harrington's relatives railed against the notion that Harrington was a murderer. They pushed police to look closer, but the case stayed closed for years.

MARK AND DONNAH WINGER

Donnah worked as an operating room technician, and Mark was a nuclear engineer. They adopted a baby girl in June 1995, when they learned Donnah could not have children. They named the girl Bailey, and initially the family seemed happy, but the emotional climate started to change just a few months later.

Donnah went to see her mother and stepfather in Florida, and took Bailey with her. When they returned from the trip, arriving at the St. Louis airport, they took a shuttle to Springfield, which would be an hour and a half ride. The shuttle was driven by Harrington.

Winger reported that Harrington, who'd been working for the company for six months, was speeding and told Donnah he had "out-of-body" experiences when driving, as if he were flying above it all. Winger said he called the company and complained to Harrington's boss.

Several days after that, Winger called police and told them Harrington attacked Donnah, and that he'd killed Harrington in self-defense.

QUESTIONS ABOUT THE SCENE

In the following years, one detective became suspicious of Winger, especially because he came to the police station a few times to look into the case, which had been considered closed.

Detective Williamson came to believe that Winger was the murderer.

On one of the occasions that Winger came to the department, he told police he was getting married again, to Rebecca, a woman he hired as a nanny five months after Donnah's murder. Rebecca adopted Bailey, and the couple had two more children.

Several years after the murder, one of Donnah's friends came forward. DeAnn Schultz told police she had been withholding information and could no longer keep it secret. Schultz said that, a month before Donnah's murder, she had started an affair with Winger, and it continued for several more months. She told police that Winger confided he wanted out of the marriage and that he had talked about killing his wife. Schultz said Winger talked about the shuttle driver, Harrington, and mentioned her possibly participating in the murder.

Under questioning, Winger admitted to the affair, but he denied the rest of Schultz's story. Her report, however, was enough to reopen the investigation into Donnah's murder.

In examining the evidence again, police noticed photographs that had been taken at the scene before Donnah and Harrington were moved to the hospital. Some of the investigators had not seen the photographs before, and those photos keyed in on just how Donnah and Harrington were sprawled. Harrington was lying in the opposite direction than Winger said he had fallen after being shot in the head.

Some of the investigators who had examined the Winger house again looked at the evidence and noticed that a few pieces did not fit. It appeared that when Harrington came to the house, he'd brought a mug of soda and a package of cigarettes with him and put them on the kitchen table. Police thought it odd for someone planning a murder to bring things like that inside. In addition, if Harrington had planned the murder, they considered it odd that he would use a hammer belonging to Winger and would not have brought a weapon of his own.

There had been no sign of a break-in, and one officer questioned why Donnah would open the door to Harrington if she feared him. Too, Donnah had left Bailey alone on her bed. In addition, Harrington's car was parked in front of the Wingers' house; he had made no attempt to conceal his presence. On the front seat, a piece of paper had Winger's name and address and "4:30" written on it.

Three people who lived in the mobile home with Harrington claimed that Harrington had received a call from Winger. Harrington told them he was going to Winger's home.

Investigators started to believe that Winger had lured Harrington to the house, shot him in the head, and then beat his wife to death.

In 2001, police arrested Winger on two counts of murder. The stain on Harrington's memory was cleared, and Winger was held on a $10 million bond.

Prosecutor John Schmidt contended that Winger lied from the

beginning of the murder investigation, including in his 911 call for help, in which he said a stranger had beaten his wife.

During the trial, Raymond Duffy, owner of the shuttle bus company Harrington had worked for, testified that Winger had indeed called to complain about Harrington. Further, Duffy said Winger wanted to talk directly to the driver. Duffy contacted Harrington, who okayed giving his phone number to Winger so things could be worked out.

Police believe Winger did not anticipate Harrington having a note on the seat of his car that listed Winger's name, address, and meeting time.

THE PROSECUTORS' CASE

By the time the trial started, Winger had four children, including Bailey.

During the proceedings, he continued to profess his innocence, saying Harrington had killed Donnah, and that he in turn killed Harrington in self-defense. Winger protested the use of the pictures taken at the scene. He said paramedics moved the bodies before those pictures were taken. The paramedics, however, denied that.

Further, Winger said he had no idea why Harrington would have a note in his car with the Winger address and 4:30 written on it.

District attorneys believed Winger, then at work in his office at the Illinois Department of Nuclear Safety, called Harrington at 9:00 A.M. the morning of the murders at his home in rural Mechanicsburg. The two men arranged to meet at Winger's house at 4:30 P.M. that day. Attorneys contended that Harrington left his home an hour before the scheduled meeting, and that Winger was already there at the house, lying in wait for him.

During the trial, defense attorneys called a blood spatter expert they'd hired to examine the scene. The expert, Terry Laber, a forensic scientist from Minnesota, testified that the blood pattern supported Winger's story.

Schultz was given immunity in exchange for her testimony

about her affair with Winger and his conversations with her. However, in the years after Donnah's murder, Schultz had attempted suicide a few times and had undergone electroshock therapy. The defense argued that she was an unreliable, unbelievable witness.

THE VERDICT AND APPEAL

The jury deliberated only thirteen hours before reaching a guilty verdict. Key in the jurors' considerations were the pack of cigarettes and drink Harrington had brought into the house, and the fact that he didn't bring his own weapon to kill Donnah.

In the sentencing hearing, Winger continued to say he was innocent. In a long speech before the judge, he continued to maintain that Harrington killed Donnah.

Winger was sentenced to life in prison, without the possibility of parole. Bailey continued to be raised by Winger's second wife, who filed for divorce.

In May 2004, Winger appealed his conviction to the Fourth District Appellate Court in Sangamon County in an effort to overturn his murder conviction. Too, he asked for more DNA tests on blood-soaked items from the murder scene, claiming they would support his innocence. The court denied Winger's appeal and request.

COMMENTARY: Mark Winger

Of all of our killers—those who actually did or caused the death—Mark Winger is certainly among the more imaginative and dramatic. In his plan to fool the police—and perhaps Agatha Christie and Hercule Poirot as well—he set up a second victim in order to get rid of the first, his wife. And it appears that at first he had the detectives in his corner, buying his tale of personal heroism hook, line, and sinker.

But once more, none of the accused subjects of this book had any real experience in constructing or carrying out the perfect crime, and those who tried made more than one cardinal mistake.

Winger is no exception.

Apparently, he didn't think to look in Harrington's car, but it was more than likely that a stranger coming to an address for the first time would have a note of some kind as to where he was going and how to get there, and who to call if he got lost. A search of Harrington's pockets would have disclosed that there was no such paper on his person. A quick look in the car, even if seen and reported by a neighbor, would not have been an unreasonable step for Winger to have taken under the circumstances, even if his story were true.

The mug of soda and the pack of cigarettes on the kitchen table, apparently without question put there by Harrington, were very out of place vis à vis Winger's story. It is astonishing in a way what it took for the detectives to see these clues as a red flag. Furthermore, the anomaly in the position of the bodies took rather a long time to puzzle the police.

The killer clue, however, was the hammer.

Unless a homicide is the result of some unforeseen rage, killers coming from outside the home inevitably bring their weapons with them. If Winger thought a hammer was a plausible instrument of murder for the occasion, he should have obtained one at some source (other than a new purchase, which might well be traced) by stealing it; the use of the household hammer cried for recognition as a huge contradiction in his story.

In truth, until DeAnn Schultz came forward and confessed to an adulterous affair, detectives were probably not looking for—and therefore not sensitive to—clues. They had written Winger off as a suspect, and committed themselves to looking elsewhere. The most common thread in this book is the paramour, often the motive, and ever the grounds for suspicion.

Allen Blackthorne

Charged with hiring the murder of his ex-wife on November 7, 1997

THE MURDER

Thirty-five-year-old Shelia Bellush was found murdered in her Sarasota, Florida, home on November 7, 1997. Her throat had been slashed twice, she had been shot in the face, and her two-year-old quadruplets were spattered with her blood.

Her thirteen-year-old daughter, Stevie, had rushed home that afternoon, excited, having discovered that a boy at school liked her and intended to ask her out on a date.

Stevie didn't immediately find her mother. She heard crying, though, and then discovered the quadruplets in the laundry room . . . with her mother's body. Blood coated the floor and the children.

Investigators uncovered numerous clues—a fingerprint, a bullet shell, and a knife. Neighbors told police they'd spotted a man dressed in combat fatigues near the Bellush house. Others said they saw a white car with Texas plates.

Tracking the car, police learned that the driver was Jose Luis Del Toro Jr., and they issued a warrant for his arrest on charges of first-degree murder. However, it wasn't until two weeks later that Del Toro was arrested— in Monterrey, Mexico.

Del Toro's fingerprints matched the one found at the murder scene. Police also reported that a gun found in Del Toro's car was used in the shooting, and there were directions to the Bellush home. Del Toro remained in Mexico for months, in an attempt to avoid extradition.

The police in Texas also arrested Sammy Gonzales, Del Toro's cousin, and Danny Rocha. Both were believed to have helped Del Toro plan the Bellush murder. None of the three had known Bellush. However, Rocha had golfed with Allen Blackthorne, Bellush's ex-husband.

ALLEN BLACKTHORNE

Blackthorne, forty-four at the time of the murder, was a successful San Antonio businessman—a self-made millionaire who'd earned his fortune selling medical equipment.

He lived in a million-dollar home with Maureen, his fourth wife, and their two children. He had a violent history with Sheila Bellush, his third wife, and was arrested in 1987 for beating her—a charge he pleaded guilty to. (He maintained it was a one-time event.) However, shortly after that incident, Sheila filed for divorce, and after the divorce, she had Blackthorne arrested for sexually abusing Stevie. He denied that allegation, and the charges were later dropped.

Blackthorne had divorced Sheila in 1988, and he was granted limited visitation of their two daughters, Stevie and Daryl. He was ordered to pay $75,000 to his ex-wife for pain and anguish, and child support payments were set at $1,250 a month. The following year, Blackthorne went to court to have the payments reduced to $350. He attempted to gain custody of the girls, and failed, and a court ordered that monthly child support payments be decreased, this time setting them at $1,100.

SHEILA AND JAMIE BELLUSH

Sheila met Jamie Bellush during the tumultuous times with her ex-husband, Blackthorne. She and Jamie were soon married, and

Sheila won custody of her two daughters. Sheila had four more children with Jamie—quadruplets.

Jamie's job took him to Sarasota, Florida, more than a thousand miles from San Antonio, and the entire family moved there six weeks before the murder. Blackthorne hired private investigator Chuck Chambers to find them.

Chambers gave the address to Blackthorne three weeks after the move.

ROCHA'S TRIAL

During Rocha's trial, it came out that Blackthorne had complained to Rocha that he believed Sheila was abusing Stevie and Daryl.

Rocha, twenty-nine at the time, also claimed that Blackthorne asked him to have Sheila "roughed up."

Prosecutors claimed Rocha was not intending the incident to help the daughters but to help himself, as Blackthorne would reward him with a partnership in a golf course.

Gonzales, the third man involved in the murder, had made a plea arrangement with prosecutors and testified against Rocha. According to Gonzales, Rocha said Blackthorne wanted his ex-wife beaten.

Gonzales said Rocha gave him $4,000 for the deed, and Gonzales contacted his cousin, Del Toro, to handle the job.

Gonzales also testified that he'd heard the deal had improved, and that Blackthorne had upped the payment to $10,000 if he got his daughters back.

The prosecution rested its case after three days, and Rocha attempted to negotiate his own plea deal. However, he failed to pass a lie detector test when asked about Blackthorne's part in the murder, and so the deal fell through.

After deliberating five hours, the jury returned a guilty verdict against Rocha, and he was sentenced to life in prison without the possibility of parole.

DEL TORO AND GONZALES'S TRIALS

After a twenty-month legal struggle, Del Toro, twenty-three, was extradited from Mexico in July 1999 when the United States agreed to waive the death penalty. He was set to go on trial for murder one year later.

While Del Toro was in Mexico, he had told Mexican police that he entered the Bellush home, hit the woman, and left. He said she was unconscious, not dead, and that someone he knew as "Jorge" later killed her. Police learned that Del Toro stayed at a Sarasota hotel the night before the murder.

In U.S. custody, Del Toro initially continued to claim that he was innocent, but then in court he admitted to stabbing and shooting Bellush in exchange for a promised $4,000.

During the case, the district attorneys presented the events of the murder. They said Del Toro used his grandmother's car to drive to Florida, stopping to buy camouflage clothes, and stopping again to get directions to the Bellush home. They contended he broke into the home and waited for Bellush arrive. Then he shot her in the face and stabbed her twice to be sure she was dead. Del Toro, they said, next called Gonzales to tell him it was finished and that he would be coming back to Texas to get his promised $4,000.

At the end of the trial, Del Toro gave a half-hour statement, in which he read poetry, said he believed in God, and apologized to Bellush's survivors. The jury found him guilty, and the circuit judge handed out the maximum penalty—two consecutive life-in-prison sentences with no chance of parole.

Gonzales, twenty-seven, pleaded guilty to the charge of conspiracy to commit murder, and was sentenced to nineteen years.

BLACKTHORNE'S ARREST AND TRIAL

Although speculation swirled that Blackthorne was involved in his ex-wife's murder, it was roughly two years after the incident before a federal grand jury indicted him. In January 2000, he was arrested at a San Antonio country club on a charge of murder conspiracy, and denied bail, as the prosecution claimed he was a flight risk.

Prosecutors needed to prove that Blackthorne was connected to the three men and that he orchestrated the murder.

During the investigation, Blackthorne railed against various allegations and refused to cooperate with investigators. He called Rocha a liar, saying he never gave him the Bellush address, and that he never asked Rocha to kill his ex-wife. (Rocha had argued otherwise.)

At the heart of the prosecution's case was Blackthorne's alleged motive to regain custody of his two daughters from Sheila Bellush. The two had fought over custody for nine years before Blackthorne had relinquished all rights in 1997—and this after supposed threats from his ex-wife that she would bring up claims he'd molested one of the girls. Sheila apparently was trying to get more child support out of Blackthorne and to terminate visitation rights, which prosecutors say further angered him.

Chambers, the private investigator who found the Bellush family in Florida at Blackthorne's request, said he was shocked to read about the murder in the newspaper. He said it had been difficult for him to find the family.

Tom and Debby Oliver, Blackthorne's uncle and aunt, had raised their nephew for a few years. They said Blackthorne paid them a visit more than a week before the murder and let them know he was still angry at his ex-wife over losing custody of the children.

The trial began in September, nearly two and a half years after Sheila's murder.

Prosecutors presented more than four hundred pieces of evidence that they maintained tied Blackthorne to the murder.

The prosecution played a 911 tape of Stevie Bellush after she discovered her mother's body. The recording was full of hysterical sobbing and children crying, and Stevie saying there was "blood everywhere" and that her mother was dead.

Stevie was thirteen at the time of the murder. Now sixteen, she was called to testify. She said her father was manipulative, and that he gave her and her sister Daryl a lot of gifts to win their loyalty. She also testified that her stepfather, Jamie Bellush, was strict and had spanked her when she was younger.

Stevie cried when she described the scene of the murder.

Rocha also testified, telling the jurors that Blackthorne wanted his ex-wife beaten and crippled and her tongue ripped out. Under questioning, he detailed his bookie business and golf hustling, and said that sometimes he made more than $10,000 a week.

The chief prosecution witness, Rocha, was serving a life sentence for his involvement in the murder conspiracy. He had failed lie detector tests and had told different versions of Blackthorne's involvement. He was the only one of the previously arrested trio who was said to have personal contact with Blackthorne.

Rocha testified that Blackthorne was as responsible as he was for the murder. He was questioned for three days, during which he said Blackthorne was the brains behind the plot and had provided the money. While his credibility was questioned, Rocha admitted numerous lies to police; however, he kept his story consistent about Blackthorne initiating the murder.

Prosecuting attorneys attempted to prove that Blackthorne was obsessed with his ex-wife and children. Their witnesses included Chambers, the private investigator Blackthorne hired, who testified that Blackthorne was straightforward and cold in telling him to find Bellush.

A former employee of Blackthorne's testified that he had asked her to go to a parking lot in Sarasota, where Sheila Bellush went to church, as he wanted her to follow Sheila home.

The prosecution played recorded telephone conversations in which Blackthorne, posing as a bookie, called a bail bond company, trying to get Sheila Bellush's new Sarasota address. Records showed phone calls from Blackthorne's house to Florida.

Daryl testified that her father also tried to get the family's new address from her, claiming he wanted to visit them at Christmas. However, Blackthorne contradicted her, testifying he wanted the address so he could protect his daughters. He said he believed the girls were being physically abused.

The girls said after their mother's death their father ceased calling to check on them.

THE DEFENSE'S THEORY

Blackthorne's defense team consisted of a half-dozen attorneys. They suggested that Sheila's husband, Jamie, might have been involved in the murder. Jamie had told police that he was at a doctor's appointment in Fort Myers, Florida, on the morning of the murder. A receptionist there said Jamie was there a week or more earlier, and he was never able to prove his claim.

Blackthorne hinted that Jamie was prone to violence. For example, police had been called to the Bellush home in San Antonio, where neighbors said the couple abused the children. Jamie allegedly hit Stevie with a belt and a spoon but was never arrested.

The defense also noted that Jamie had three life insurance policies on Sheila, and that he would profit by her death. Jamie admitted that he collected a little more than $300,000, which he invested for the children's college funds.

Defense attorney Richard Lubin claimed Rocha was trying to blame Blackthorne for the murder and save himself. Lubin drilled Rocha about the various stories he plied authorities with. Lubin got Rocha to admit that the prosecution spent more than forty hours prepping him for the trial. Further, under Lubin's questioning, Rocha said Blackthorne never ordered the murder, just a beating in exchange for backing in a sports bar.

The defense contended that Rocha ordered the killing to improve his standing with Blackthorne. Lubin showed a letter from a federal prosecutor that stipulated a good word would be put in for Rocha, perhaps moving him from a prison in Florida to one in California, nearer his family. During the trial, the defense had Rocha read selections from letters he wrote in jail and sent to friends. The letters asked the friends to implicate Blackthorne in the murder. In one letter, Rocha wrote: "Either Allen walks or I do."

The defense put Blackthorne on the stand, a move that surprised prosecutors and the media. Blackthorne told the jurors that he met Sheila in the fall of 1992 and married her the following year. During the marriage, he legally changed his name last name from Van Houte to Blackthorne because he disliked his father and wanted to distance himself from the man. He testified that he missed his daughters Stevie and Daryl and that he'd given up parental rights a few months before his ex-wife was killed.

Blackthorne said he was innocent of the charges and that he was "numb" and "in shock" when he learned of his ex-wife's murder. He testified that he'd only once threatened his ex-wife, and that was when one of his girls fell out of a window. He told the jurors: "If anything happens to my kids, I will kill you." He firmly denied Rocha's allegations about hiring someone to kill Sheila.

Blackthorne testified that he did not like his ex-wife, but that he would not want her killed, as she was the mother of his two daughters. He said: "I wouldn't want her hurt." In addition, he said he was happy to be with his new wife, Maureen, with whom he had two sons.

Maureen Blackthorne testified in her husband's defense, saying he didn't want anything to do with Sheila Bellush. She admitted that their marriage was not perfect, that she was not happy with her husband's gambling and that she had asked him to stop. Her testimony signaled an end to the defense's case.

In closing arguments, Lubin described Rocha, the prosecution's key witness, as a liar and manipulator. He contended that without Rocha, the prosecution did not have a case.

THE VERDICT

The verdict followed three weeks of trial and thirty hours of deliberation, and came after news that Del Toro had confessed to the murder a few hours before. When the jury of four women and eight men found Blackthorne guilty of two counts—conspiring to commit murder-for-hire and arranging an act of domestic violence across state lines—he took the news stoically.

BLACKTHORNE'S APPEAL

In August 2000, Blackthorne's attorneys tried to get a U.S. Circuit Court of Appeals to force another trial or to acquit him. Lead attorney Lubin alleged errors were made in the trial. Among the problems he cited were that prosecutors failed to disclose a report made by the lead investigator, and excessive publicity prevented Blackthorne from getting a fair trial.

The report that Lubin attacked revealed twenty points that could have aided the defense, including pointing to contradictions in statements from Rocha, the prosecution's key witness. In addition, Blackthorne's attorneys contended that the court itself committed errors, including not allowing the man who gave Rocha a polygraph test to testify.

In May 2002, the Fifth U.S. Circuit Court of Appeals upheld the conviction and prison term.

COMMENTARY: Allen Blackthorne

Allen Blackthorne is all too typical of those who hire a supposed "hit man"—more often a "con man"—who then delegates the "job" to a friend for a small cut of the fee, who then gets his friend to do the actual dirty work for an even smaller "cut" of the murder money. This usually ends up with the triggerman being very poor, quite ignorant, and not very bright. All of these terms apply to Jose Luis Del Toro Jr., who clearly executed the victim, Blackthorne's ex-wife, Sheila Bellush. It was certainly clever of him to drive his grandmother's car, sporting Texas plates in Sarasota, Florida, to the scene of the crime, and to leave his fingerprints there as well. Keeping the murder weapon handy for the police to find was also thoughtful.

Because the victim was an ex-wife, the "secret lover" was not a factor in Blackthorne's case. However, the "mastermind"—Rocha—was the homicide manager of Blackthorne's choice, and inevitably contributed heavily to his undoing.

It is of some interest to note that Blackthorne was not convicted of murder, even though as a principal he could have been found guilty of the same crime as his agents (Rocha, Gonzales, and Del Toro) if the jury found that he ordered and paid for the "hit." But this case was tried in federal court, and murder itself is almost always a state crime, except where murder is committed on federal (or federally controlled) real estate. When the federal courts punish someone for murder, it is often charged as a denial of civil rights, or an act in furtherance of a racketeering or continuing criminal enterprise charge, both federal statutes used in mob cases.

In this case the charge of "principal" was converted to "conspiracy," and the second charge—arranging an act of domestic violence across state lines—was federal because there was interstate involvement.

One other matter of interest—because it is so often thought to be an unfair edge—is that being rich did not help Blackthorne in the end.

He got a very good run for his money from lead counsel Richard Lubin and chief investigator Patrick McKenna—both among the top in the country—but even talent this strong could not overcome Blackthorne's own ineptitude.

Michael Schiavo

Legal battles to let his wife die begin in 1998

The personal tragedy of Michael Schiavo's wife, Terri, slipping into an irreversible coma, became front-page news across the country. What Michael had hoped to keep a private family matter—deciding to end her life support—became a public and political debate that involved high-profile lawyers, religious leaders, local and national politicians, and character assassination.

The legal fight included fourteen appeals and many hearings, petitions, and motions in Florida courts, as well as five suits filed in Florida's Federal District Court.

TERRI SCHIAVO

Theresa Marie Schindler was born December 3, 1963, in Pennsylvania. She would die at age forty-one on March 31, 2005, after having been disconnected from her feeding tube.

Terri was the oldest of three children. Her younger brother, Robert, and sister, Mary, grew up with her in a suburb of Philadelphia, Pennsylvania. She attended Archbishop Wood Catholic High School and Bucks County Community College. She met Schiavo in a sociology class at the college in 1982, and claimed he was her first boyfriend. After five months, they became engaged, and were married on November 10, 1984, in Our Lady of Good Counsel Church.

In 1986, the couple moved to Saint Petersburg, Florida, and Terri's parents moved to the city a few months later. Terri found work as an insurance claims clerk for Prudential, and Schiavo managed a restaurant.

TERRI'S COMA AND THE FIGHT TO END HER LIFE

Michael Schiavo said he came home at 2:00 A.M. on February 25, 1990, went to bed, and said good night to Terri. He recalled that she had kissed him. About two and a half hours later, he said he heard a thud in the hall outside the bedroom, went out into the hall, and found Terri on the floor.

He said at first he thought she'd just tripped but, when he turned her over, she was unconscious. He shook her to try to wake her up, and when that had no effect, he called 911. Then he said he called Terri's brother, who lived in the same apartment complex.

Schiavo said tests revealed that Terri's potassium level was very low, hinting at bulimia, and that she had suffered a heart attack.

She never regained consciousness.

Doctors who later examined brain scans contended that Terri was in a "persistent vegetative state," and that there was no brain activity. Spinal fluid had built up where her cerebrum used to be.

Schiavo recounted numerous times to the media how he sought help for Terri, meeting with several doctors, including a team in California. He even took her to California, where a medical team tried to use implanted electrodes to stimulate brain activity. Later, he took her to Bradenton, Florida, to a rehabilitation clinic specializing in brain and spine trauma. She underwent various tests and therapies that produced no discernable results.

Schiavo said he hired an aide to take Terri to parks, malls, and museums in the hopes that seeing something there might spark a reaction. He would have her hair styled and makeup put on in an attempt to gain a response from her . . . but nothing worked.

Schiavo reported that nurses attempted "swallowing tests," in the event Terri could be weaned off the feeding tube, but to no avail.

Finally, Schiavo hired George Felos, an attorney famous for a landmark Florida case that established a person's right to refuse unwanted medical treatment.

During this time, the Schindlers continued to talk to the press about their daughter, sometimes intimating that Schiavo was responsible for her condition, and ultimately for her coma.

MALPRACTICE CASE

In November 1992, Schiavo filed a medical malpractice suit against doctors he claimed had misdiagnosed her. He and Terri had visited several doctors, as they were trying to conceive. Terri was missing her period but was not pregnant, Schiavo reported. During this time, he said, no doctor had taken a blood sample, which he believes would have tipped people off to Terri's bulimia and low potassium level. Schiavo was awarded more than $1 million, which he said he spent on Terri's medical and legal expenses.

SCHIAVO AND THE SCHINDLERS

In the first few years of Terri's coma, Schiavo remained on good terms with Terri's parents, Robert and Mary Schindler; however, a fallout occurred regarding her care and future. He'd been living with them but moved out, and they began accusing him of not doing enough to help Terri.

In 1994, Schiavo asserted that he did not believe Terri could recover and that she would not want to live the way she was. He asked that treatments for any infections be stopped. Some medical personnel and Terri's parents voiced their opposition, and treatments continued.

Four years later, Schiavo asked that the feeding tube be removed, in an effort to end Terri's life, while the court had established that she was in a persistent vegetative state and had little chance of recovery. Legal battles ensued between Schiavo and Terri's parents. He reported being forced to move because of threatening letters, phone calls, and e-mails. He also claimed that at one point Terri's parents offered him $700,000 to drop the matter and leave Terri's fate in their hands. (They were not wealthy people, but they'd received money from various right-to-life groups and supporters.)

Terri's parents and siblings fought constantly with Schiavo to keep Terri alive, contending that she had a level of awareness, recognized them, and wanted to live. Her brother, Robert, repeatedly told the media that Terri was aware, would try to talk, and that she was responsive during his visits.

In March 2000, Terri's parents filed a motion that would allow their daughter to be fed by hand. This, under Florida law, was not considered a life-prolonging measure. They filed another such motion in 2005. Pro-life groups and individuals flocked to the Schindlers' side.

TERRI'S LAW AND FINAL APPEALS

In September 2003, the Schindlers petitioned the court to stop the removal of Terri's feeding tube. The petition included affidavits from the Schindlers, a nurse, and a doctor. Judge George Greer found against them, writing: "The petition is an attempt by Mr. and Mrs. Schindler to relitigate the entire case. It is not even a veiled or disguised attempt. The exhibits relied upon by them clearly demonstrate this to be true."

The following month, Terri's feeding tube was removed, but the Schindlers' pleas reached the Florida legislature, which passed a measure dubbed "Terri's Law." It was signed by Florida governor Jeb Bush, and allowed the governor to intervene in the case—which is what he promptly did. The governor ordered Terri removed from the hospice and taken to a hospital, where her feeding tube was surgically reinserted.

Terri was later returned to the hospice, and an "ad litem" guardian, Dr. Jay Wolfson, was appointed for her to represent Terri's "best interests" and report to the governor. This did not remove Schiavo as Terri's guardian.

The Florida Supreme Court would later overturn Terri's Law.

During December 2003, Wolfson visited Terri daily and submitted a report that stated he supported other doctors' findings that she was in a persistent vegetative state. Wolfson also stated that Florida law allows for removing feeding tubes in instances of persistent vegetative states.

Next, the Schindlers filed a motion for relief from judgment pending medical evaluations, asking that Terri be given new swallowing tests. This was packaged with nearly three dozen affidavits from specialists, therapists, speech pathologists, and doctors recommending the tests.

Judge Greer also denied this motion and set a date to remove the feeding tube: March 18, 2005. Greer would also deny a petition for intervention by the Department of Children and Families.

At the same time, the Schindlers' attorney challenged Schiavo's right to be Terri's legal guardian.

That attempt failed, and Schiavo remained his wife's guardian.

TERRI'S DEATH AND AUTOPSY

Terri was given last rites before the feeding tube was removed, and a drop of wine was placed on her tongue.

Schiavo was at Terri's side when she died. Her parents had been denied access to her during the final hours; however, they were allowed in the room after Schiavo left, about one-half hour after Terri's death.

The medical examiner for Pinellas and Pasco Counties performed an autopsy that indicated extensive brain damage, which supported the earlier diagnosis of persistent vegetative state. In addition, there was significant damage to Terri's nervous system. The examiner ruled that the damage to her brain and nervous system could not have been repaired with any amount of treatment.

The Schindlers held a memorial for Terri and complained publicly that they had not been told where their daughter's ashes were going to be buried. (They were notified after the service.)

Terri's ashes were buried at the Sylvan Abbey Memorial Park in Clearwater, Florida, in June 2005.

SCHIAVO REMARRIES

In late January 2006, Schiavo married Jodi Centonze in a private ceremony in Safety Harbor, Florida. Reporters were not allowed inside the church. The couple, who met in a dentist's office, started a relationship after Terri was placed in a nursing home. They have two young children.

Schiavo contended that he could have divorced Terri and married his girlfriend years earlier, but that would have meant relinquishing control over Terri's situation. He continued to fight to have Terri's feeding tube removed while keeping company with Jodi, who often washed Terri's clothes and visited with her.

TIME LINE

1990. At 5:30 A.M., February 25, Terri, twenty-six, collapsed from a heart attack. Her heart stopped long enough to cause severe brain damage. She was able to breathe on her own, but required a feeding tube to stay alive.

Schiavo was appointed as her legal guardian.

1991. Schiavo entered the nursing program at Saint Petersburg Community College, saying he wanted to better care for his wife. He later became a respiratory therapist and ER nurse.

1992. Terri's father, Robert Schindler, claimed that Schiavo was responsible for Terri's condition.

Schiavo was awarded $250,000 from a malpractice settlement with one of Terri's doctors. In a separate case, Schiavo was awarded $1 million in a malpractice judgment, $700,000 of which was placed into a trust fund for Terri's medical bills.

1993. The Schindlers attempted to have Schiavo removed as Terri's guardian.

1995. Schiavo met Jodi Centonze in a dentist's office and they began dating.

1998. Dr. Jeffrey Karp evaluated Terri and determined that she was in a "chronic vegetative state" and could not improve.

Schiavo petitioned the court for the first time to have Terri's feeding tube removed.

2000. Judge George W. Greer of the Florida Circuit Court ruled the feeding tube could be removed.

2001. Dr. Ronald Cranford tested Terri's brain function. It was a court-ordered exam, and it revealed that her cerebral cortex had been destroyed, that more than half of her upper brain had been destroyed, and that there was significant damage to her lower brain.

Terri's feeding tube was removed for the first time. However, two days later it was reinserted by order of Circuit Court judge Frank Quesada. An indefinite stay was set by the second Circuit Court of Appeals.

2002. A trial was scheduled to determine if new treatments might help Terri regain cognitive functions. Five doctors were chosen to provide their opinions. Two were chosen by the Schindlers, two by Schiavo, and one by the court. Schiavo's and the court's doctors concluded that Terri was still in a persistent vegetative state. However, the Schindlers' doctors claimed that Terri was in a "minimally conscious state."

Jodi gave birth to Schiavo's first child.

2003. Judge Greer again ruled that the tube could be removed. It was removed for the second time in October.

"Terri's Law" passed in the Florida legislature, and Governor Jeb Bush ordered the tube to be reinserted.

2004. "Terri's Law" was declared unconstitutional by the Florida Supreme Court.

Governor Jeb Bush appealed to the U.S. Supreme Court.

Jodi gave birth to Schiavo's second child.

2005. The U.S. Supreme Court rejected Bush's appeal.

The Schindlers approached the Second District Court of Appeals to grant Terri a divorce from Schiavo, citing his adultery, having two children with another woman.

Throughout early March, nearly three dozen complaints were made, alleging Terri was in pain from dental work, that she hadn't been given enough dental work, that there wasn't enough light in her hospice room, and other claims of abuse. Investigators from the Department of Children and Families ruled there was no mistreatment.

The feeding tube was removed for the third time on March 18.

On March 21, Congress passed a bill that was signed by President George W. Bush. This transferred the jurisdiction of Terri's case to Judge James Whittemore of the U.S. District Court.

Whittemore, on March 23, declined to grant a restraining order. The Schindlers appealed, and a panel of the U.S. Circuit Court of Appeals turned them down.

Terri died on March 31 at the age of forty-one. Schiavo was at her bedside and was accompanied by his brother, two attorneys, and hospice workers.

Terri's body was cremated on April 4, despite the Schindlers' wishes.

On June 15, autopsy results were publicly released, showing Terri was blind and that her brain was half the normal size.

Terri's ashes were interred at the Sylvan Abbey Memorial Park in Clearwater, Florida. Terri's marker reads: Born December 3, 1963, Departed This Earth February 25, 1990, At Peace March 31, 2005.

Governor Jeb Bush, on June 17, asked a state prosecutor to investigate Terri's 1990 heart attack to determine how much time had elapsed between when she collapsed and when Schiavo called for an ambulance, thus casting suspicion on Schiavo's role. The prosecutor found no wrongdoing on Schiavo's part and recommended no further action. Governor Bush dropped the matter.

Schiavo formed a political action committee on December 7, TerriPAC.

2006. Schiavo and Jodi Centonze were married in Espiritu Santo, Florida.

COMMENTARY: Michael Schiavo

Except for the fact that some people very cruelly suggested that Michael Schiavo had some sinister and selfish purpose when he insisted that he wanted his wife, Terri, to die because she was hopelessly in an irreversible coma, this case should not strictly belong in this book. And although this is not one of them, some of the most tragic homicide cases we ever see result not from hatred, greed, or malicious purpose, but from a very deep and unrelenting love. Usually dubbed "mercy killings," they frequently involve older people who no longer have much conduct with life or any of the living due to Alzheimer's or some other disease of the mind, and whose existence is so pathetic that someone close to the unfortunate terminally ill person can no longer stand to see them suffer.

Because the Terri Schiavo case was so bitterly fought by her husband on the one hand and her parents on the other, and because its tentacles reached out to involve the Florida and federal courts, and the governor and legislature of that state, it is a painful illustration of how deeply divided is this nation on the subject of euthanasia, the intentional killing of a terminally ill patient for merciful purposes. While we regularly "put to sleep" pets and crippled racehorses who are injured or aged beyond recovery, to allow individuals the right to decide when another should be allowed (or forced) to expire will probably be controversial well beyond the life span of anyone alive today. The essence of the dispute is in part no doubt religious, and in larger part the ongoing fear that this would be an awesome power to hand to anyone—even judges, where it is normally now very reluctantly exercised, as in Terri's case—because it could be so easily abused for all the wrong, nonmerciful purposes.

James "Jeff" Cahill

Charged with murdering his wife
on October 28, 1998

What began as a domestic dispute in the spring of 1998 would escalate into murder the following fall. Jeff Cahill's subsequent trial would shock and mesmerize the local community and would renew arguments statewide about the death penalty.

THE SCENE OF THE BEATING

In early April 1998, Jeff and Jill Cahill signed a separation agreement; however, they continued to live together at their home in Spafford, Onondaga County, New York. The couple was in financial straits, and Jill was reportedly saving so she could afford to move out. On April 21, Cahill reported that he and his wife got into an argument, and that she stabbed him several times with a kitchen knife. He said he told police that, in defense, he grabbed a Louisville Slugger baseball bat and hit her in the head.

During the attack, Jill allegedly screamed out to their two young children who were in the house, begging them to call the police. Police found Jill on the kitchen floor, covered in blood and writhing in pain. Her left temple was indented from being hit with a baseball bat.

Initially, Cahill, thirty-nine, told police the story of Jill's attacking him with a kitchen knife and his defending himself by hitting her with a baseball bat. He had some cuts and scratches to show for it.

Next, he said he taped a garden hose to the tailpipe of his car, intending to kill himself with carbon monoxide fumes. He told police he changed his mind when he saw a rosary hanging in the car.

He came inside the house and waited for police and paramedics.

Cahill and Jill were taken to separate hospitals. Cahill was treated for minor injuries and released, then went to the police department for questioning.

Jill, forty-one, was in a coma in the hospital for six months and was showing some signs of improvement, when she was murdered that October.

Cahill was charged with the crime.

In July 1999, defense attorneys argued that Cahill could not possibly obtain a fair trial in Onondaga County because there had been so much publicity and notoriety surrounding the case. Too many people had already formed opinions about it, they said.

The defense subsequently petitioned the trial court for a change of venue. (Attorneys had previously made an attempt for a change of venue in the spring.) The attorneys claimed that most of the five hundred prospective jurors were familiar with the case because of the publicity, and some of them certainly had already made up their minds about it.

JILL'S MURDER

Cahill reportedly entered University Hospital after visiting hours on October 27. According to several staff members, he was sporting a wig and glasses, and was posing as a maintenance worker. He even had a mop and a false name tag to complete his disguise. Cahill allegedly poisoned her, and then left.

A nurse who stopped in Jill's room shortly thereafter found Jill gasping for breath. The nurse saw bruises around Jill's mouth and a white powder—later identified as cyanide—on her chest. Jill died the following day.

An autopsy revealed that potassium cyanide was administered through her mouth or feeding tube.

The police quickly arrested Cahill for murder. Investigators obtained search warrants and recovered files from his home computer that showed Cahill had researched "cyanide" and "ordering potassium cyanide."

Sources reported that letters were found on the computer sent from an East Syracuse company named General Super Plating to Bryant Laboratories, placing orders for potassium cyanide.

In addition, police found a burned wig and a bottle containing potassium cyanide on Cahill's property. The potassium cyanide was in a hollow space inside a cinder block next to a shed in the yard. Investigators located witnesses who saw Cahill intercept the cyanide delivery at General Super Plating in July 1998.

CAHILL'S TRIAL

On November 19, 1998, a grand jury indicted Cahill on two counts of first-degree murder. One charge stated the defendant had murdered his wife to stop her from testifying against him on the assault charge. The other charge alleged that Cahill murdered his wife while committing a burglary (this stemming from breaking into the hospital room). The grand jury also indicted him on two counts of murder in the second degree, burglary in the second degree, aggravated criminal contempt, and criminal possession of a weapon in the fourth degree.

A little more than one month later, the DA's office filed an intent to seek the death penalty and to consolidate the murder and assault charges. In January 1999, the motions were granted.

According to juror questionnaires, more than 80 percent of prospective jurors had heard or read about the case from television and newspapers. The defense twice attempted to obtain a change of venue, but both times was turned down. When officials reviewed the media coverage, they determined it was not prejudicial or overly sensational.

In addition, the defense argued that the police performed an improper search, as the warrant was not specific enough. It stated the search was to be for toxic or caustic materials in the Cahill house or "within any unattached garage or storage shed." It did not mention outside the storage shed.

The search was deemed fair.

Following Jill's beating, the Onondaga County Family Court placed the two Cahill children with their maternal grandparents and aunt. In addition, prior to Jill's murder, the Family Court and Onondaga County Court issued orders of protection against Cahill that prohibited him from seeing his children or entering University Hospital, where Jill was being treated.

Prosecutors called more than sixty witnesses during the eight days of the trial.

THE DECISION

The jurors found Cahill guilty of two counts of murder in the first degree (intentional) and one count of assault in the first degree, the latter charge arising from when he assaulted Jill with a baseball bat, the incident that put her in the coma.

Prosecutors said they would seek the death penalty if Cahill was convicted. They said they believed he should face a death-penalty trial, because New York statutes allow for anyone convicted of "intentional murder" to be eligible.

One of the first-degree findings was based on Cahill's eliminating a witness to a crime—his wife, Jill—and on murdering Jill. The other first-degree charge involved murder committed during the course of felony burglary in the second degree. Burglary in the second degree is committed when someone enters a building, in this instance a hospital room, with the intent to commit a crime.

The jurors deliberated only five hours before recommending that Cahill be sentenced to death on both counts.

THE DEATH PENALTY ISSUE

Defense attorneys appealed Cahill's conviction to the New York Court of Appeals.

The Court of Appeals subsequently decided that aggravating factors were not proved in the murder case, and so did not qualify under the death penalty statute. Cahill was instead convicted of murder in the second degree, which did not carry an option of a penalty of death.

The court ruled that the jury's conclusion was incorrect, that Cahill did not kill his wife to prevent her from testifying against him. The judges in the majority opinion decided that to convict an individual of murder under the witness-elimination rule, prosecutors must prove that the elimination of the witness was the substantial motive for the killing. The judges believed the jurors did not properly weigh the evidence regarding that charge. The court's majority opinion stated that the evidence pointed to Cahill's poisoning his wife because the marriage was ruined.

In addition, the Court of Appeals countered the jury's conclusion that Cahill committed burglary by entering his wife's hospital room. Prosecutors had used both reasons in seeking the death penalty.

The case was sent back to the local court for resentencing, which was scheduled for January 2004.

Cahill was resentenced to twelve to twenty-five years for assault in the first degree, the maximum allowed by law, and twenty-five years to life for murder in the second degree. The terms were to run consecutively, yielding a total sentence of thirty-seven years to life in prison.

JILLY'S LAW

In May 2004, legislation was passed in New York that would give courts more options in setting bail for defendants. Known as "Jilly's Law," it allowed judges to take into account whether a defendant presents a danger to an alleged victim or to others in the community, or if the defendant has a history of violence against an alleged victim. The law was named in memory of Jill Cahill. At the time of her murder, her husband was out on bail.

COMMENTARY: James "Jeff" Cahill

There is little wonder that James Cahill's case aroused renewed outcries for reinstatement of the death penalty. It is difficult to imagine a more reprehensible or premeditated homicide than the one involved here. In a country where fairness is held to be almost divine, and there is usually sympathy for the underdog, attacking a patient in a coma—which the killer had earlier inflicted—rates with the lowest of the low.

Since the police would first and foremost look at Cahill, who had dented Jill's head with a baseball bat, one might consider his venture into the hospital as sheer stupidity. But it was much worse than that. While his assault with the bat might have been the result of a flash of rage, the cunning, disguised visit to the hospital was quite a different matter, despite the fact that he would get caught was all but inevitable. Furthermore, the use of cyanide as the instrument of murder was right out of a bad (and old) movie. Leaving physical traces of cyanide on the victim's chest was certainly clumsy, but to a mind like Cahill's, a minor circumstance.

The jury's determination that Cahill should be put to death is no surprise, given the nature of his conduct. But the action of the Court of Appeals—New York's highest court and therefore its "court of last resort"—is instructive, because it shows the added degree of caution with which appellate courts will scrutinize a conviction to which the death penalty is attached. Almost certainly, mindful of the awful finality of an execution, appellate judges apply a higher standard of proof than in other cases, where a wrong may at least have a chance of being righted. Such an attitude is clearly reflected in the historical death-penalty decisions of the United States Supreme Court. In 1935, in Powell v. Alabama, *a capital case involving young black men convicted of raping a white woman in a heavily racist community in Alabama, the court ruled that anyone on trial for his or her life must have a lawyer to defend him or her, as a matter of due process of law.*

In 1942, in Betts v. Brady, *that same court ruled that those not facing the death penalty were not entitled to an appointed lawyer. In 1963, in* Gideon v. Wainwright *(argued by appellate counsel Abe Fortas, who later became a Supreme Court Justice himself), the court ruled that everyone charged with a felony must have counsel appointed for their defense, almost thirty years after only capital defendants had such an entitlement.*

Fans of the death penalty should note, however, that commendable though intensified appellate scrutiny may be when the accused's life is on the line, it is not enough. A whole spate of men have been rescued from death row in the past ten or so years due to the near infallibility of DNA evidence—thirteen in Illinois alone. This unfortunate history gives rise to some chilling thoughts: How many defendants did our court system mistakenly execute before DNA was on the scene, and how many are we executing wrongfully today because DNA was not a factor in the case?

Rae Carruth

Charged with soliciting the murder of his girlfriend and her unborn child on November 16, 1999

THE MURDER ATTEMPT

Carolina Panthers football player Rae Carruth and his pregnant girlfriend, Cherica Adams, went to the late show the evening of November 15, 1999, watching *The Bone Collector* at the Regal Cinemas in Charlotte. After the movie, Carruth, twenty-six, and Adams, twenty-four, left in his Ford Expedition and went to his home, where Adams's car was parked. They decided to go to her apartment in separate vehicles, so Carruth headed down Rea Road, Adams driving behind him.

Shortly after 12:30 A.M., a Nissan Maxima pulled alongside Adams's car, and shots were fired. Adams was struck with four bullets. As she watched the Maxima drive away, she called 911 on her cell phone, and frantically told the operator that she had been shot. The call lasted ten minutes, and in it she explained to the operator that Carruth was in front of her and that she believed he had something to do with it.

Police and an ambulance arrived at the scene at 12:45 A.M., and only Adams's car was in the area.

She was taken to Carolinas Medical Center, where emergency room doctors performed a Caesarean section and delivered Chancellor Lee Adams about two months early.

When Carruth arrived at the hospital, he declined meeting with Charlotte-Mecklenburg police investigators. However, he consented to a search of his home and car.

Nine days later, on Thanksgiving, he was arrested and charged with attempted murder and conspiracy to commit first-degree murder. Carruth's bond was initially set at $1.5 million, but district judge Jerome Leonard doubled that, and Carruth's lawyers were not able to get the bail reduced.

Van Brett Watkins, Michael Eugene Kennedy, and Stanley Abraham, all acquaintances of Carruth's, were also charged in the shooting.

TELEPHONE CALLS LINK CARRUTH TO KENNEDY

Phone records showed that a call was made from Carruth's cell phone to Kennedy's cell phone at 11:51 P.M. on November 15.

At 12:03 A.M., November 16, a call was placed from Carruth's home to Kennedy's cell phone.

At 12:07 A.M., a call was made from Carruth's home to the home of Carolina Panther Hannibal Navies.

Two minutes later, another call was made from Carruth's home to Kennedy's cell phone.

At about the same time, Adams made a call from her cell phone to her apartment. According to Adams's cousin Modrey Floyd, who said he answered the phone, Adams asked him to tidy up the apartment because Carruth was coming over.

At 12:21 A.M., a call was made from Kennedy's cell phone to Carruth's old cell phone.

One minute later, a call was made from Kennedy's cell phone to Carruth's current cell phone.

Phone records also showed that at 12:27 A.M., a call was placed from Carruth's cell phone to a girlfriend in Atlanta. This was the longest of the conversations, lasting sixteen minutes.

AFTERMATH OF THE SHOOTING

On December 6, a grand jury indicted Carruth, Watkins, Kennedy, and Abraham for attempted murder, shooting into an occupied vehicle, assault with a deadly weapon, and conspiracy to commit first-degree murder.

The following day, December 7, Carruth posted bond. He was released with the understanding that if either the baby or Adams died, he would turn himself in. Carruth repeatedly told police he was miles away when the shooting occurred.

One week later, Cherica Adams died, and charges against all four men were upgraded to murder. Carruth did not turn himself in, however. He fled to Tennessee, hiding in the trunk of a friend's car.

CARRUTH'S CAPTURE

The FBI captured Carruth the next day in a motel parking lot in Wildersville, Tennessee. They had received a tip to his location by his bail bondsman.

Carruth provided a statement to the FBI, claiming he had nothing to do with the shooting.

On December 16, Adams's mother was awarded temporary custody of her grandson, Chancellor. A paternity test proved Carruth was the father.

Three days later, Carruth waived extradition and returned to South Carolina, where he was jailed without bail. This same day, the district attorney's office announced it would seek the death penalty.

A few days before that, Carruth had hired attorney David Rudolf of Chapel Hill. Rudolf was renowned for high-profile cases.

On New Year's Eve, Chancellor was released from the hospital and went home with his grandmother.

LEGAL PROCEEDINGS BEGIN

In early January a grand jury was called and indicted Carruth, Watkins, Kennedy, and Abraham for murder and conspiracy to commit murder.

JANUARY 14. Carruth offered to pay $3,000 in monthly child support for Chancellor. This was about the same amount he claimed he paid in support for his six-year-old son in California.

MARCH 20. Saundra Adams, Adams's mother, sought control of Carruth's assets for Chancellor.

APRIL 18. Carruth requested visitation rights for Chancellor.

MAY 16. Carruth was ordered to sell his home and liquidate his retirement account to pay child support.

MAY 28. The district attorney's office offered plea agreements to Carruth, Watkins, Kennedy, and Abraham. The agreements would have guaranteed long prison sentences, but would have negated the threat of the death penalty.

JULY 5. David Rudolf, Carruth's attorney, told the court that Carruth would not accept a plea arrangement, as he was innocent of the charges.

JULY 31. Watkins pleaded guilty to second-degree murder in an arrangement to testify against Carruth.

CARRUTH'S TRIAL

Jury selection began in October, and defense attorney Rudolf claimed that prosecutors were biased against black men by excluding them from the jury. Eight of eleven black potential jurors were excluded, and the judge ordered prosecutors to list reasons other than race for dismissing them.

The DA's office answered, citing a variety of reasons including that their ages were too close to Carruth's, meaning they might be too sympathetic to him. Assistant District Attorney David Graham said three blacks had been selected to the jury, proof that there was no bias.

The judge reviewed the reasons for the exclusions and rejected the defense's claim.

The final jury selected included three black women, two white women, and seven white men. The four alternates included one black man and three white women.

Rudolf also lodged a complaint about leaks to the news media, which he said were hampering his client's right to a fair trial. *The*

Charlotte Observer had printed two stories containing information about transcripts that had not been made public. One of the articles detailed the call Adams made to 911, in which she told the operator Carruth was at the scene and drove away.

Opening statements in the trial lasted more than two hours.

Prosecutor Gentry Caudill told the jury that Adams had made a deathbed statement to police and hospital personnel that pointed a finger at Carruth. Prosecutors had contended early on that Carruth wanted Adams and the baby dead so he would not have to pay child support.

Caudill said: "Cherica Adams wasn't supposed to be an eyewitness to what the defendant had done to her and to her son. She wasn't supposed to, but she did."

Rudolf praised Caudill's opening, but was quick to attack the state's case. He told the jurors there was no motive, its main witness was a liar, and the prosecution's version of what happened made no sense. He showed a chart with Carruth's finances, saying Carruth earned more than $600,000 a year and could easily pay child support. Carruth had no motive to have Adams killed, he said.

Rudolf explained that Watkins, a drug dealer, killed Adams to punish Carruth, who would not fund a marijuana deal. Rudolf wrote on a board a quote attributed to Watkins before Adams died: "If he had just given us the money, none of this would have happened."

Rudolf told the jury: "The shooting was the result of anger and rage and violence by Van Brett Watkins after Carruth refused to give him money. The truth of this case is that the shooting of Cherica Adams had absolutely nothing to do with the fact that she was pregnant."

Carruth was known to be a kind and gentle person, Rudolf said, and Watkins was filled with anger and violence, especially toward women. Rudolf said a guard reported Watkins as saying of Adams, "I hope the bitch dies."

Rudolf said that, on the day of the shooting, Carruth certainly did not act like a man who was ordering a hit on his girlfriend.

Carruth played video games and visited with friends, then went out to a movie with Adams. It would not make sense for Carruth to be out in public with her, Rudolf added, if he was intending to have her killed.

THE PROSECUTION'S PRESENTATION

The prosecution's case would cover eleven days and would include more than two dozen witnesses.

Prosecutors played the recording of the 911 call Adams made. In it, she said she believed Carruth was responsible. She cried and moaned and pleaded for help. She said Carruth was "in the car in front of me," and that he slowed down when a car pulled alongside of hers and someone in it opened fire. She gave part of the license plate number of Carruth's vehicle, then helped give directions to where she was.

District Attorney Caudill called various emergency medical personnel to the stand. A nurse in the Carolinas Medical Center, Tracy Willard, testified that she held a clipboard while Adams wrote notes about the shooting. Willard read from the notes for the jury: "He was driving in front of me and stopped in the road and a car pulled up beside me and he blocked the front and never came back." Willard said she asked Adams who was blocking her, and Adams wrote "Rae."

In reading more of the notes, Willard said Adams mentioned her and Carruth going to the late show of *The Bone Collector*, and that Adams wrote, "Before we left his house, he called someone and said we were leaving now." Willard said a policeman in the room asked Adams who Carruth had called, and she wrote "Hannibal Navies," who the couple saw at the theater.

Nicole Michaels, a paramedic on the scene, testified that initially Adams was alert, but that she quickly deteriorated, with her blood pressure dropping. The baby's heartbeat was dropping, too, Michaels said, and he was delivered by Caesarean section when they arrived at the hospital.

One witness, Farrell Blalock, testified that Adams's car ended up in his front yard. He said he watched police and paramedics at the scene. He told the jury: "As soon as the policeman opened the door, the lady inside, she said, 'I'm pregnant, and I've been shot.' The policeman asked her who did it, and she said, 'My husband, I mean, my boyfriend.' " Blalock said he did not hear her name Carruth.

Blalock said he'd been reading the Bible when he heard gunfire. He called 911 and looked outside, seeing Adams's car. He was walking out to it about the time paramedics arrived. He told the jurors he prayed for her survival.

MICHAEL KENNEDY

Kennedy, twenty-five at the time of the trial, had made no plea arrangement with the district attorney's office, yet he testified for them and waived his Fifth Amendment right to self-incrimination. Kennedy said he played a role in the murder, but Carruth paid Watkins to do the killing.

He told jurors about a conversation he had with Carruth the day before the shooting. Kennedy said: "He was telling me about this girl he had got pregnant. He said she was trying to juice him for money." He said Carruth told him he didn't want to pay any more child support.

Kennedy said Carruth paid Watkins to beat Cherica to the point she would lose the baby. Kennedy said he didn't want anything to do with it, but that Carruth threatened him, saying he already was involved because he knew about it. Kennedy said: "He told me if I didn't I would be next." He further testified that he agreed to drive Watkins to where he would buy a gun with money Carruth had given him.

Kennedy told the jurors he was the driver on the night of the shooting. He testified: "Watkins told me to pull up beside her car. So I pulled up beside her car, and he started shooting at her car. I heard her screaming."

Carruth was in his SUV at the shooting scene, Kennedy said. He said that Carruth believed Adams had set him up and tricked him into getting her pregnant. Kennedy said Carruth told him that Adams bought baby books, and that he'd consulted a nurse friend who told him Adams might have planned their sexual encounter for when she was ovulating.

Kennedy testified that Carruth claimed he'd paid someone to beat up Adams so she would miscarry, but the beating hadn't happened yet. He added that he heard Carruth give Watkins suggestions for times and places he could beat up Adams. Kennedy said he once went to Adams's apartment complex with Watkins and Carruth.

Kennedy admitted he took part in helping Watkins get a gun. (He contacted a man who he knew had a gun for sale, and said that, with his friends Abraham and Watkins, he went there and bought the gun and bullets.) He said he told Abraham about the plan, and that Abraham wanted immediately to go home. Kennedy said he pressed his friend and said he needed him to stay.

The three of them parked near the theater, Kennedy said, and waited for Adams and Carruth to come out, but they didn't see the couple, and received a call from Carruth saying they'd driven to Carruth's house and were now on their way to Adams's apartment in separate cars. Soon after that, they saw Carruth's SUV, followed by Adams's car. Kennedy explained that they followed the car along a dark road.

Kennedy testified: "Rae went over a hill then down in a dip. He stopped his car, she stopped her car behind his, we stopped behind her." Kennedy said he then pulled alongside Adams's car and Watkins started shooting. He said Carruth started driving again, and then he drove away, too, dropping Watkins along a highway where he'd left his truck, and taking Abraham to a grocery store where he could call for a taxi.

When police interviewed him a week after the shooting, Kennedy said he did not tell them everything, such as about buying the gun. However, Kennedy had admitted to previous convictions for weapon possession and to being a crack cocaine dealer.

Rudolf cross-examined Kennedy, keying in on discrepancies in his testimony. Rudolf pointed out that it seemed Kennedy changed his testimony several times until it finally matched the state's theory behind the shooting. Further, Rudolf pointed out, according to police records Kennedy had said earlier that he was not threatened to participate, yet testified that Carruth told him he would be next if he didn't help. Kennedy countered that more than a year had passed since the shooting, and so some things were muddled to him. However, he said some things were more clear. "Since I've been in jail I had time to think, so I remember a lot of things that happened," Kennedy said.

At one point Rudolf asked: "If you hadn't bought the gun, this murder would've never occurred, would it?"

Kennedy replied, "If Rae would've never threatened me and gave me the money for the gun, it would've never occurred, sir."

ADAMS'S FATHER

Jeffrey Moonie, Cherica Adams's father, told the jurors that Carruth's behavior seemed odd after the shooting. Moonie said he never heard Carruth ask about how Adams or the baby were doing. Carruth sat in the waiting room, and a woman rubbed his shoulders.

Moonie said he asked Carruth what had happened, and Carruth said he didn't know, that they'd gone in separate directions after the movie.

He said it looked like his daughter and Carruth were a couple, but that Carruth became less supportive after he was injured during the football season.

CANDACE SMITH

Smith, who took the stand under a grant of immunity, reportedly had a confrontation with Adams a few weeks before the shooting. The two women had argued when Adams saw Carruth with Smith at a restaurant after a Panthers football game. A security guard at the restaurant intervened to break up the quarrel.

Smith, a former stripper who once dated Carruth, testified that she was the woman in the waiting room rubbing Carruth's shoulders. She told the jurors that Carruth said he hated Adams and had considered having her beaten up so that she would lose the baby.

However, Smith said Carruth denied planning the shooting.

On the day of the shooting, Smith told the jurors, Carruth called her asking to borrow her car. She declined, but agreed to meet him for breakfast. Smith said that as she was driving to breakfast, Carruth called again and said he was headed to the Carolinas Medical Center. She said she would meet him at the hospital.

Smith testified that Carruth swore her to secrecy and confessed to the murder plot while she was sitting with him in the hospital waiting room, and that he wished that Adams would die. "He said, 'I can't get in trouble, can I? Because I didn't actually pull the trigger.'" She added that Carruth wondered if the police would test for gunpowder on his car and clothes, which would clear him.

In addition, Smith reported that Carruth told her he drove in front of Adams and put on his brakes to slow her down. She said Carruth watched the shooting before he drove away.

Defense attorney Rudolf argued that Smith was testifying out of jealousy and that Carruth was dating several women at once and was not interested in a permanent relationship with any of them.

Smith admitted that Carruth was a ladies' man who kept a few dozen photos of women he was dating. Smith also said that she and Carruth occasionally saw each other after Carruth knew Adams was pregnant. Smith asserted that Carruth talked to her about the situation, that he didn't want to pay more child support, and that he had asked Adams to have an abortion. She said Carruth mentioned paying someone to kick Adams in the stomach so she would have a miscarriage.

Smith testified that when she saw pictures of Carruth's codefendants, she recognized them, though she did not know their names at the time she'd met them. Watkins visited the strip club where she worked, she said, adding that she'd seen Kennedy and Abraham with Carruth several times. She said that, at first, she kept her promise to stay quiet about the shooting. But she said she worried that she might be arrested for withholding information, and so she hired a lawyer and agreed to testify.

Rudolf aggressively cross-examined her, and played tapes of interviews she gave to police on the morning of the shooting and then more than a year later to a private investigator who had been hired by Carruth. Rudolf questioned if she testified because she had hoped for a permanent relationship with Carruth, and figured that was denied when Adams became pregnant.

Smith admitted to Rudolf that she was disappointed about the pregnancy and about Carruth's becoming distant during that time.

CHARLES SHACKLEFORD

Former NBA standout Charles Shackleford was also called to the stand. Although Shackleford was married and had three children, he told the jurors he had had a yearlong affair with Smith. He testified that, in one of his conversations with Smith, she told him that Carruth admitted to his part in Adams's shooting.

Shackleford, who played for the Charlotte Hornets and Dallas Mavericks, testified that he received a call from Smith at the hospital. "She said that he basically confessed to her at the hospital what had happened." He said Smith told him Carruth didn't want to pay any more child support.

Shackleford said he knew Adams through another friend, and had seen her only a handful of times. One occasion was at a rap concert when Smith called Adams names and told Shackleford not to talk to her.

He recalled telling police investigators that some of the conversations about Adams and Carruth were "fuzzy" and vague. Shackleford could not remember times or dates of various conversations.

Under cross-examination, Shackleford said he was giving Smith thousands of dollars for rent and car payments, while she was secretly still seeing Carruth.

Rudolf pressed Shackleford, "She was able during this whole time period to keep you uninformed about what she was doing with Mr. Carruth?"

Shackleford replied: "I wasn't really watching her like that. I have a life."

TANYA FERGUSON

Tanya Ferguson, called as a prosecution witness, turned out to be supportive of Carruth. She told the jurors he was a "very caring person" and that on the night Adams was shot he was his regular happy-go-lucky self.

Ferguson said she and her boyfriend, Hannibal Navies, saw Carruth and Adams at the movie theater that night. She testified that Carruth was relaxed and appeared to be getting along well with Adams. She said they all left the theater together. Ferguson said Carruth asked if he could drop by Navies's house later to play a video game. She added that Navies and Carruth were video game addicts and would hold tournaments with other players.

Carruth arrived at the house at 12:30 A.M., Ferguson said. (That was several minutes after Adams had been shot.) She said when she opened the door to let Carruth in, he was talking on his cell phone to a girlfriend of his in Atlanta.

Ferguson said Carruth talked about Adams's pregnancy, and that he seemed pleased she was having a boy. He'd continued to play video games when Ferguson said Navies went to bed. Ferguson recalled that she'd left her cell phone on a table, and she said she did not make the three calls the phone company attributed to her cell phone.

According to phone company records, calls were made to the Villager Lodge, where Watkins lived, and to Kennedy. Ferguson's cell phone looked identical to Carruth's.

Early in the morning, she testified, Navies woke her and said that Adams had been shot. Ferguson said she went with Navies to the hospital, Carruth following them because he said he did not know how to get there. Carruth had turned instantly serious, she said, and appeared to be in shock.

OTHER PROSECUTION WITNESSES

Police officer Kevin Wallin told the jurors that he spoke with Carruth in the hospital waiting room after the shooting. He said Carruth asked if the hospital was surrounded by police and that if he was arrested, would his head be covered. Carruth asked if police would check for gunpowder in his car. Wallin said he overheard part of a conversation Carruth had with Smith. In it, Carruth said he would give up women when this was all over.

Police officer Peter Grant testified that Adams had told him Carruth was responsible for the shooting and that Carruth had slowed his car so she had to stop when another car pulled alongside her and someone in it started firing.

Telephone company employees detailed the times of calls that were made between Carruth, Adams, Smith, Watkins, Abraham, and Kennedy around the time of the shooting.

Dwight Perry, the owner of a service shop, told the jurors that Carruth brought his SUV in to be cleaned on November 24, one day after Carruth had been questioned by police. Perry said Carruth asked to make a few calls from his phone. Records show that one call was made to Watkins's room at the Village Lodge. Perry testified that Carruth was a regular customer and a gentleman.

Dr. Michael Thomason of Carolinas Medical Center told the jurors that Adams was struck by four bullets and suffered serious bleeding. Thomason, director of trauma services, said Adams lost six pints of blood, essentially more than her body would contain, and that her heart just kept pumping the blood out of her body.

Thomason testified that transfusions kept her alive, even as she continued to bleed internally. He said the bullets essentially ripped her pancreas in two and shredded parts of her intestines. There were holes in her stomach and liver, and a bullet missed her baby by only an inch or two. Adams was awake when she was brought to the emergency room, and was immediately given morphine, Thomason said, adding that with the help of a nurse, Adams wrote three pages of notes that pointed the finger at Carruth.

Medical examiner James Sullivan testified that Adams died of "multiple organ system failure."

FBI agent Mark Post told the jury that when Carruth fled after Adams died, the FBI found him at a motel in Wildersville, Tennessee. Carruth had been driven there by a friend, Wendy Cole. She had checked into the motel, and agents found no trace of him there. Cole gave the FBI permission to search the hotel room, Post said. He added that she gave them hints to his location, throwing her car keys on the bed and telling them he could be in the area. He said she kept looking on the bed where her keys were, and he finally asked her if Carruth was in the trunk. She asked the agents not to tell Carruth she had given him up, Post said.

Post testified: "She placed the key in the lock of the trunk." She announced to Carruth that the FBI was with her. Carruth responded that he had no weapons.

Post said eventually they found him in the trunk of Cole's car, where he had apparently hid for twenty-four hours. "He was laying on his side, and put his hands where I could see them. His pants were down to his knees." Post said he helped Carruth out of the trunk. In the trunk, agents found two bottles filled with urine, candy wrappers, and Cole's purse, which had almost $4,000 in it.

THE DEFENSE'S STAND

Carruth had been out on $3 million bail for Adams's shooting, and had been told to surrender himself if she or the baby died. He fled when she died, and prosecutors contended that was a sign of his guilt. The defense, however, said Carruth was upset over Adams's death and needed time to think before turning himself in.

Defense attorney Rudolf pointed out that the FBI did not find any clothes for Carruth in the trunk, suggesting he did not intend to flee, and was indeed going to surrender.

Rudolf continued to maintain that Adams had been shot because Carruth refused to finance a drug deal for Watkins, and that the incident had nothing to do with Carruth's trying to duck child support payments. Rudolf told the jurors that Watkins, who admitted shooting Adams, did so for his own reasons, and not as a favor to Carruth.

Rudolf said that Kennedy, who testified against Carruth, was not credible. He was an admitted drug dealer who'd been in trouble with the law multiple times. Kennedy had been charged in the past with assault, and was implicated in a drug dealer's death, though charges were dropped. It was Kennedy's drug deals that could have led to Adams's death, Rudolf suggested.

Rudolf called to the stand police officer William Ward, one of the investigators in the Adams case. Ward testified that one of the prosecutors stopped an investigation into Kennedy's drug dealings when Kennedy agreed to testify against Carruth. Ward said he asked if he should press Kennedy about drug dealings, and the prosecutor walked away.

Witnesses testified that when Kennedy was interviewed, notes were not always taken, and he was not always recorded. Rudolf pointed out variations in Kennedy's testimony during the trial and reports he first gave to police. One witness agreed it was possible that Kennedy, in the year between the shooting and the trial, could have read newspaper accounts and made his testimony fit with the prosecution's claims about the case.

Rudolf alluded that the prosecution attempted to keep damaging information about Kennedy away from the defense and the jury. Kennedy had testified that he, Watkins, and Carruth drove to Adams's apartment once, after he'd picked Carruth up at a body shop. The body shop owner did not remember Kennedy's black car, but he remembered the men driving a white Ford Expedition. Rudolf said prosecutors knew that particular part of Kennedy's testimony was wrong, but they allowed him to tell the lie in court anyway.

During cross-examination, the prosecution said Kennedy was correct about the body shop and the car Carruth was having repaired there, a red Mercedes.

Carruth's banker, Erica Crawford of Bank of America, testified that Carruth showed no signs of having money problems. He had never been overdrawn. Crawford said that one month before the shooting, Carruth asked her to give a $1,260 check to Adams.

HENRY LEE

The criminologist who testified at the O. J. Simpson trial, and whose testimony is attributed to helping get Simpson an acquittal, was permitted to speak for the defense via videotape because he could not be in Charlotte during the days he was originally scheduled to testify. Lee had successfully cast doubts on how the Los Angeles Police Department had handled evidence regarding the Simpson trail, and that footprints at the scene had suggested more than one person killed Ronald Goldman and Nicole Brown Simpson.

Lee, who is considered one of the foremost criminologists in the country, testified for the defense. (He would also later testify at Michael Peterson's murder trial.)

Lee explained that examining the angles of the bullets in Adams and in her car shows that Carruth's SUV could not have been directly in front of her car. Lee argued that a diagram presented by prosecutors and showing Carruth's SUV blocking Adams's car could not possibly be correct.

Lee explained that three bullets entered Adams's car at a ninety-degree angle, suggesting that the shooter's car was parallel to hers. But the final two bullets illustrate that Adams's car was ahead of the shooter's car. Lee suggested that Adams's car was moving forward, which could not have happened if Carruth had been blocking her, and there was no indication that Adams's car hit anything in front of her.

Prosecutor Caudill got Lee to agree that Adams's car could have moved slightly ahead of the shooter's car, but not far enough to strike Carruth's SUV. Too, Lee agreed that the shooter could have changed positions or that Adams's body could have shifted.

CAROLINA PANTHERS

Leonard Wheeler, of the Carolina Panthers, testified in Carruth's defense. Wheeler, who was known for his community service, said Carruth had volunteered to help him at youth outreach and charity bowling programs. Wheeler testified that people try to take advantage of football players because of their money. He said he was careful in choosing his friends.

He said, "Coming into the NFL, you're a player who never had any money. There are many people who want to be associated with you. People all of sudden become your friends who were not your friends. It's easy to get caught up with it."

Wheeler said he was one of several teammates with Carruth the day before the shooting. They were playing a video football tournament at William Floyd's house.

Floyd also testified, describing Carruth as a "fun-loving guy" who liked to tell jokes.

Muhsin Muhammad, a Panthers wide receiver, said Carruth seemed excited about being a father and was making plans to maintain a close relationship with Adams. Muhammad said he was surprised to hear that Carruth had been accused of murder.

In his testimony, Muhammad recalled saying, "Are you sure we're talking about the same Rae? . . . Rae was the type of guy who avoided conflict, he wasn't the type to argue." Muhammad shared a hotel room for three seasons with Carruth when the Panthers were on the road. He said he never knew Carruth to be violent, and that on several occasions Carruth was a guest in his home.

Muhammad said that Carruth often spoke with him, and that on one of those occasions, Carruth told him that he was looking forward to having a son that he would be involved with. Muhammad said Carruth had fathered a child when he was playing with the University of Colorado, and that while he dutifully paid child support, he hardly ever saw his son.

Muhammad said he told Carruth to participate in this child's life if a paternity test indeed proved he was the father.

Hannibal Navies said that when Carruth showed up at his

house after the late movie, he did not act upset or unusual. However, Carruth's demeanor changed after getting the news about Adams being shot. Navies testified: "He was very quiet. He basically had nothing to say at all."

Navies said Carruth never complained about supporting his child in California (six years old at the time of the trial); however, Carruth was sometimes concerned that the mother might not be spending the money appropriately and that it might not be going to the child.

Navies was a teammate of Carruth's when the two attended the University of Colorado. They were acquaintances then, as Carruth was two years older, but Navies asserted that when he was drafted by the Panthers, Carruth showed him around Charlotte and helped him get settled. Navies told the jurors he lived with Carruth from June to October 1999 while he was purchasing his own house. During that time, Navies said Carruth was always laughing and energetic.

He admitted that Kennedy was at Carruth's house on two or three occasions, and that he met Watkins the day of the shooting; he was washing Carruth's car. Navies said he also knew Smith, one of the prosecution's witnesses. He said Smith appeared at the house one day, screaming and knocking on the door. She had a box cutter with her, and Carruth went outside, telling Navies to come check on him if he wasn't back in several minutes. Navies said Carruth defused the situation, and that he told Carruth not to see Smith again.

Head team trainer John Kasik said the Panthers staff had been certain Carruth would return to playing, as his injury earlier in the season did not seem severe. Kasik explained the injury to the jury and detailed the physical therapy treatments Carruth received. He said Carruth was scheduled to play the next game but that, after the arrest, they suspended him without pay. When Carruth jumped bail, Kasik said, the team fired him.

Marty Hurney, director of football operations, testified that Carruth was a first-round draft pick in 1997 and had had a stellar rookie season with forty-four receptions. The following year, Carruth missed most of the season because he broke his foot. In

October 1999, Carruth suffered an ankle sprain, but it was not serious. Hurney testified that Carruth's four-year contract was for $3.7 million, and that after that contract was up he would likely have made more money.

Barbara Harrison, director of community relations for the Panthers, said Carruth always acted respectfully. She told the jurors that in February 1999, he came into her office looking for volunteer work. Carruth said he would like to teach T-ball to inner-city children. She said she helped him become the head coach of a YMCA team.

WATKINS TESTIFIES FOR THE DEFENSE

Originally, prosecutors wanted Watkins to testify on their behalf and cut a plea arrangement with him that would spare him the death penalty. However, Watkins's comments to police officers and jailers weakened his potential testimony.

Instead, Rudolf called him to the stand and asked him about his long rap sheet and psychiatric records. Rudolf read to the jury a report from Shirley Riddle, a corrections officer. Riddle reported that Watkins told her Carruth backed out on financing a drug deal. Riddle claimed that Watkins said he and Kennedy were looking for Carruth when they saw Adams, who made an obscene gesture at him and would not tell them where Carruth was.

Riddle said Watkins claimed he started shooting.

Watkins, however, denied making the statements to Riddle. At one point, he suggested Rudolf work out a plea deal for Carruth. Watkins would not admit to killing Adams over a botched drug deal.

Riddle later was called to testify and told the jurors that Watkins made a confession to her that Carruth was not involved in the shooting. She said she tried to report the confession to her superiors, but it went nowhere.

OTHER WITNESSES FOR THE DEFENSE

Ronald Guerette, a private investigator working for the defense, testified that he analyzed more than three thousand pages of phone records. Guerette said he believed the series of phone calls between Carruth, Watkins, and Kennedy seemed like a "classic, classic drug transaction," rather than the arrangement of a murder.

Guerette told the jurors that Watkins, Kennedy, and Carruth exchanged many phone calls during the weeks before the shooting, and that those calls were not listed in the prosecution's reports. Further, Guerette said the pattern and length of calls looked like Carruth was returning Watkins and Kennedy's calls.

He supported the defense's belief that Adams was shot in retaliation for a fouled drug deal. Guerette said Kennedy's purchasing the gun shortly before the shooting demonstrated it was not a planned hit.

Adrian Barnett, an accountant, testified that Carruth's net worth at the time of the shooting was $368,000. He said that Carruth was living well within his means, earning about $55,000 a month, while keeping his monthly living expenses to $9,500.

Erika Worthy, Carruth's former financial manager, told the jurors that Carruth held a disability insurance policy with Lloyd's of London. That meant if he suffered a career-ending injury, the insurance company would pay out a tax-free $1 million. Worthy said Carruth was always polite when he spoke to her. Worthy testified that Carruth always paid his monthly child support payments for his son in California and had set up a trust fund for him.

Dr. Gary Pellom, an anesthesiologist, testified that the drugs Adams was given in the emergency room could have affected her ability to remember the events of the shooting. Pellom was considered an expert witness regarding drugs such as the ones administered to Adams.

Dr. Elizabeth Loftus, a psychologist and memory expert, testified that when people are under stress, their memory can be distorted. Loftus said that at one point Adams claimed Carruth had stopped in front of her, later she said he'd slowed in front of her, and another time she said Carruth blocked her in front, all different versions. Loftus also said that Adams's recollections could have been tainted by her family's visiting in the hospital and discussing their suspicions about Carruth.

Michael Griffin, a police officer who escorted Watkins to a court appearance prior to Adams's death, was one of the strongest defense witnesses. He testified that in his presence Watkins said "I hope the bitch dies," and that Carruth would never be able to play football again.

Melvin Fontes, Carruth's high school football coach, called Carruth modest, intelligent, and a leader on and off the field.

Starlita Walker also testified to Carruth's character. She told the jurors that her seven-year-old son was mentored by Carruth. They met Carruth at a barber shop, and he took an instant like to her son, inviting him to join a T-ball team he coached. She said Carruth took her son out bowling, for pizza, or to a movie once a month.

Morris Whittaker, another character witness, a radio station employee, said Carruth approached him to help start a charity program for underprivileged boys in Charlotte. Whittaker said he helped plan a bowling party and video game tournament with Carruth.

In all, more than three dozen witnesses were called by the defense.

THE DEFENSE RESTS

Defense attorney Rudolf once again told the jurors that Adams was shot because a drug deal went sour, and that Watkins shot her in a moment of rage. Rudolf said their stance is backed up by testimony from Riddle, a jail guard who claimed Watkins confessed to her.

Rudolf showed the jurors a photograph of baby furniture Carruth had purchased for Adams's son. Carruth was looking forward to the birth, the attorney said, and was not trying to avoid child support.

CLOSING STATEMENTS

Although Adams's 911 call had been played for the jury on the first day of the trial, prosecutors replayed it during summations.

Caudill told the jurors that in that recording, Adams told everyone that Carruth was guilty. Carruth lead her into a trap, stopping his SUV in front of her car so Watkins could shoot her. But there was a snag in Carruth's plan, Caudill said. Adams lived long enough to make the 911 call and then later to make notes in the hospital.

Caudill said that defense witnesses painted Carruth as someone of good character, yet he had drug-dealer companions and frequented strip clubs.

Rudolf argued that the prosecution's case did not make sense and that there was a lack of evidence to convict Carruth. He said: "Rae Carruth is innocent of the charges. He is innocent of the charges."

The police tainted the testimony of some witnesses, including Carruth's former girlfriends, Rudolf contended. Officers fed them information about the case, he said.

Rudolf said there were many points of reasonable doubt, including that Carruth hired Watkins to kill Adams. Enough evidence of a failed drug deal existed to cast reasonable doubt, he said, adding that Watkins had confessed to a jailer that he killed Adams in a fit of rage.

THE VERDICT

After eighteen hours of deliberation, the jury found Carruth guilty of conspiracy to commit murder and shooting into an occupied vehicle. The jury acquitted him of capital murder, which could have carried a death sentence.

Rudolf asked the judge to set aside the jury's verdict, but the judge upheld their decision. Then Rudolf asked the judge to sentence Carruth for the minimum of ten years. Instead, Carruth received closer to the maximum of twenty-five.

Carruth was sentenced to nineteen to twenty-three years at the Nash Correctional Institution in Nashville, North Carolina.

Watkins was sentenced to a forty- to fifty-year term.

Under a plea arrangement, Kennedy was sentenced to twelve to fourteen years.

Abraham served eighteen months and was released from a minimum-security prison in 2001.

COURT OF APPEALS

Carruth's attorneys appealed his conviction and sentencing, and the North Carolina Court of Appeals agreed in part. The court ruled in August 2003 that Adams's notes were not correctly introduced as evidence. That was not enough of an error, however, to grant a new trial. Therefore the court upheld Carruth's conviction and sentencing.

COMMENTARY: Rae Carruth

The jury system in America is often attacked on a number of grounds; among them is the claim that juries make mistakes in believing the wrong witnesses, drawing the wrong inferences from circumstantial evidence, and—worst case—sending the wrong people to succumb to the "Executioner's Song." Defense lawyers live in fear of the fact that there is virtually no remedy to fix a factual error by a jury; if they have wrongfully acquitted a guilty man, that is the end of the case. If the jurors have wrongfully convicted an innocent man, there is ordinarily a very narrow opportunity to change the result. Appellate courts exist to review mistakes by judges, not juries, unless those mistakes are obvious. There is no record of a jury's deliberations, and jurors are generally rendered legally incompetent to testify as to why a certain result was reached, or even how each juror voted as the deliberations went along.

All of that said, grizzled defense lawyers often marvel at the degree of accuracy some juries demonstrate as they pick and choose from various options on the verdict form, matching what the accused actually did to the crime for which he should be punished.

It would seem that this is what may have happened in the case of Carolina Panthers star Rae Carruth. Although there was some evidence that Carruth was a principal in the killing and thus guilty of capital murder, there was also ample room for reasonable doubt from the many contradictions in the testimony. Carruth was given the benefit of that doubt.

The largest puzzle in the case arises from what is known in legal circles as "the time line." While the available proof falls short of establishing a classic alibi, such as "I was with the pope in the Vatican in Rome when the murder occurred in North Carolina," backed by Vatican witnesses, plane

*and hotel receipts, and stamps in the accused's passport, facts and circum-
stances operating together may preclude the accused from having had any
opportunity to commit the crime. The Carruth case is somewhere between
these two, depending on how much you credit the testimony of teammate
Hannibal Navies, and his girlfriend, Tanya Ferguson. It would appear
that the jury may have believed them, for if they had supported the contention that Carruth had indeed blocked Adams's escape path when the
shooter in the Nissan opened fire—a claim that had some strong eviden-
tiary support—it is likely that Carruth would have been convicted of murder in the first degree. That this close call was resolved in favor of Carruth
can clearly be attributed to the excellent work by a high-caliber defense
lawyer, David Rudolf of Chapel Hill. The important time line is as follows:*

*1.   At 12:27 A.M. on November 16, Carruth calls from his cell phone
to a girlfriend in Atlanta. That call continued—according to phone
company records—until 12:43 A.M.*

*2.   Hannibal Navies—backed by Ms. Ferguson—said that Carruth
appeared at his door at 12:30 A.M. to play video games, and that his
demeanor was pleasant and relaxed. Navies's apartment is two or so
miles from the scene of the shooting. Unless Carruth had taken tutor-
ing from a top-flight acting school, this would be a difficult face to
wear if one knew that within minutes one's pregnant girlfriend was
about to be gunned down.*

*3.   12:31 A.M. Cherica Adams indisputably called 911 to say that she
had been shot while driving her automobile. This call lasted for ten
minutes, during which time Cherica said that Carruth was "in front
of her" and she "believed he had something to do with it." This is a
terribly damning piece of evidence. In legalese, it is variously called an
"excited utterance" or a "spontaneous exclamation." Such statements
are thought to be inherently credible because one in the middle "of the
action," as Cherica was here, is unlikely to fabricate a story that could
ordinarily not have been preplanned. As such, declarations of this sort
are and have been for hundreds of years a classic exception to the rules
forbidding "hearsay" evidence.*

*4.   On the other hand, it is most important to note that at this very
moment Carruth was equally indisputably still talking to his other*

girlfriend in Atlanta, a curious phone conversation to pursue if the mother of one's son-to-be is being repeatedly shot at less than fifty feet away. It is significant that no "Atlanta girlfriend" was produced by either side who did or not hear gunshots over the phone. It is clear that if she had remembered a loud noise similar to a firearm being discharged through her earpiece as she talked to Carruth, the prosecution would have called or forced her to the stand. While the defense would have benefited from this one piece of testimony, there might have been many other things this young lady could have said on cross-examination that would not have been helpful to Carruth.

Apart from the issue of whether he participated in the shooting by assisting the triggerman, Carruth cooked himself with his conduct. His phone calls to Kennedy and Watkins might have been about a drug deal, but that seems a bit of a stretch, no matter how skillfully David Rudolf sought to prove that theory. Those calls might also be last-minute preparation. The 12:07 A.M. call to Hannibal Navies—no doubt asking if Carruth could come over to play video games—could well have been a plan to set up an alibi, which it did. This is a strange hour to make and follow up such a request, and a severe imposition on a friend, at best. On the other hand, the victim's conversation with her cousin, Modrey Floyd, instructing him to clean things up because Carruth was "coming over," lends support to the fact that Adams at least believed that Carruth would do so.

Jumping bail and hiding in a trunk for twenty-four hours does little to bolster innocence. Further, Carruth's lack of affection at the hospital hardly helped, and his decision to get a shoulder massage from a stripper-lover in the waiting room indicates an outrageous insensitivity to Adams's plight. On the other hand, Carruth may have benefited from the fact that the prosecution allowed Watkins—a cold-blooded killer—to plead guilty to second-degree murder, and thus avoid the death penalty. In any event, the result Carruth got from the jury was more than fair it would seem, but refreshing evidence that at least some jurors (a minority, I fear) honor the standard of "reasonable doubt."

Kenneth Fitzhugh

Charged with murdering his wife
on May 5, 2000

The local headlines read "Music Teacher Slain." Initially, authorities believed fifty-three-year-old Kristine Pedersen Fitzhugh died from falling down the basement stairs of her Palo Alto, California, home. However, the next day the police said Kristine was murdered, and fourteen days after that they arrested her husband of thirty-three years.

THE MURDER

The school district reported that Kristine went home between two of her classes, but did not show up at the Addison Elementary School for her afternoon session. School district officials called her husband, a real estate developer, who went with two friends to the house and noticed the front door was open. Fitzhugh called the police shortly before 2:00 P.M., frantic that he'd found his wife at the bottom of the stairs. The police and fire department paramedics could not revive her.

The police immediately investigated and initially treated it as an accident.

Neighbors wondered if Kristine had been killed by a burglar, as there had been several burglaries in the area recently. Police considered that possibility. They met with her relatives, friends, co-workers, and neighbors, and tried to reconstruct her last day.

Police determined that after her class at Duveneck Elementary School 11:00 A.M. Kristine bought muffins at a nearby coffee shop on her way home. When a FedEx driver stopped at the house shortly after noon, there was no answer. (Kristine missed her 1:00 P.M. class.)

Investigators believe that Kristine was in the kitchen when she was killed. They found a half-eaten muffin, a half-empty cup of coffee, and class materials sitting on the kitchen table. They speculate that Fitzhugh, fifty-six, struck her with a blunt object, then strangled her and tugged her body down the stairs and staged the scene, putting dry cleaning around her to make it look as if she fell while carrying the clothes.

KENNETH AND KRISTINE FITZHUGH

At the time of the murder, he worked as a self-employed real estate consultant out of his home, and part-time as a paralegal. He once served as a Boy Scout leader, and had no criminal record.

She was a well-loved, part-time music instructor for the Palo Alto Unified School District and at the Cesar Chavez Academy, and memorials in her honor were made to the Palo Alto Ravenswood Music Collaborative.

Kristine had met Fitzhugh in 1964 when he was playing a pipe organ at the San Diego County Fair. She was sixteen, four years younger than Fitzhugh. They married two years later.

THE AFFIDAVIT

According to a police affidavit, Fitzhugh said he had left the house around 10:00 A.M. and was driving down a highway when he got a call on his cell phone from the school district about his absent wife. In the affidavit, he stated that he tried to call Kristine at home but there was no answer; however, according to records received from the phone company, he never called his home from his cell phone.

The affidavit, compiled by Detective Mike Denson of the Palo Alto Police Department and filed in the Santa Clara County Superior Court on May 19, 2000, states: "On May 5, 2000, Kenneth Fitzhugh Jr. killed his wife, Kristine Fitzhugh, by beating her over the head with a blunt object and strangling her. This vicious assault occurred in the kitchen of their home located at 1545 Escobita Avenue, Palo Alto, California. During the assault, the victim lost a substantial amount of blood. Mr. Fitzhugh attempted to clean up the victim's blood, which had dripped onto the kitchen floor and furniture. He then moved her body and 'staged' it at the foot of the basement stairway adjacent to a brass ship bell. Later he brought friends to the scene so that he would have witnesses to the 'discovery' of his wife's body. He attempted to mislead investigators by suggesting that the victim had been killed when she fell down the basement stairs and hit her head."

Denson's affidavit further states that the washer and dryer in the laundry room had blood spatters on them. The carpeted landing on the basement stairway had a wet bloodstain, and a large brass ship's bell blocked a portion of the landing. There was also blood on dry cleaning bags and school papers that were near Kristine's body. "The basement floor had a large pool of wet blood consistent with the location of the victim's head when resuscitation efforts were attempted," Denson wrote. In estimating the time of Kristine's death, he wrote: "I believe that the time of the victim's death was between 12:08 P.M. (the time the FedEx driver knocked on the door) and 1:41 P.M. (the time of the '911' call)."

Regarding the discovery of Kristine's body, the affidavit states: "Two female friends of the victim told investigators that Mr. Fitzhugh arrived at their home on May 5, 2000, around 1:30 P.M. driving his blue Suburban. He told them that his wife had not shown up for class and he wanted to go by his house to see if she was there. They rode with Fitzhugh to his Escobita Avenue home. They noticed that the front door was ajar and remained in the car while Mr. Fitzhugh went inside. They saw him go upstairs and heard him calling out Kristine's name. Mr. Fitzhugh looked around downstairs and then came back outside and told them he need [sic] help because his wife was injured. One of the women went downstairs with Mr. Fitzhugh. She observed Kristine Fitzhugh's body lying at the base of the stairs. Her head was on the landing, near the ship's bell and her legs extended up the stairwell. There were several pieces [sic] clothing in dry cleaning bags and school papers under her body. One woman called '911' and told the Palo Alto Police Department dispatcher that a person was injured inside the residence located at 1545 Escobita Avenue." The Fire Department arrived quickly and attempted to resuscitate Kristine, but she was already dead.

Also according to the affidavit, Fitzhugh told firemen that his wife must have slipped while carrying the dry cleaning down the stairs. He said that when he first discovered his wife, her head was at the bottom of the stairs next to the ship's bell, and her feet were above her on the stairs. He said that some dry cleaning was under her head and one of her shoes was located farther up the stairs. As a result, firemen initially believed that the death was accidental.

Denson wrote: "I was assigned the investigation and arrived at the residence at approximately 3:00 P.M. on May 5, 2000. I observed the condition of the house, and in particular the stairwell area where the victim had been found. . . . On the dining room table, I observed the victim's purse, keys, an uneaten muffin, and a bottle of water. On the kitchen table was a half-eaten muffin, a half-full cup of coffee, a notebook, some school papers, and an orange marker. It appeared to me that the victim had been sitting at the kitchen table immediately before she died."

Fitzhugh told Denson that he and his wife woke up at 6:00 A.M., read the newspaper, drank coffee, and then went jogging. He said Kristine left for her class at 10:00 A.M., and he left an hour later and drove to a vacant lot and walked around the undeveloped property for about an hour. He was considering it as a building site for a potential client, and that he did not talk to anyone while he was there. Fitzhugh further said he had an appointment to pick up friends in Palo Alto at 1:30 P.M. to run some errands. He said he left the vacant property, and while driving received the call about his absent wife.

The affidavit states: "Fitzhugh said he continued to drive to the home of two friends of his and Kristine's in Palo Alto. Once at the house he told them that his wife had not shown up for her 1:00 class, and that he wanted to go back to his house to see if she was there. They agreed and he drove them to his residence on Escobita Avenue in his blue Suburban. When they arrived, Fitzhugh said his wife's car was parked in the driveway and the front door to the house was ajar. He went inside while the two women waited outside in his Suburban. He said that he first looked upstairs and called out her name. He then looked for her on the on the [sic] first floor. When he noticed that the door to the stairwell leading to the basement was ajar he looked down the stairwell, he saw his wife lying near the bottom landing. Her body was on top of some dry cleaning, her hands were clutching some items, and her face was touching a large brass ship bell. He said he did not immediately go down the stairs. Instead, he went back outside and told the women that he 'needed some help.' They all came inside, and one of the women went down into the basement with Mr. Fitzhugh. The other woman called 911. He said that he and one of the women attempted CPR on the victim. They continued to give CPR until the personnel from the Fire Department arrived at around 1:40 P.M. He said he realized that his wife was dead while he was giving her CPR but nevertheless he continued until Fire Department personnel took over."

Denson asked Fitzhugh if he could search the house to determine if a burglar had broken in. Fitzhugh agreed, but insisted on being present. Denson wrote: "While at the home an officer told me that a bloody paper towel and a pair of bloody running shoes had been found in Mr. Fitzhugh's Suburban. The Suburban was sealed and impounded. I asked Mr. Fitzhugh if he could show me where the running shoes he had worn that morning were located. He took me upstairs to a closet in the master bedroom. I observed an empty space in a row of shoes that were lined up on the floor of the closet. He told me his running shoes should be where the empty space was. He described the running shoes to me. I informed him that his running shoes had been found in his Suburban, and showed him a picture of the recovered shoes. He had no explanation as to why they would be in the vehicle. He further stated that he had no explanation for why they would have his wife's blood on them. He also could not provide an explanation for the bloody towel. Subsequently, Mr. Fitzhugh left the house and went to pick up his son at the airport. In an interview conducted several hours later, Mr. Fitzhugh told me that perhaps his wife's blood had gotten on the shoes when she cut her left hand a week or two before while gardening. He said the [*sic*] he applied direct pressure to her wound to stop the bleeding, and suggested perhaps that explained the blood on the shoe. He still could not explain how his running shoes got into the Suburban, or why they would have blood on the sole."

Denson met with the coroner, Dr. Gregory Schmunk, and with forensic pathologist Dr. Diane Vertis.

Dr. Vertis conducted the autopsy and reported "three impact wounds" on the top of Kristine's head, and three more on the back of her head, indicating she had been hit with a blunt object. There was also a puncture wound behind Kristine's ear that penetrated into her brain. Further, it appeared Kristine had been strangled and punched, as she had two black eyes. There was a defensive-type injury to a finger, as if she had held up her hand to block a blow. Dr. Vertis and Dr. Schmunk contended that these wounds were the cause of death and were not consistent with a fall down the stairs.

The affidavit states: "These wounds were consistent with the assailant attacking Ms. Fitzhugh from behind with a blunt object and the victim at least briefly attempting to fend off the attack. The injuries were consistent with an attack that included the assailant having grabbed Kristine's neck, attempting to strangle her with one hand, while punching her face with the other. In all likelihood, they believed Ms. Fitzhugh was dead before she was moved to the basement."

Denson reported that more than seventy spatters of blood were found in the kitchen, and they could be the result of blood flying off an object that was used to beat Kristine. Luminol tests were done May 10 to find blood that was not otherwise noticeable or that had been cleaned up.

After looking at the Luminol results, Denson wrote: "Evidence of blood was located on the kitchen chair that was found next to the half-eaten muffin and Ms. Fitzhugh's music papers (Exhibit 1b and 2b). Evidence of blood was found on the kitchen wall (Exhibit 3b). Evidence of a large area of blood was revealed on the kitchen floor (Exhibit 4b). A luminous path of blood led from the kitchen to the top of the basement stairs (Exhibit 5b). Evidence of a pool of blood was detected on the top of basement stairs (Exhibit 5b and 6b). Apparent in Exhibits 4b and 5b are distinctive patterns that appeared to me to be consistent with the soles of Mr. Fitzhugh's running shoes. Within the luminous images in Exhibits 4b and 6b, there appeared a pattern consistent with someone having wiped up blood."

DNA test results matched Kristine's blood to blood found on Fitzhugh's shoes and shirt that were in his Suburban.

Police attempted to validate Fitzhugh's story and alibi. Denson, in the affidavit, states, "A fellow police officer told me that he drove to the location to 2101 Sneath Lane, San Bruno, and determined that it was a vacant lot adjacent to a business called the Family Golf Center. The officer told me he spoke to employees of the Family Golf Center. He spoke to a manager of the facility. She told him that she knows Kenneth Fitzhugh and had an on going [sic] long-term friendly business relationship with him. She has spoken to him on several occasions. She said that Mr. Fitzhugh he [sic] had been involved in getting the city building permits for the facility. She pointed out the vacant lot to him (2101 Sneath Lane). The lot was adjacent to the office and was clearly visible from the office. The manager told Officer Souza that due to the nature of their relationship, it would be unusual for Mr. Fitzhugh to be on or near the property and not come into her office and speak with her or other employees. She told him that if he had been at the property on May 5 between 11:45 A.M. and 12:45 A.M, she would have seen him."

THE INVESTIGATION
AND PRELIMINARY HEARING

In searching for a motive to the murder, police probed Fitzhugh's financial situation. According to records, the Fitzhughs refinanced their home several times and Fitzhugh applied to refinance again the day before the murder. Moreover, Fitzhugh had a record of bouncing checks.

Kristine had a $48,000 life insurance policy, with her husband listed as the beneficiary. According to the policy, that amount would double if her death was ruled an accident.

Fitzhugh's lawyer, Thomas Nolan, questioned how police handled evidence at the scene. Nolan contended that investigators could not prove whether the blood traces they noted were recent or old.

Prosecuting attorneys stated that Fitzhugh killed his wife in the kitchen and arranged her body on the stairs to make it look like an accident.

Fitzhugh pleaded not guilty. The trial was expected to begin that summer, but was postponed because his lawyer was working on another murder trial. Too, his attorney's son was competing in the Olympics in Australia, and Nolan intended to watch.

THE CELL PHONE CALL

During the preliminary hearing, prosecuting attorneys mentioned Fitzhugh's statement that he was traveling south on Highway 101, near the exit to Woodside Road in Redwood City, when he received the call from the school district about his wife's absence. However, a representative of GTE Wireless, Fitzhugh's cell phone provider, said that according to records the call was handled by an antenna on University Avenue in Palo Alto and that if Fitzhugh had been near Woodside Road, another antenna would have handled it.

Attorney Nolan got the representative to admit that he could not specify the range of the antenna in Palo Alto and that he could not produce maps showing the range of other antennas in the area.

THE TRIAL

In his opening remarks, Nolan told the jurors that Fitzhugh was traumatized by his wife's death and that in his state of shock he did not remember putting his bloody shirt and shoes in his Suburban. Nolan explained that Fitzhugh had gone to the Suburban after finding his wife's body, to check on the two family dogs that were in there. Fitzhugh put the clothes and shoes in the car at that time.

Further refuting police evidence, Nolan said there wasn't enough blood in the kitchen to show that Kristine was killed there, and the blood found in the kitchen by Luminol could have been from animals, even from food such as steak.

Prosecutors began their presentation with a videotape tour of the Fitzhugh home, complete with images of Kristine's body on the stairs.

Patrick Morris, a Palo Alto Fire Department captain, testified that Fitzhugh was calm at the scene, and seemed "detached."

Gaelyn Mason, a schoolteacher and family friend, testified that she and Carolyn Piraino were with Fitzhugh when he went home looking for Kristine. She said she performed CPR, and Piraino called 911. Mason and Piraino had been with Fitzhugh because they were going to pick up casino tables for Mason's upcoming birthday party.

Mason said Fitzhugh was wearing a shirt with a white collar and loafers when they discovered Kristine's body. Mason and Piraino testified that Fitzhugh's face and hands were covered in blood after he checked on his wife, and that they saw him go into the bathroom to clean up. They joined him several minutes later in the living room.

Fitzhugh's attorney contended that in the time between when Fitzhugh cleaned up and met the women in the living room, he went to the Suburban and put the shirt and shoes in it, not realizing what he was doing.

Coroner Schmunk testified that he did not find enough blood

around Kristine's body to indicate she'd died on the stairs. Too, Schmunk said her head injuries were the result of being struck by something such as the arm of a chair or a piece of wood, not from a fall.

Nolan asserted that police contaminated the murder scene and that their investigation was shoddy. Further, he challenged the coroner's credentials in discussing blood spatters, and pointed out that if reports Kristine had been beaten were true, no murder weapon was found.

A MOTIVE FOR MURDER

Prosecutors claimed that Fitzhugh killed his wife for the life insurance money and because she was going to tell their oldest son that his biological father was another man who used to be a family friend.

During the trial, Robert Brown testified that he'd had an affair with Kristine, which resulted in a son, Justin. Brown told the jurors that Kristine had invited him to Justin's upcoming graduation from the University of the Pacific in Stockton. She was going to tell Justin soon that Brown was his biological father. However, Kristine was murdered two weeks before Justin's graduation.

Brown admitted under defense questioning that he had a criminal past, including auto theft, and was disbarred as an attorney. Too, he said he'd had bouts of drug abuse.

Brown said he met Kristine in the late 1960s. She was already married to Fitzhugh, and the three of them got together for dinners and weekends. They jointly purchased real estate, stock, and boats, and through the years, Brown told the jurors a secret romance bloomed between him and Kristine. Their child, Justin, was raised by the Fitzhughs. Brown said he suspected Justin was his, and put him in his will in 1996. However, he wasn't certain until after Kristine's death, when DNA tests were done.

SHAKY FINANCES

Prosecutors presented evidence that, at the time of the murder, the family's finances were in ruins, with only $20,000 in liquid assets. Four days after the murder, Fitzhugh made a loan application in which he claimed a monthly income of $16,500. In the previous year's tax statement, Fitzhugh listed his annual income at approximately $30,000.

Fitzhugh testified that the $16,500 monthly figure was based on if he worked full-time and charged his typical consulting fee of $90 an hour.

The prosecution showed the jury a graph of the Fitzhughs' finances in the two years prior to Kristine's murder. The Fitzhughs had three investment accounts worth almost $400,000 in early 1998, which dropped to about $11,000 in May 2000.

Fitzhugh countered that while the accounts had dwindled, their home increased in value to more than a million dollars.

THE DEFENSE'S CASE

Fitzhugh's attorney, Nolan, said he believed an intruder killed Kristine and that police missed evidence because they focused on Fitzhugh. While DNA tests revealed that Kristine's blood was in the kitchen, they also revealed the presence of DNA belonging to a man that was not Fitzhugh.

One of the defense witnesses, Thomas Moore, was a lawyer who worked in a home office next door to Fitzhugh's house. He told the jurors he saw Fitzhugh on and off between 10:00 A.M. and 11:30 A.M. on the day of the murder. Experts believe Kristine was killed between 12:08 P.M.—when the FedEx driver got no response at the house, and 1:30 P.M.—when Fitzhugh and two friends arrived and found the body.

The defense hired a forensic pathologist to perform a second autopsy on Kristine's body. The pathologist, Thomas Rogers, testified that Kristine died from strangulation and blows to the back and the front of the head, matching the findings of the previous autopsy.

The defense also called a forensic scientist, who disagreed with investigators's claims that Kristine was killed in the kitchen. James Norris, the director of forensic sciences for the San Francisco police, told the jurors that police and paramedics contaminated evidence in the kitchen and tracked blood around. Norris said there did not appear to be blood found between the kitchen and the basement, making it unlikely that the body was taken from the kitchen to the basement. However, he admitted it could have been done if the body had been wrapped in something.

THE FITZHUGHS TESTIFY

Fitzhugh's oldest son, Justin, testified that his father called him at college to give him the unfortunate news of his mother's death. Justin, twenty-three, told the jurors that his father explained to him that it was an accident. He said he had no idea that Fitzhugh was not his biological father. However, he admitted that he had a better relationship with Brown than his younger brother, John, did. John is Fitzhugh's biological son.

Fitzhugh told the jurors that he was also unaware that Justin was not his biological son. Defense attorney Nolan pointed out that fact contradicted the prosecutors' claim that Fitzhugh killed his wife to prevent her from telling Justin about Brown, his biological father.

Fitzhugh added that he discovered Brown was Justin's biological father eight months after the murder, when he was in jail. Fitzhugh said he was devastated, and that he later told Justin, "I am still your dad."

CLOSING ARGUMENTS AND THE VERDICT

The prosecution wrapped up its two-hour presentation against Fitzhugh by saying: "The blood of Kristine Fitzhugh leads us to the killer." Her blood was on Fitzhugh's shirt, which had been stuffed under the seat of his car, and on his shoes, also found in the car. The jurors were shown a tape of Fitzhugh being interviewed by police on the day of the murder. In it, Fitzhugh pounded his fists on a table and said his wife died because she wore a pair of high-heeled shoes on the stairs.

The prosecution tried to discredit Fitzhugh's alibi of surveying vacant property at the time his wife died.

The defense contended that police focused too much on

Fitzhugh and not on the possibility of an accident or the result of a burglary. Defense attorney Nolan told the jurors that the prosecution was wrong in what they thought were motives. He said there was no proof Kristine told Fitzhugh that he wasn't Justin's father.

Nolan painted a scenario in which Kristine came home and surprised a burglar in the basement. She tried to run up the stairs, but he pulled her down and her head struck a large brass bell.

The jury deliberated only three days before finding Fitzhugh guilty of second-degree murder. A Santa Clara County Superior Court judge sentenced him to fifteen years to life, making him eligible for parole in 2015. In addition, Fitzhugh was ordered to pay $10,000 in restitution and $4,000 to cover counseling fees for Justin.

COMMENTARY: Kenneth Fitzhugh

For those who wish to dispose of their wives or sweethearts, and then blame the death on a "fall down the cellar stairs," the Fitzhugh case is a lesson showing why this is a bad idea. Falls on a staircase happen accidentally, and are not uncommon among those who are elderly or infirm.

These trauma cases give the police and medical examiners a database containing a list of those injuries that are likely to arise from such an accident. Injuries of this sort are very difficult to create by using a blunt instrument or other weapon, even if one were to have access to these databases, which Kenneth Fitzhugh decidedly did not. It is doubtful that the idea of the cellar stairs occurred to him until after he had killed his wife in a burst of anger; on the facts, this was simply a clumsy effort to create an attempted cover-up. The puncture wounds on her head, bruises on her face, and especially the defensive wound on her finger were all red flags that proclaimed to a trained investigator that the victim had been in a fight of some kind—the kind for which staircases are not known.

Fitzhugh compounded the frailty of his staircase story by trying to construct a false alibi. Among the explanations he gave for his actions at about the time his wife was killed, the most damning was his claim that he had called his wife at home when she failed to appear at her job but got no answer. People not in the business of crime—or the detection of crime—have little appreciation for the mountain of information available through telephone company records. Perhaps Fitzhugh thought that if one asserted that an attempted call received no answer, there would be no record because there was no charge. Wrong indeed! Since he did get a call from the victim's employer, the school district, asking about his wife, an innocent man would have called home looking for his wife. A guilty man would have known that such a call would be pointless, since she was already dead. A clever and sophisticated guilty man would have made the call anyway, just to create a telephone record consistent with his alleged innocence.

The claim that while out jogging he'd spent "about an hour" inspecting some property for a client—which claim was later contradicted by people who would have seen him had he been there—was, again, not too bright. It is pretty much defined as the time he went home after his exercise, got in a fight with his wife, injured her fatally, and then tried to make it look like an accident. His decision to pick up two of his wife's friends to maneuver them into helping him "discover" the body must have seemed shrewd to him at the time; in fact, it wound up biting him rather severely, as any sensible person might have predicted.

Lastly, killers who think themselves to be cagey will never, never learn that it is all but impossible to get rid of trace evidence of human blood. The plethora of television shows dealing with scientific crime detection demonstrate again and again that blood is all but ineradicable, but many people just "don't get it." To compound the case against him, Fitzhugh's laughable explanation about the bloody clothes in his motor vehicle was a coup de grâce for the prosecution.

One cannot help but conclude that it was a conscientious jury that spent three days reaching a verdict of guilty. There really, on the evidence, was little choice.

Richard Sharpe

Charged with murdering his estranged wife on July 14, 2000

The press had the proverbial field day with the case of the million-aire cross-dressing dermatologist who stabbed his wife with a fork, and later shot her at her Wenham, Massachusetts, home, near Gloucester. Sharpe admitted to police that he killed her, but he claimed insanity since he wasn't really aware of what he'd done.

RICHARD AND KAREN SHARPE

The Sharpes had known each other since childhood, started dating while in their teens, and married three months after graduation from Shelton High School in Connecticut. Their first child, Shannon, was born shortly before the wedding.

Sharpe enrolled in college, intending to study medicine, and Karen entered nursing school. In 1985, the family moved to Boston, where Sharpe was studying at Harvard Medical School. He was quick to establish his own dermatology practice, taught at Harvard on the side, and later formed two small medical companies. (One of the companies turned into a chain of hair removal clinics, LaseHair, and would yield Sharpe $2 million.)

On the surface the couple looked happy, but close friends were aware of their troubles. In the spring of 1991, Sharpe came home to find his wife with another man. Kathy asked him for a divorce and, in a fit of anger, Sharpe stabbed her in the forehead with a fork.

Karen fled the house that night, taking Shannon, now a teenager, with her. She contacted police, and they picked up Sharpe. He was later taken to an asylum, where doctors diagnosed him with major depression and a personality disorder.

Two days after the incident, Karen recanted her complaint and Sharpe came home.

Later, Karen filed to end their twenty-six-year marriage. (The divorce was not yet final at the time of the murder.)

In court papers, Karen cited physical and emotional abuse. She reported to friends that Sharpe frequently acted oddly, that he liked to cross-dress, and that he went to a LaseHair clinic and had all of his body hair removed. She added that he sometimes stole her birth control pills, that he prescribed himself hormones, and that he stole their oldest daughter's underwear. She took out a restraining order against him because she feared his erratic behavior and bad temper.

The night of the murder, Karen spent a few hours with friends and her brother and his girlfriend on a chartered boat in Boston Harbor before going home. According to police reports, Sharpe showed up at the Wenham house shortly before midnight, stepped into the entryway, and shot Karen in the chest with a hunting rifle that was never found. The bullet caused massive internal damage and shattered her spine. The shooting was witnessed by Karen's brother, his girlfriend, and a babysitter.

Sharpe fled the scene to New Hampshire and disposed of the gun. Police found him at a motel thirty hours after the murder. He had registered under his own name and paid with a credit card, making it easy to track him. Police found an empty six-pack of beer in the room, along with a newly purchased clothesline that had been knotted into a noose.

PICKING THE JURORS

Jury selection was a lengthy process, and some potential jurors were dismissed because they said they had problems with cross-dressers, and might be biased. (A few said they were re-pulsed by pictures of Sharpe in drag.) At one point, when Sharpe claimed he was assaulted in jail, selection was halted. He was taken to the emergency room at Lawrence General Hospital. There, Dr. Patrick Curran treated Sharpe and disagreed that he'd been seriously injured. Sharpe remained at the hospital to be evaluated as a precaution, which suspended court proceedings.

Sharpe said guards had attacked him, and he was certain he'd suffered a concussion, among other injuries. His attorney told court officials that his client was in pain after having been slammed against a wall. The attorney said the incident left Sharpe disori-ented and not competent to continue in the courtroom. He would need time to recover, the attorney said.

Prosecutors and jail officials blustered at Sharpe's report. A spokesman for the sheriff's office said Sharpe started the struggle in the jail, pushing an officer who spun him around, put him against a wall, and handcuffed him. The spokesman said that, at the time, Sharpe did not complain of injuries or request medical help. (The complaints came the following morning, before he was scheduled to go to court.)

It took four days to seat a jury of nine women and seven men, four of whom would be named alternates prior to deliberations.

Once the trial began, the jurors were bussed to Sharpe's home just outside of Gloucester. They looked only at the outside of the house. From there, they were driven to Karen's house in Wen-ham, one-half hour from Sharpe's house.

THE TRIAL BEGINS

The facts of the murder could not be disputed, since Sharpe pleaded not guilty by reason of insanity. What was disputed, however, was Sharpe's sanity. Prosecutors would have to prove him sane if he were to be found guilty and sentenced. The de-fense would have to show enough evidence that he was not.

Prosecutors called Sharpe's friends and business associates, who testified he seemed rational and alert earlier on the day of the murder. Others called to the stand said that in late June and early July Sharpe told them he was interested in buying a gun. One said he was trying to find someone who would search his wife's belongings.

Both Sharpe and Karen were reported to have had affairs during the marriage. The defense claimed Karen's infidelity hit him hard, particularly when he found his wife with a man who was one of the contractors on a home they were building. That sent him "over the edge," defense attorney Joseph Balliro said.

WITNESS TESTIMONY

Kristen Dormitzer, a college student, was babysitting for Alexandra and Michael Sharpe, who were aged four and seven at the time of Karen's death. Dormitzer testified that Karen had just returned from a dinner cruise with her brother and his girlfriend when Sharpe showed up at the house.

She told the jurors, "The door opened and a man poked his head in the door and said, 'Is Karen here?' Karen looked at him and said, 'Richard, you know you're not supposed to be here.'"

Dormitzer added: "He pulled a gun from behind his back." Karen screamed and tried to run. But there was an "explosion" of sparks and the gun Sharpe was holding went off. Dormitzer said she grabbed the children, and the three of them hid in a shower stall until police arrived.

The jurors listened to the 911 call James Hatfield, Karen's brother, made right after the murder. On the tapes, Hatfield said: "The shooter is still on the premises as far as I know, and there's somebody here who might be dying in my arms."

Hatfield testified that he initially chased Sharpe, then returned to Karen's side and called 911. "I went back to try to save my sister," he told the jurors.

Another witness for the defense was Connie Behnke, a close friend of Karen's. She testified that Sharpe called Karen fat and ugly and disrespected her. After his wife filed for divorce, Behnke said Sharpe called Karen and asked his wife to reconcile with him. She said Sharpe claimed Karen stole money from him.

A gun collector from Gloucester testified that Sharpe approached him three weeks before the murder, trying to buy a gun. The collector said he told Sharpe he didn't have any for sale.

Richard Fonte, president of LaseHair, said Sharpe did not act strangely the day of the murder, and that earlier in the day he had engaged others in complicated discussions about finance.

Paula Hiltz, who was in a romantic relationship with Sharpe, told the jurors that on the night of the murder they had gone out to dinner and danced. (She testified that Sharpe drank as many as eight glasses of red wine.) Before going home, she said the two of them went to her ex-boyfriend's house, where she needed to close some windows that she'd left open. She said Sharpe was so drunk that he had trouble walking in the house. Hiltz said she did not believe that Sharpe was insane; however, on the night of the murder, he was "not in his right mind" because of medicine he'd taken and all the wine he'd drunk.

Sharpe took the stand in his own defense. He testified to the jurors that he had a notion of bringing his family back together, which is why he went to Karen's house that night with a loaded gun. He said he'd taken medicine, drunk wine, and could not remember much of the shooting or just why he had killed her.

Sharpe told the jurors that his mental problems started in his childhood. He said he began cross-dressing as a young teenager, feeling safer at home dressed in his sister's clothes. While he still lived with his parents, he said, he started buying women's clothes and going out in drag.

Over the years he became more interested in cross-dressing, though he did not often dress in full drag (however, he admitted that on hundreds of occasions he would wear women's underwear or clothes; he called it relaxing, fun, and erotic). He said he took female hormones to relieve stress, and that he had had a half-dozen cosmetic surgeries, including liposuction and a "nose job."

Sharpe explained that he and Karen married despite their parents' objections. He said marrying so young didn't stop either of them from excelling—Karen as a nurse, and he earning first a master's degree in engineering and then completing medical school. Sometimes, he said, he worked two jobs to pay all the bills, and was known to work as many as ninety hours a week.

He admitted that he and Karen fought and that he attacked her with a fork when he saw her with another man in their home. On another occasion he struck her so hard he knocked a tooth loose and she went to the emergency room. Sharpe also admitted to several affairs of his own.

He said he could not remember many of the details about the shooting. He testified: "I have no idea what the hell was going through my mind. I really don't."

Sharpe said he remembered going out to dinner with Hiltz, then driving to his wife's house in Wenham. He testified that he loaded the gun, walked onto the front porch, and opened the door.

He told the jurors that Karen said she would call the police and reminded him about a restraining order. He said he remembered the gun going off, the noise rattling him. He said he ran and threw the gun away along the highway. He called the next thirty hours a blur, though he did remember buying some beer and a clothesline. He said he wanted to kill himself. He told prosecutors he could not remember the route he drove to reach the New Hampshire motel.

Sharpe said he was abused as a child, and his brothers supported that claim to the jury. His older brother, Robert, told the jury about Sharpe's unbalanced temper, and that Richard became furious one day when his wife brought home dinner from the wrong fast-food restaurant. He said Sharpe took the bucket of chicken and threw it against the wall.

Sharpe's brother Ben said he had to throw Sharpe out of his restaurant after he started a disturbance one New Year's Eve.

Sharpe's sister, Laurie Monopoli, also called him unstable. She testified that once Sharpe urinated in a wine bottle and then recorked it so one of his brothers would drink it.

DUELING DOCTORS

Psychiatrists for the prosecution testified during the trial that Sharpe was sane when he killed his wife, and was not experiencing a psychotic episode.

One psychiatrist, Dr. Malcolm Rogers, told the jury that Sharpe's behavior was threatening but not crazed. Rogers said that Sharpe's having stolen a gun only hours before the crime and disposing of it afterward showed that he understood what he was doing and that he could understand the difference between wrong and right. In addition, he said Sharpe's tendency to cross-dress did not indicate mental illness. "It is a choice . . . it is harmless," Rogers testified.

Rogers said Sharpe appeared to be a narcissistic, controlling person, and that he shot his wife because she was leaving him and would take some of his fortune with her. Rogers admitted he gave little credence to Sharpe's unfortunate childhood.

Defense psychiatrist Dr. Kenneth Ablow testified that he'd diagnosed Sharpe with major depression, a personality disorder, and that he was not criminally responsible for the murder. Ablow told the jurors that Sharpe was abused as a child and that he started dressing in women's clothing during his teen years to avoid his father's insults. Sharpe's mental problems began at an early age, Ablow said.

Sharpe had claimed he killed his wife while he was in a haze of drugs and alcohol. A psychiatrist for the defense supported that claim, arguing that those factors, plus Sharpe's mental state, led him to kill Karen, and that he did not have a "true understanding" of what he was doing.

THE SENTENCE

The jury deliberated for only twelve hours before reaching a unanimous decision.

Sharpe was found guilty. After the sentence was announced, he shouted: "I have a right to talk!" He said he loved Karen and that he was sorry for what he did.

Sharpe was sentenced to life in prison, without the possibility of parole.

REACHING A SETTLEMENT

Sharpe, while in prison, agreed to a $5 million settlement to Karen's estate. His children Michael and Alexandra would receive most of the money. Shannon Sharpe, the couple's oldest daughter, was awarded custody of the two children, in conjunction with Karen's sister and brother-in-law.

SHARPE'S CONTINUING SAGA

One of Sharpe's fellow inmates reported in the spring of 2002 that Sharpe offered him $100,000 to murder the assistant district attorney who had prosecuted him. Sharpe was promptly charged with solicitation to commit murder, and shortly after that he tried to hang himself from his shoelaces. He made a second attempt in the fall of that year, and was put in the Bridgewater State Hospital.

COMMENTARY: Richard Sharpe

Of all of the accused husbands, ex-husbands, and boyfriends described in this book, the only one who stepped up to the plate immediately and told the world that he had killed his wife is Richard Sharpe. Acting as his own lawyer, and thus having a fool for a client, he also asserted that he should not be held to account for his cruel act because he was legally insane. He was not, unfortunately for him, so insane that he was unable to flee the scene and lodge himself in the neighboring state of New Hampshire, where he consumed a six-pack of beer.

Because Sharpe had one of the best lawyers in the country—Joseph J. Balliro of Boston, who had been defending homicide cases for more than forty years—it was unfortunate for Sharpe that he committed himself to a defense strategy before he had the benefit of legal advice. When he had finished macerating his case, there was little Balliro could do for him. Since this is the only case in this compendium where the defense of insanity was locked in at the outset by the defense and tried to a jury, a few words about the insanity defense may be useful.

There are two defenses in criminal cases where the accused admits he committed the crime but asserts that he should not be found guilty or punished. The first is entrapment, where the defendant says in essence: "I did it, but I would not have acted this way except for the persuasion of Fred, and because Fred works for law enforcement, I was trapped into doing it." This is an extremely difficult defense and it rarely succeeds. In some "sting" operations, however, where the cops go too far and actually entice an otherwise lawful person into participating in criminal conduct, a jury may acquit as a way of punishing the cops.

The defense of insanity is also very difficult, and very unpopular with juries. To be found "not guilty by reason of insanity," one must prove that either (1) one did not know the nature and quality of one's act (that is, one thought—because of some mental aberration—one was cutting up an orange, rather than the victim's throat), or (2) if one knew what one was doing, one didn't know that it was wrong (one thought the victim was the devil, who was about to kill one unless one struck first). In some jurisdictions there is a third prong added to the test: if an accused knew what he was doing and knew that it was wrong, but acted as a result of an "irresistible impulse," he may be acquitted. When one reads about "temporary insanity" as a defense, the "irresistible impulse" is probably in play. A fair example might be a father who has just seen his child slaughtered. It is too late for self-defense or defense of a third person, but a killing under those circumstances would likely persuade a jury to find that one was indeed temporarily insane.

Applying these rules and principles to Sharpe, he had only one thing going for him: he was unquestionably mentally ill. His history was quite consistent with that of a violently sick person. "Insane" is not a medical term or a recognized illness.

But it is painfully clear that he knew that Karen was his wife and a human being, and that her chest was not an orange, when he shot her. It is also plain that his flight to New Hampshire was strong evidence that he knew what he had done was very, very wrong. There were no facts that would have supported an argument that he acted on an "irresistible impulse," even if the law permitted that defense in his case. As in Fitzhugh, there was not a great deal for jurors to argue about. It appears that they had little trouble in reaching a verdict of first-degree murder with, no death penalty option to consider.

But had Balliro been a magician, rather than just an outstanding lawyer, and had somehow persuaded the jury that his client was legally *insane, Sharpe would not be much better off. Such people are not returned to the community but are housed in secure institutions that are prisons in most every sense of the word. They do not get out, with rare exception.*

Robert Blake

Charged with murdering his wife on May 5, 2001

This celebrity case was spread across four years and countless newspapers and tabloids. It featured a revolving door of defense attorneys, television interviews, and talk of hit men and conspiracies, and like the O. J. Simpson case, there was also a civil trial in which the public got to hear the testimony all over again.

THE MURDER

Bonnie Lee Bakley was murdered May 4, 2001, while she sat in a car near Vitello's, a restaurant in Studio City, California. From the beginning of the investigation, Blake said he escorted Bakley to the car, then returned to Vitello's to retrieve a gun he had accidentally left behind. When he returned to the car, he discovered she'd been shot. The gun he carried, which he had the proper permits for, was not the murder weapon.

Almost a year later, following an extensive police investigation, Blake was charged with one count of murder with the special circumstance of lying in wait, and two counts of soliciting murder. Detectives believed that Blake first tried to hire someone else to do the killing, but after that failed, shot Bakley himself.

Blake's former personal bodyguard, Earle Caldwell, was charged with conspiracy in the crime, though that

was later dismissed. There were many delays before the trial got under way in late 2004 and wrapped up in the spring of 2005, nearly four years after the murder occurred.

Born Michael James Vijencio Gubitosi in 1933 in Nutley, New Jersey, his name was changed to Bobby Blake in 1942. Blake's acting career started at the age of five when he landed a role in Our Gang comedies. To modern audiences he is perhaps best known for portraying Tony Baretta, a tough cop with a well-trained pet cockatoo. (He won an Emmy for the role in 1975.)

Blake married Bonnie Lee Bakley in November 2000, after learning through a paternity test that he had fathered her daughter Rose.

He appeared in more than fifty movies between 1942 and 1997, including *China Girl* (1942), *The Return of Rin Tin Tin* (1947), *Screaming Eagles* (1956), *Town Without Pity* (1961), *PT 109* (1963), *The Greatest Story Ever Told* (1965), and *Lost Highway* (1997).

He also appeared on *Saturday Night Live, The Tonight Show, Hollywood Squares, The Mike Douglas Show, The Merv Griffin Show,* and in various episodes of the television shows *The F.B.I., Naked City, Bat Masterson, Alcoa Presents: One Step Beyond, Billy the Kid, The Californians, The Cisco Kid, The Roy Rogers Show, Fireside Theatre, Zane Grey Theater, Twelve O'Clock High, The Rebel, Death Valley Days, Rawhide, Slattery's People, Have Gun—Will Travel, Ben Casey, Laramie, Wagon Train, The Richard Boone Show, The Roseanne Show,* and *Hell Town.*

Before marrying Blake, Bakley was involved with Christian Brando (the son of Marlon Brando). She met Blake at a California nightclub and started up a casual relationship. Bakley was occasionally investigated by police for running various scams, including mail-order pornography, where she would get money from men she'd met via newspaper personal ads.

She initially named her daughter, born in the summer of 2000, Shannon Christian Brando, but renamed her Rose Lenore

Sophia Blake after a DNA test confirmed that Blake was the father.

More news reporters attended Bakley's funeral than did family and friends. Blake attended the funeral with an adult son and daughter from a previous marriage, and his infant daughter, Rose. During the service, held almost three weeks after the murder, Blake thanked Bakley for Rose and promised to give the girl a good life.

Some of Bakley's relatives did not attend, citing that Blake went against their wishes of wanting her cremated. Furthermore, they said they did not want to associate with Blake, who they believed killed Bakley.

Bakley was buried at Forest Lawn Memorial Park, at Blake's request, so Rose could visit her mother's grave. Some family members had wanted her buried in New Jersey.

DELAYS AND MORE DELAYS

It took almost four years from the night of the murder to get the case to court. The LAPD's investigation took a year before police believed there was enough evidence to indict Blake. Next, Blake fired three lawyers over the course of preliminary hearings, which further delayed matters.

Blake's first attorney was Harland Braun, who quit when, against his advice, Blake set up an interview with Diane Sawyer of the ABC network. (The interview was later stopped by the sheriff's department.) Another of Blake's attorneys, Jennifer Keller, also asked to be removed from the case, citing Blake's constant desire to talk to the media.

Attorney Thomas Mesereau, who took the lead counsel role after Braun quit, eventually also backed away, claiming there were "irreconcilable differences" between him and Blake.

Replacing Mesereau was Gerald Schwartzbach, a veteran criminal trial lawyer who would stay with Blake through the end of the trial.

CIRCUMSTANTIAL EVIDENCE

Prosecutors admitted to the jurors from the beginning that the evidence they presented against Blake was largely circumstantial.

There were no fingerprints on the murder weapon, and six fingerprints on Blake's car, on the driver's side door and window, could not be identified. Blake did not have blood on him the night of the murder.

Prosecutors speculated that Blake was withdrawing money to pay for a hit man, as a spokesman for City National Bank said the actor had been put on a "suspicious activity report." Between September 2000 and March 2001, Blake withdrew $126,000, mostly in increments of $5,000.

THE PROSECUTION

Sean Stanek, a witness for the prosecution, testified that Blake hammered on his door shortly after 9:30 P.M. on May 4, 2001. The actor was yelling that someone had beaten up his wife. Stanek added that he thought Blake might have done it, but that his hands were clean. Stanek said he called 911 and went to Blake's car, finding Bakley shot instead of beaten. Blood was pouring from her wounds; she was gurgling but didn't answer Stanek when he asked if she could hear him. Stanek, a director, said that while he tried to help Bakley, Blake did not touch the body but just shouted questions, such as: "What happened to her?" Blake did not act like a grief-stricken husband, he said.

Stanek testified that Blake told police he carried a "piece" because Bakley was afraid of people who might want to hurt her because of her pornography ventures. He gave police the gun. Stanek also said he was concerned that Blake might have been involved in the murder, and he asked police to search his own house. He said he thought Blake might have planted the murder weapon in his house. However, the police did not find anything.

Blake wailed loudly when a police detective told Blake his wife was dead from gunshot wounds. Detective Michael Coffey testified that he was the one to break the news, and he thought that Blake did not sound sincere when he cried, as there were no tears.

Also testifying were Rebecca Markham and Andrew Percival, who lived in the neighborhood of Vitello's. They said they were walking that evening when Blake passed them a little after 9:30 P.M. Markham said it was 9:41 P.M. when they got to their home, which was half a block from the Stanek home, where Blake hammered on the door.

Blake had left Vitello's at 9:30 P.M., and the 911 call from Stanek came ten minutes later.

Given the time frame, prosecutors said Blake could not have walked with Bakley to the car, returned to the restaurant to retrieve his gun, then made it back to the car to find Bakley shot and run to Stanek's. Further, no one at the restaurant recalled Blake's returning for his gun.

Another prosecution witness, LAPD detective Martin Pinner, told the jurors that on the night Bakley was murdered, Blake had said during a police interview that he wanted to draw up a will. Blake told his attorney, present at the interview, that he wanted to make sure his infant daughter, Rose, did not end up with Bakley's family, and that he feared for his own life. Pinner also testified that Blake called Bakley's family "crazy people."

LAPD detectives testified to the jury about their observations of the murder scene. One pointed to dried blood in the car and vomit near the Dumpster where the gun was found. Prosecutors assert that Blake was so rattled about killing his wife that he threw up in the men's room of the restaurant and afterward near the Dumpster.

Witness Lisa Johnson told the jurors that one of Blake's former employees plotted with the actor to plant cocaine on Bakley. Earle Caldwell, a former bodyguard of Blake's, used to date Johnson. Johnson testified that the day following Bakley's murder, Caldwell called her and and asked her to remove some things from his apartment, saying he was concerned that police might search his place. Those items included a computer, notes, receipts, and an Altoids tin in the freezer that was filled with translucent brown rocks. A year after the murder, Caldwell was charged with murder and conspiracy to commit murder. Those charges were later dropped for insufficient evidence.

Roy "Snuffy" Harrison, a retired Hollywood stuntman, was another witness for the prosecution. Harrison said he considered himself a close friend of Blake's since meeting him in the 1970s on the *Baretta* set. Harrison testified that he put Blake in contact with two other former stuntmen—Gary "Whiz Kid" McLarty and Ronald "Duffy" Hambleton. He said he didn't know why Blake wanted to meet the stuntmen.

BAKLEY'S DAUGHTER TAKES THE STAND

Holly Gawron, Bonnie Lee Bakley's daughter from a previous marriage, told the jurors she met Blake in the summer of 1999. She went with her mother from Arkansas to California for a visit. Gawron had been living with her mother in Little Rock.

Blake and Bakley were dating at the time. Bakley was also dating Christian Brando.

Gawron testified that Blake came to their hotel room and was not pleased to find her there. Gawron said she left, and, when she returned an hour later, Blake was gone.

That fall, Gawron said her mother was happy to be pregnant, and they discussed how to break the news to Blake. Gawron testified that she answered the phone once, and the caller was Blake, who cursed at her.

Gawron also told the jurors that she and her brother discovered cocaine in her mother's car in December 2000, the month after Bakley married Blake. Gawron said her mother had never used cocaine.

BLAKE'S EX-WIFE'S TURN

Sondra Blake Kerr, who was married to Blake for twenty years, testified that in January 2001 she saw Blake on the street and congratulated him on his new life and marriage. She said that Blake took her hand and told her: "The baby's real, the marriage isn't." She told the jurors that Blake pressed her against a wall and said he wanted to talk to her later in private, that the marriage was a big mess.

However, Kerr said she did not meet with him later.

PROSECUTORS POINT TO THE EVIDENCE

The jury was shown several items taken from the murder scene, including Bakley's cell phone and a purse containing $300. The prosecution discounted Blake's theory of a mugging because neither the purse nor the money had been taken. Further, they questioned why Blake would run to a friend's home to ask for help, rather than calling 911 on his wife's cell phone. However, the defense pointed out no one had proven that Blake knew about the cell phone.

Other evidence included a 9 mm Walther P-38, the murder weapon, that was found the morning after the murder in a Dumpster about a dozen feet from where Bakley's body had been. The gun was German, dated to WWII, and could not be traced. There were no readable fingerprints on it. Police reported that it was found with the hammer pulled back and a live round in the chamber.

Blake's hands had been tested for gunshot residue. (He had earlier surrendered a gun he was carrying to police.) The defense asserted that the trace amounts of residue on Blake's hands could have resulted from handling his own gun.

THE ISSUE OF GSR

Gunshot residue (GSR) experts told the jury that tests on Blake's hands could not prove he had fired a gun that night. And though tests on sweatshirts found in Blake's car also showed the presence of GSR, it could not be proven that the clothes were used as a silencer. (Police did not test the spot in the restaurant where Blake said he'd accidentally left his own gun.)

Some items Blake was wearing at the time were also tested, and GSR particles were found on his boots, T-shirt, blue jeans, belt buckle, and socks. The experts testified, however, that such particles can remain on clothes for a considerable period of time. Prosecutors pointed out that photographs of the scene show Blake running his hands through his hair, setting his hands against the grass, and holding glasses of water, activities which could have cut the amount of GSR found on his hands.

Experts also testified that the GSR on Bakley and her clothing was no help in determining how far away the shooter stood.

JURORS AT THE MURDER SCENE

The jury toured the area where the murder occurred, walking along the street twice and studying various points of reference, such as the location of the restaurant, where the Dumpster had sat, and where Blake's car had been parked. Although jurors took notes, they were not permitted to touch anything or discuss the scene among themselves.

The jurors walked to the Stanek home, where Blake banged on the door and called for help. Then they walked to the home of the couple who said Blake passed them on the street. They also walked through Vitello's and looked at the booth where Bakley and Blake had sat.

BLAKE'S ROCKY RELATIONSHIP WITH BAKLEY

Various witnesses testified about Blake and Bakley's relationship. One witness said Blake was trying to find people who would investigate Bakley's illegal ventures. Another witness, Robert Renzi, told the jurors that Blake offered him $10,000 to "help him." (Renzi had met Blake about six months before the actor married Bakley.) Under defense questioning, Renzi said he assumed he was supposed to use legal means, and that Blake had not asked him to do anything illegal. Renzi testified that Blake was not getting along with Bakley and that she conned people to get money.

Renzi said he met with Blake at least twenty times and that Blake told him about letters and nude photos that Bakley had sent him. He maintained Blake also told him that she was on probation for credit card fraud in Arkansas, that she was violating her probation, and that she dabbled in mail-order porn scams.

Renzi recalled Blake's wedding for the jury. He testified that Blake called him to say he was getting married one night and would Renzi come over. Renzi said he was busy, and Blake countered that it would not take much time. The ceremony was over quickly, Renzi said, adding it was clear Blake didn't like Bakley and was marrying her for Rose's sake.

Renzi also testified that Blake loved Rose and did not want Bakley to be involved with the child. He said he contacted Luis Mendoza, a former FBI informant and friend, and asked him to come from Florida to Los Angeles to help in the matter of Bakley.

Mendoza, a boat dealer, told the jurors he had contacts at the FBI and U.S. Customs office and that he tried to get those contacts to arrest Bakley. Mendoza said those contacts were not interested in pursuing the matter. Mendoza testified that when he met with Blake, the actor painted Bakley as a bad person, and he wanted Rose away from her. He admitted that Blake did not specifically ask him to do anything illegal.

William Welch, who once worked as a private investigator for Blake, testified that the actor had told him he tried to pay his wife to get out of his life. Bakley would not accept the money, he said. Welch also testified that Blake talked about killing Bakley before the baby was born. Welch, a retired LAPD detective, said he declined to participate and that Blake called him later and said he'd changed his mind and was not going after Bakley.

Welch told the jurors that when he worked for Blake, on and off for a dozen years, he performed background checks on various people. Welch said he was aware of Bakley's mail-order porn scam, and that she would send photos of herself to predominantly older men and run up charges on their credit cards. Welch told the jurors he suggested a background check on Bakley, which involved an Arkansas private investigator who accumulated a thick file on her.

Welch testified that the file included such tidbits as Bakley's having false Social Security cards traced to at least four states; in addition, she was using seventeen aliases. Welch said he suggested having Bakley arrested for parole violation, as she had no legal permission to be in California, but Blake countered that his wife had had a relationship with the parole officer, so nothing would come of such an attempt. Instead, Blake came up with a scheme to plant drugs on his wife and contact the LAPD. Welch said he refused to play a part, and that he did not contact the police about the scheme or Blake's previous comment about killing her.

Neither did Welch call the police after Bakley's murder. He testified that he was going on a fishing trip and expected to be called when the LAPD found his phone numbers at the Blake home.

LOOKING AT OTHER SUSPECTS

Though police considered Blake their main suspect in Bakley's murder, they investigated others, including Christian Brando, as well as those men from whom Bakley had bilked money.

The defense contended that dozens of other men might have had motives to murder Bakley because of her mail-order scams whereby she would get men to send her money for nonexistent medical bills and other expenses.

Ronald Ito, an LAPD detective, told the jurors that police investigators pursued leads from letters and photographs. Ito testified that more than five hundred letters were examined, and five or six of those aimed threats at Bakley. The writers of those letters were cleared after investigations, he said.

Police received a few hundred calls and e-mail messages offering clues to the Bakley murder, Ito said. One clue involved a prostitute named Cherry, who was allegedly with a man near the murder scene. However, she was never located.

Ito testified that Christian Brando was also looked at, but he was in Washington when the murder took place, and his alibi was sound.

TWO MORE STUNTMEN TESTIFY

Gary McLarty, a semiretired movie stuntman, told the jurors that a few weeks before the murder Blake had offered him $10,000 for the deed. McLarty testified that Blake complained Bakley took advantage of him and spent his money, and that he had sex with her once and that led to Rose.

Further, McLarty testified that Blake showed him materials related to Bakley's mail-order endeavors, and suggested a few murder scenarios. McLarty said in one of those scenarios Blake and she would go to dinner, and he would leave her in the car afterward so that someone could shoot her.

He said Blake did not name the restaurant.

McLarty said he met Blake in the 1970s while working as a stuntman on the *Baretta* television show. McLarty testified that Blake showed him a guesthouse behind Blake's Studio City home and said Bakley stayed there. McLarty said Blake suggested he sneak in and kill her while she slept, and that he used the word "pop," as in "pop her."

Another potential scenario was Blake and Bakely taking a road trip and someone killing her while they walked by a river.

McLarty said he refused to participate.

The defense argued that McLarty was delusional because of his history with drugs (at one time he had committed himself to a hospital). He admitted to lying under oath in the preliminary hearing two years before, when he maintained that he had rarely used drugs. Furthermore, the defense believed that McLarty learned about the murder details from reading the tabloids. McLarty admitted following the stories, but he denied using information from them when he talked to police after Bakley's murder.

Another retired stuntman, Ronald "Duffy" Hambleton, told the jurors he thought he was getting together with Blake to talk about a movie. This was roughly two months before Bakley's murder. However, he testified that he soon realized Blake wanted to talk about getting rid of his wife instead. Like McLarty, Hambleton testified that Blake discussed different murder scenarios.

Hambleton, who said he met Blake in the 1960s at a gym, said he refused to get involved and that Blake said he would do it himself.

The defense questioned Hambleton's drug use and his initial meetings with police, when he denied that Blake asked him to kill Bakley. Hambleton countered that he lied then, but told the police the truth when they questioned him again in the fall of 2001.

THE DEFENSE'S STAND

Lidia Benavides, Blake's housekeeper, testified that nearly three weeks before Bakley was murdered, she twice noticed a stranger sitting in a car across the street. She spoke to the jury through a Spanish interpreter, describing the car as old and ugly, very unlike the cars usually in the neighborhood. Benavides worked for Blake three years before the murder. She admitted getting $1,000 from the *National Enquirer* for her story, but said the final printed story was filled with lies.

The defense spent time questioning relatives and friends of the stuntmen who'd earlier testified for the prosecution. The defense pointed out their significant drug use and hallucinations, and that Blake never directly asked the men to kill his wife.

Other witnesses included patrons who were at Vitello's restaurant, where Blake and his wife dined the night of the murder. Several patrons testified Blake's behavior was normal, in contrast to patrons the prosecution called earlier who claimed Blake seemed nervous.

Prosecutors argue that Blake did not love his wife, and that he killed her when he could not find someone to do it for him. He wanted full custody of their infant daughter, Rose.

Captain Kevin Bailey of the Los Angeles Fire Department told the jurors that he spoke with Blake for a few moments on the night of the murder. Bailey said he did not notice anything unusual about Blake's behavior, and that at one point Blake appeared physically sick from the ordeal.

THE DEFENSE'S EXPERT

Investigators would have found more gunshot residue on Blake's hands if he killed her, testified Celia Hartnett. Hartnett was one of the chief forensic scientists and director of the laboratory for Forensic Analytical in Hayward, California.

Hartnett said there would have been more than ninety particles on his hands, rather than the five they found. Furthermore, she told the jurors that none of the particles they found were considered "highly specific," a term for particles resulting from discharging a gun. Hartnett's laboratory conducted an experiment with the murder weapon and found more than two thousand particles on the hands of the test shooter. She said Blake's handling of his own gun that night could have caused the GSR particles on his hands.

CLOSING THE CASE

Prosecutors told the jury that despite the lack of direct evidence pinning the crime to Blake, they had proven beyond reasonable doubt that he killed Bakley. They said that when Blake could not hire someone to do the deed, he pulled the trigger himself.

The defense argued that there were no eyewitnesses, a lack of physical evidence—in particular that the gun could not be linked to Blake. And while Blake was not fond of Bakley, she was Rose's mother and he would not kill her. Other men had motives for killing Bakley, the defense continued, because she had been bilking money out of them through her mail-order business.

The jury, seven men and five women, requested a read-back of witnesses' testimony during deliberations, focusing on Blake's alibi. Then they acquitted Blake of the murder, also finding him not guilty of one count of solicitation of murder. The jury did not reach a verdict on the second count of solicitation of murder, and that charge was dismissed.

Blake wept when he heard the verdict.

THE CIVIL SUIT

Blake was ordered to pay $30 million in damages to Bakley's children when a jury found him liable for Bakley's murder. The jury deliberated eight days before deciding that Blake likely caused her death. Rose Blake was scheduled to receive $7.5 million of that, with the rest divided among Bakley's other four children.

Unlike in Blake's criminal trial, the civil jury did not have to reach a unanimous decision. Of the twelve jurors, ten agreed Blake was liable, and nine agreed to the $30 million sum. Four of Bakley's children filed the wrongful death suit nearly three years earlier, in April 2002.

During the civil proceedings, Blake continued to maintain his innocence. Although he did not testify during the criminal trial, he testified for seven days in the civil trial. He told the jurors that he left Bakley alone in the car and returned to Vitello's. She was shot through an open window. He said he returned to find her unconscious and bleeding from two gunshot wounds.

Former stuntmen testified that Blake asked them to kill Bakley for him. No prints were found on the pistol police recovered from a Dumpster. The pistol was determined to be the murder weapon.

Some jurors after the trial reported that Blake was antagonistic on the stand and that his recollections were not consistent.

COMMENTARY: Robert Blake

The case against prolific actor Robert Blake is a puzzler in many respects. It seems likely that he had little use for Bonnie Bakley, and would not have been overly disconsolate if she were out of his life, so long as their little girl remained safe with him. On the other hand, he was good enough to marry her for the benefit of the child, even though she didn't know whose child it was until a DNA test was run. He did take her out to dinner at a decent restaurant on May 4, 2001; if he did so as part of a plan to have her shot to death in the front seat of his car while he was only a few steps away, that was a dumb plan indeed; Robert Blake does not strike one as a dumb person. The question confronting his jury was whether he had arranged (paid) for someone to shoot her. He apparently had no history of personal violence toward her.

Burning questions arise, nonetheless. Perhaps most important was the series of cash withdrawals over a six-month period, totaling $126,000. Proof that one used cash is always a blow to the defense in a criminal case. Cash is clumsy, dirty, risky (if some unsavory persons know you have it on you or in your home or place of business), and anonymous. Except in law enforcement sting operations where serial numbers from the bills have been photographed and recorded in advance of the transfer, tracing cash is usually difficult, often impossible. It is—expecially when used by those who have access to charge accounts, bank accounts, and credit cards—very often the instrumentality of crime. It is an almost daily occurrence that public officials (in one instance, a vice president of the United States) are reported to have taken clandestine cash payments for some corrupt deal or other. Blackmailers and extortionists insist on cash. Without it, the Mafia would have withered and died in its infancy.

Not only the generation of cash in a significant amount by bank withdrawals but also the manner of those withdrawals makes Blake's conduct perplexing. If there was a legitimate reason for these withdrawals (and there are but very few), it never surfaced. What is plain, however, is that the withdrawals were intended to go unnoticed.

The proliferation of cash in criminal enterprise has caused the government—albeit decades after it should have done so—to monitor banking transactions involving $10,000 or more. To deposit or withdraw this amount, one must fill out a federal form called a CRT (cash transaction report) at the bank. At a minimum, this is apt to generate a visit by the IRS, and perhaps other federal agencies as well. It appears that Blake was careful to keep each individual transaction at or below the $5,000 level.

Then there is the matter of the "gun in the restaurant" story. Those who have official permits to carry concealed pistols are generally very, very careful not to leave them laying around like cell phones, especially at a booth in a restaurant. Blake, whose thespian roles on TV and in motion pictures must have given him a good deal of familiarity with firearms, seems an unlikely person to have been that careless. Oddly coincidental with his unusual act of forgetting his weapon and going back alone to the restaurant to get it was the more unusual circumstance that his wife was murdered by someone during the few minutes he was supposedly away from their automobile. Add in the fact that no one in Vitello's saw him return, and the story has a stench.

On the other hand, the self-styled "hit men" who testified against him—for some queasy reward, to be sure—were by all appearances a sorry lot. These were not people who had pulled the trigger—as in Rae Carruth's case—but people who were allegedly asked to do so and declined. Blake could not be tied to the shooting itself, nor to the weapon that caused death. And it was certainly clear that Bonnie Bakley was not *long on conscience, had a criminal attitude, and may well have made some serious enemies in the porn world. If a killer paid by someone else was stalking her, killing her under circumstances where Blake would necessarily be a prime suspect was a clever bit of devious thinking.*

The short of it all seems to be that—at least in the criminal trial—the system functioned as designed. Despite the malodorous circumstances discussed above, there was at least reasonable doubt, and the jurors voted as the judge guided them to do if they were not "really sure" that Blake was a culprit in the murder. Defense lawyers would be a happier lot if the average jury followed the law as closely as this one did. Unfortunately, that has not—over the years—been the case.

Michael Peterson

Charged with murdering his wife
on December 9, 2001

THE MURDER

On December 9, 2001, shortly before 3:00 A.M., Michael Peterson said he found his wife, Kathleen, lying at the bottom of their back staircase in a pool of blood.

He called 911.

He told police he'd been drinking with her in the backyard.

He said she had apparently slipped on the stairs and hit her head.

Terry Wilkins, a Durham, North Carolina, police sergeant who responded to the call, reported that Peterson was covered in blood, was visibly upset, and appeared to be confused.

The medical examiner at the scene initially believed that Kathleen's death was an accident. However, after an autopsy, the office attributed her death to blunt force trauma and noted it did not appear to be the result of a fall down the stairs.

Peterson's trial would last three months. More than five dozen witnesses would be called, and more than eight hundred pieces of evidence would be introduced.

TIME LINE

DECEMBER 7, 2001. Kathleen took a day off from Nortel and went Christmas shopping with Peterson. That evening, they attended a party.

DECEMBER 8 AND 9. Peterson deleted hundreds of files from his computer in the early afternoon, and then went to the YMCA. He later rented the movie *America's Sweethearts* from Blockbuster. Christine Tomassetti arrived to accompany Peterson's son, Todd, to a party. Helen Prislinger, one of Kathleen's coworkers, called to tell Kathleen she was e-mailing her a file for work. The Petersons watched the movie and then at midnight had a drink outside by the pool. Kathleen went inside before Peterson, and he told police he found her shortly before 3:00 A.M. at the bottom of the staircase. His 911 call was at 2:41 A.M.

DECEMBER 10. Police labeled Kathleen's death suspicious and got a search warrant for the Petersons' home.

DECEMBER 11 AND 12. Police searched the home and seized more than sixty items, including computers.

DECEMBER 17. Peterson hired David Rudolf to defend him.

MICHAEL PETERSON

Born in the fall of 1943, Peterson moved frequently with his family during his early years. He graduated with a degree in political science from Duke University in Durham, North Carolina, in 1965, then entered law school, but soon dropped out for lack of interest. In 1966, he found work at the U.S. Department of Defense, researching material to support an increased U.S. military force in Vietnam, and from there he enlisted in the marines and was sent to Vietnam to fight.

Following the war, Peterson spent the next eleven years working as a government consultant, part of that time in Gräfenhausen, Germany, where he started work on what would be his first novel. His first wife, Patricia, taught at an elementary school on a U.S. Air Force base there. A nanny found their neighbor and friend Elizabeth Ratliff dead in 1985. (Elizabeth's husband, George, had died of a heart attack a year and a half earlier while on a mission in Grenada.) Peterson became legal guardian to Ratliff's daughters, Margaret and Martha, who moved in with the Petersons and their two sons, Clayton and Todd. Shortly before the extended family moved from Germany to North Carolina in the late 1980s, Peterson and Patricia divorced.

In Durham, Peterson worked in earnest on his writing. He authored three novels that were based on his time in Vietnam: *A Time of War*, *The Immortal Dragon*, and *Charlie Two Shoes and the Marines of Love Company*. The income from the novels helped purchase a manor in the Forest Hills area in 1991. Peterson's writing career later expanded to include a column for the local paper, the *Herald-Sun*.

Peterson became involved with Kathleen Atwater, a Nortel executive he met because Martha and Margaret were friends with her teenage daughter, Caitlin. Peterson married Atwater in 1997, extending the family further.

In 1999, Peterson ran for mayor of Durham. He had tried to use his columns and community work as a springboard into politics, but news surfaced that a Purple Heart he had received came from a car accident in Japan, and not through combat in Vietnam, as he'd claimed.

KATHLEEN HUNT PETERSON

Born Kathleen Hunt in early 1953, Kathleen was the first female student accepted at Duke University's School of Engineering. She earned bachelor's and master's degrees, then worked for a variety of companies before settling with Nortel in Durham. She became active in the Durham Arts Council and the American Dance Festival.

Kathleen married Peterson in a ceremony at his manor.

PETERSON'S TRIAL

Prosecutors contended that Peterson killed his wife with a fireplace tool called a "blow poke," disposed of it, and staged the scene to make it look like an accident before calling 911. Because so much time had passed, some of the blood at the scene and on Peterson's clothes had dried, thereby alerting police, prosecutors said.

The defense maintained that Kathleen, who had been drinking, blacked out or slipped and hit her head on molding at the bottom of the steep staircase. She came to, slipped in her blood, and hit her head a second time and died. Defense attorneys believed the police so contaminated the scene of the fall that their evidence was tainted and unreliable. In addition, the defense pointed to evidence lost between the house and the trial as part of a shoddy investigation and an inept case by the prosecution.

OPENING STATEMENTS

Durham County District Attorney James Hardin Jr. told the jurors: "They say it was an accident that was caused by a couple of falls in the staircase. We say it was not. We say it was murder." (Hardin knew Peterson before the trial through Peterson's bid for office.)

Hardin said a fall down the stairs did not kill her; she was likely struck with a fireplace poker that had disappeared from the house. Hardin had elected not to seek the death penalty, but to go after life in prison on his bid for a first-degree murder conviction.

Defense attorney David Rudolf told the jurors that prosecutors were too single-minded in going after Peterson, and that investigators were slow to look into the death.

In a ninety-minute statement Rudolf said city police had a vendetta against Peterson because of numerous columns he had written for the newspaper that criticized the poor rate of solving crimes. "There's no doubt it affected the way Durham police viewed him," Rudolf contended.

Then he played a recording of Peterson's 911 call to police. The tape was filled with sobs and stammering.

POLICE AND PARAMEDICS TESTIFY

Paramedic James Rose said he'd never seen so much blood on a call before, and that some of it appeared dry, which made him suspicious. Rose testified that he and his partner reached the Peterson home at about 3:00 A.M. December 9, 2001. That amount of blood was unusual for a fall, he said.

In cross-examination, however, he admitted he'd only responded to one fatal fall before, and that victim had not been drinking.

Rose told the jurors Peterson was upset, sobbing, and unable to answer simple questions.

Jayson Crank, a Durham firefighter who was at the scene, also testified to seeing dried blood; however, he admitted to not putting it in an initial report.

Corporal J. C. McDowell, of the Durham Police Department, testified that something about the scene didn't seem to fit in her eyes. She told the jurors that after she saw how much blood was around Kathleen's body, she called for crime scene technicians.

She asserted: "It didn't look consistent with someone falling down steps."

The defense pointed out that McDowell and other officers did not keep people from contaminating the scene, and that blood was tracked elsewhere in the house as a result.

Yellow police tape was not put up until approximately twenty minutes after officers were on the scene, when Corporal Scott Kershaw arrived and took over. Kershaw testified that he posted police at the front door to limit traffic in the house.

Fran Borden, a retired police sergeant, had been asked by the department to go to the Petersons' house. At the time, Borden said, he'd been told he would be looking into the death of a woman who fell out of a wheelchair and down a staircase.

Borden told the jurors that he was immediately suspicious when he saw blood on a kitchen cabinet and drawer handle. In addition, he said there was too much blood around Kathleen's body and that her head and spine seemed to be aligned, despite the alleged fall down the stairs.

He testified: "I squatted in the stairwell and looked up the stairs, trying to visualize every possible scenario how this woman could have come down those stairs, landed in the position where she landed, and where did all that blood come from. It didn't jibe. It didn't fit."

Rudolf argued in his cross-examination that Borden was not aware of all the facts, particularly that Kathleen likely hadn't fallen down the entire flight of stairs and that the scene had already been contaminated because the police had traipsed through the house.

Sergeant Emanuel Paschell was in charge of the homicide detectives called to the Peterson house. Paschell said that police obtained a warrent and searched the house and grounds for a possible weapon, but found nothing. Five teams of six officers searched. He told the jurors: "We didn't find anything we considered a weapon."

Corporal Kim Gregory testified that Peterson was belligerent when police arrived at his home at 6:00 P.M. December 12, 2001, with a second search warrant. The wake for Kathleen was that night, and Peterson missed it, staying in his home while police searched.

A forensic meteorologist, William Haggard, testified about weather conditions the night of Kathleen Peterson's death.

Prosecutors showed the jurors a videotape police took of Kathleen's body at the bottom of the staircase. Hardin played the tape again, this time with a crime scene technician discussing what was being shown.

Crime scene technician Dan George told the jurors he collected clothes, watches, blood, hair, glasses, computers, and other items from the home. He said the hair and blood were particularly important. He admitted that police did not take three blood-covered towels that were under Kathleen's head.

During Rudolf's cross-examination, George agreed that the scene could have been contaminated. George admitted that police did not photograph bloody footprints in the kitchen. (The footprints were revealed with the chemical Luminol, suggesting the blood had been wiped up before police arrived.)

THE AUTOPSY REPORT

Dr. Kenneth Snell, the medical examiner who watched Kathleen's autopsy, testified that he initially believed she died from falling down the stairs; however, he said he changed his mind after looking at her wounds in the morgue. Snell said the seven wounds on Kathleen's head suggested death from a beating rather than from a fall. In addition, the autopsy showed broken cartilage in Kathleen's neck, indicating someone might have tried to strangle her.

Forensic pathologist Deborah Radisch testified that separate impacts caused the seven lacerations on the back of Kathleen's head. Radisch said there were defensive wounds on the body, suggesting Kathleen tried to fight off her assailant. She had a fractured cartilage in her throat, Radisch added. Kathleen's skull had not been fractured, but some of the cuts split the scalp to the skull.

Radisch told the jurors she reviewed close to three hundred cases between 1991 and 2003 in which people died of a fall in North Carolina. Those individuals had one or two lacerations on their head, not seven, she said.

BLOOD SPATTERS

Peter Deaver, a blood spatter expert called by the prosecution, testified that he had analyzed bloodstains at crime scenes since 1988, and that he had examined evidence in sixty cases.

However, Rudolf questioned Deaver's credentials and said that he did not have the experience of the defense's spatter experts.

Deaver explained how bloodstains are analyzed, and that "cast-off" spots occur when a weapon is used and blood sprays from that weapon. He said he saw cast-off patterns, and based on those patterns he believed Kathleen was struck in the stairwell by someone standing outside the stairwell, and that the weapon was a blunt object. Deaver said the blood evidence pointed to Kathleen's being struck at least three times, and that she might have hit her head when she fell.

In addition, Deaver said that, based on the blood on Peterson's clothes, he had to have been crouching near a "blood source," such as Kathleen. This would account for the small blood drops inside his shorts.

Deaver told the jurors that it appeared someone smeared blood near Kathleen in an effort to clean it up, and that bloody marks on two steps appeared to have been made by something similar to a fireplace poker.

Rudolf challenged that assertion, indicating that if someone had hit Kathleen with a fireplace poker in the stairwell, the poker would have marked the door frame or the walls.

PETERSON'S FINANCES

Prosecutors revealed that about six months after Kathleen died, Peterson cashed in her 401K, worth nearly $350,000. In addition, Hardin told the jurors that Peterson could gain $1.4 million from Kathleen's life insurance policy, provided he won legal challenges from Kathleen's daughter.

The defense argued that Kathleen was worth more alive than dead, as she earned $145,000 a year and would continue to have stock options and increased earnings in her 401K.

Raymond Young, an agent with the North Carolina Bureau of Investigation, testified that the Petersons were spending more than they were earning. Young told the jurors that the Petersons had a net worth of about $1.6 million, but had $142,000 in credit card debt.

The defense countered, however, that Peterson's finances were not investigated until a month after Kathleen's death, when he had already started paying legal bills, and that the net worth was likely $500,000 higher than Young presented.

DURHAM'S WINTER WEATHER

Peterson was wearing a T-shirt, police officers said, and claimed he had been alone in the backyard by the pool for perhaps forty-five minutes.

December is chilly even in Durham, weather experts testified.

Meteorologist William Haggard testified that the temperature was between 51 and 54 degrees in the early morning hours of December 9, and that a typical person would be comfortable in the T-shirt and jeans Peterson was wearing at 66 to 72 degrees. Haggard said he took the temperature readings from an airport thirty miles from the Peterson house.

WINEGLASSES

Prosecutors suggest that Kathleen had not been drinking, and that Peterson poured wine into two glasses, then poured the wine down the sink to throw off investigators. Peterson's fingerprints were found on one wineglass, but there were only partial prints on the second glass, and they could not be identified.

However, Rudolf pointed out that the autopsy showed Kathleen's blood alcohol level at .07. She must have had more than her hand on a glass, Rudolf said.

THE MALE ESCORT

Brent Wolgamott, a former male escort, testified that he had an e-mail relationship with Peterson, though he never met the man. Wolgamott, twenty-eight, charged men $150 an hour for sexual acts. He told the jurors that between August 30 and September 5, 2001, he exchanged about two dozen e-mails with Peterson, and that the e-mails were to set up a sexual encounter. However, Wolgamott said he stood Peterson up, and Peterson never contacted him again.

Peterson found him through a Web site, Wolgamott said.

In the e-mails Peterson mentioned he was happily married and cared for his wife.

Prosecutors showed the jurors hundreds of pornographic images pulled from Peterson's computer. The pictures were recovered deleted files and included partially clothed men, and men performing sexual acts.

THE OTHER WOMAN ON THE STAIRS

Elizabeth Ratliff was found dead at the bottom of her stairs on November 25, 1985, in Germany, not far from the Peterson residence. She was a second grade teacher at the U.S. Department of Defense School, and she'd made arrangements for Peterson to be named the guardian of her daughters if something happened to her.

While there was a considerable amount of blood at that scene, German and American investigators ruled it as an accident brought on by a cerebral hemorrhage.

Prosecutors suggest that there were too many similarities in the stairway falls to be coincidence. Ratliff's body was exhumed from where it had been buried in Texas, and North Carolina medical examiners performed an autopsy and found lacerations on Ratliff's head that were ruled indicative of a beating rather than a fall.

Aaron Gleckman, an associate medical examiner and a consultant on Ratliff's autopsy, testified that he found nothing to indicate that Ratliff had suffered a cerebral hemorrhage. Gleckman told the jurors that he believed Ratliff died from being hit on the head, and that she was murdered.

Rudolf pointed out that Gleckman had worked less than two years in the medical examiner's office and that his findings contradicted an autopsy the army had previously performed just after her death.

Cheryl Appel-Schumacher, who taught preschool in Germany and who was a close friend of Ratliff's, testified that she and her husband cleaned up a lot of blood around the staircase in the Ratliff house.

She also told the jurors that Peterson took charge at the scene.

Her husband, Tom Appel-Schumacher, testified: "There was blood up the staircase wall. There appeared to be a lot of blood spattered in different places around the foyer area." He said that he and his wife cleaned it up so the girls would not see it.

Amy Beth Berner, who had worked as a substitute teacher in Germany, testified that she was suspicious when she saw all the blood on the floor and the walls. She told the jurors that she called the area a crime scene and told people not to walk on the stairs.

Peterson had walked Ratliff home the night before, after she'd had dinner with his family. Prosecutors said they believed he was the last person to have seen her alive.

THE DEFENSE'S TURN

Peterson's son, Todd, had returned home from a party to discover his father hovering over Kathleen's body. Rudolf told the jurors Todd practically had to pry his father away from the body.

Several witnesses Rudolf called to testify refuted the prosecution's claims and their interpretation of the evidence.

Dr. Jan Leestma, a neuropathologist, testified for the defense that Kathleen fell down the stairway twice. Leestma told the jurors that the cuts on Kathleen's head, even though numerous, could indeed have been caused by her falling. He asserted experts for the prosecution "misread" the wounds and that they were not from multiple strikes, but from a single impact against the stairs.

Radisch, who testified for the prosecution that the cuts on Kathleen's head were the result of blunt force trauma, was incorrect, Leestma said. He testified: "Kathleen Peterson's injuries were the result of a fall, and not the result of a beating."

Leestma explained the cuts did not appear to be caused by a cylindrical weapon, such as the fireplace blow poke that had been suggested. They also did not seem "consistent" with a beating death.

Christina Tomassetti, who had gone to a party with Peterson's son, Todd, arrived back at the home with Todd shortly after Peterson had called 911. She testified: "Michael Peterson was shaky and covered in blood. He was very upset and mumbling 'Oh my God.'"

Henry Lee, a renowned forensic scientist, testified for the defense about the blood spatters. (Lee had also testified at the trials of O. J. Simpson, Scott Peterson, and Rae Carruth.) Lee said that there were thousands of pieces of blood spatter at the scene.

Lee suggested that Kathleen writhed in pain before she died, diluted the blood evidence with urine, and coughed up blood, to explain some of the spatters on the lower part of the stairway walls.

In a demonstration for the jurors, Lee squirted red ink onto posterboard from various angles to illustrate how blood spatter occurs. He dropped ink from an eye dropper from different heights to show how blood drops vary based on angles and speed. Finally, he rammed his ink-stained hand onto the posterboard to show impact spatter.

Lee testified that much of the blood on the wall had been coughed up by Kathleen and, to illustrate, took a mouthful of watered-down ketchup and coughed it out at the posterboard.

Major Timothy Palmbach, the director of the Connecticut Division of Scientific Services, testified that the scene at the Peterson house was contaminated and police did little at the time to protect any evidence.

Palmbach, who sometimes works with Lee, said he had analyzed more than three hundred crime scenes for the Connecticut police. He maintained that there were many errors made the night Kathleen was found. Several pieces of evidence were not collected, he said, such as bloody towels that had been under her head, and her glasses. Her shoes had not been individually bagged, as is standard procedure, Palmbach stated, and there were not enough photographs taken, especially of the blood spatters.

THE BLOW POKE

Throughout the trial, prosecutors alleged that Peterson beat his wife on the head with a blow poke that had been given to Kathleen fifteen years prior. But police did not find it during their searches of the residence, and neither was any similar murder weapon found.

But as the trial was winding down, Rudolf produced the blow poke, a hollow, brass fireplace poker. He told the jury it had been found over the weekend. It had been sitting all along in the Petersons' garage.

Rudolf said a professional photographer had taken pictures, to show its location, and that it was encrusted with dust, dead insects, and webs—evidence it had sat there for some time. He pointed out that it was not damaged, as it would have been had it been used to hit Kathleen over the head.

CLOSING STATEMENTS

Hardin told the jurors: "These walls are talking. Kathleen Peterson is talking to us through these walls. She's screaming at us for truth and justice." He pointed to photos of the bloodstained walls in the stairwell where Kathleen was found.

Hardin said that Kathleen suffered thirty-eight injuries over her face, back, head, hands, and wrists. Even if she'd fallen twice, that seemed excessive. "That makes absolutely no sense."

Freda Black, who had assisted Hardin in the prosecution, said Peterson lied when he said his wife died from falling down the stairway. "It doesn't fit right here in your gut," she said.

Black continued: "We have never told you that we are absolutely certain that it was the blow poke that killed Mrs. Peterson." However, she added prosecutors believe Peterson used something similar.

Also similar, she said, was the death of Ratliff in Germany. "Do you really believe that lightning strikes twice in the same place?" she posed. Black said Peterson knew how to make his wife's murder look like an accident because it had worked in Germany years before.

Prosecutors revisited the motives for the murder, such as Kathleen's finding out about her husband's bisexuality, and discovering pornographic material and e-mails.

Rudolf began his closing argument by playing a tape of Hardin's opening statement that said prosecutors had an identical weapon to the one Peterson used to kill his wife, a blow poke.

"The missing weapon isn't missing, and wasn't used in a murder," he told the jurors.

Rudolf spent more than three hours discussing the case and listing all the reasonable doubts that should cause the jury to exonerate Peterson.

Rudolf questioned the credentials and credibility of the state's expert witnesses. He asserted that Kathleen probably knew her husband was bisexual, and the two of them still got along romantically and were in good financial shape. He said that discounted the prosecution's theory of either sex or money problems being a motive for murder.

There were traces of alcohol, Valium, and antihistamine in Kathleen's system, Rudolf said, the combination of which could have made her dizzy and could have contributed to her fall. He said: "If that's not reasonable doubt in and of itself, I can't imagine what a reasonable doubt could be."

He ended his closing statements by playing the tape of the 911 call Peterson had made the early morning that Kathleen died.

THE GUILTY VERDICT

The seven women and five men on the jury deliberated fifteen hours over the course of five days before rendering a guilty verdict.

Peterson was sentenced to life in prison.

PETERSON'S APPEAL

Chapel Hill attorney Tom Maher filed an appeal for Peterson two years after the very day that the jury found him guilty of murder. Maher's brief was nearly one hundred pages and claimed that Peterson did not get a fair trial.

Maher contended the court was mistaken to allow evidence from the 1985 death of Ratliff. Prosecutors had introduced that evidence, and had Ratliff's body exhumed, to show it was similar to Kathleen's death; however, since there was no proof that Peterson killed Ratliff, the evidence should not have been allowed.

In addition, Maher said Peterson's bisexuality was not relevant to the case, and that testimony from a male escort—who Peterson never met in person—had prejudiced the jury.

In the defendant's appellate brief, filed in the North Carolina Court of Appeals, Maher wrote the following in his conclusion:

This trial involved a seemingly simple question: Did the State prove beyond a reasonable doubt that Kathleen Peterson was beaten, rather than injured in a fall. To answer this question, however, jurors had to assess whether blood stains at the scene and on clothing were produced at the time of Mrs. Peterson's death, or the product of poor scene processing. Jurors also had to assess the competing expert views on the significance of blood stains. Finally, jurors had to assess the significance of the injuries themselves, and the lack of significant injuries often seen in beating cases. The jurors' ability fairly to evaluate this evidence, and the expert testimony presented by both sides, was crucial to a fair determination of the charge against Defendant. This ability, however, was fatally tainted by exposure to improperly obtained evidence, and to extensive evidence that had no legitimate role in the trial.

Jurors, in essence, were asked by the State to speculate about Defendant's supposed role in the death of Elizabeth Ratliff, about whether Defendant's bi-sexuality played a role in an unproven fight, and to speculate about whether there was a financial motive to the seemingly motiveless crime. In addition, jurors were told in closing argument that they could trust the prosecutor and witnesses who worked for the city, county, and state because the prosecutor personally knew that they would not risk their reputations on an unfounded prosecution, and because the witnesses worked for the jurors and therefore were trustworthy. Exposure to this evidence, and these arguments, fatally undermined the ability of jurors to make a fair assessment of the case, and Defendant's conviction must be reversed.

In January 2006, the state attorney general's office issued a one-hundred-page response to Peterson's appeal. In it, the office stated Peterson received a fair trial and that Judge Orlando Hudson did not make a mistake in allowing the evidence into trial, as that evidence suggested possible motives for the murder. Further, Ratliff's death showed a "reasonable connection" to Kathleen's death.

The North Carolina Court of Appeals decided in September 2006 to reject Peterson's appeal for a new trial.

ANOTHER TRIAL FOR PETERSON

Caitlin Atwater, Kathleen's daughter from her first marriage, filed a lawsuit seeking the benefits from her mother's life insurance policy and the benefits package her mother had accrued while at Nortel.

In September 2004, Prudential Insurance settled with Atwater, awarding her and her father, Fred Atwater, Kathleen's first husband, the $1.4 million proceeds from a life insurance policy. The percentage split between the two was not made public.

When Kathleen purchased the policy, she had named her first husband as the beneficiary. However, she changed that to Peterson when they married. In May 2004, Peterson signed away his claim to the proceeds.

Atwater filed a suit against Nortel in June 2004, claiming it wrongly paid almost $400,000 to Peterson after he had been indicted for murder. In September, Nortel settled the suit with Atwater out of court.

Atwater also filed a wrongful death suit against Peterson, alleging that he caused her mother's death. In the summer of 2006 she accepted a $25 million settlement; however, Peterson is destitute.

Peterson was declared indigent after his murder trial, and Atwater's attorney said the civil suit should ensure that Peterson does not profit from Kathleen's death. For example, if Peterson, who authored other novels, wrote a book while in prison, he would not see any profit from it if Atwater was successful with her suit.

Rudolf, who had been occasionally consulting with Peterson, has said the appeals in the murder case should be dealt with before the civil suit.

COMMENTARY: Michael Peterson

Michael Peterson was unquestionably a former marine who had spent time in the combat zone, and a successful novelist, and if he did in fact kill his wife, as the jury found, he is the first of our suspects who may indeed possess formidable acting talents. His performance on the 911 call appears to have been quite convincing—at first, at least.

Despite the usual able and well-prepared defense put forward by David Rudolf (of Rae Carruth fame), the prosecution had a strong case to present. That case became—in my view—unwinnable when evidence was received of his alleged "same and similar acts" with respect to the death of Elizabeth Ratliff in Germany years before. While Peterson was never given a chance to have a judicial decision as to whether he had in fact murdered Mrs. Ratliff, his North Carolina jury was in effect given an opportunity to make that judgment, in following and accepting the argument that "lightning doesn't strike twice." (A time-worn maxim, but in fact lightning has demonstrably struck the same spot more than once on many occasions.) The fact is, it is far from clear that Mrs. Ratliff was murdered at all, and there was no evidence tying Michael to that murder if there was one.

The evidence concluded with strong disagreement among the expert pathologists as to with what Kathleen Peterson was struck and how many times. Clearly at the eleventh hour Rudolf exploded the notion that the "blow poke" was a murder weapon. One is given to wonder how the police, with two searches accomplished, could have missed the very "blunt instrument" they claimed they were looking for. If one accepts the prosecution's evidence on the point, and murder was done, then it must have been committed in a rage; seven blows, none of which fractured the skull or was fatal, raises recollections of the manner of death of Dr. Sam Sheppard's wife, Marilyn. On a similar note, the alleged fatal tumble down the stairs is reminiscent of the facts in the case of Kenneth Fitzhugh.

The matter of Peterson's alleged bisexuality is troubling. Trial judges are required to balance "the probative value" (the tendency of the fact to prove a significant issue) of controversial evidence against its potential to prejudice the jury. This was indeed a close call, for one can only speculate that the victim even knew of Michael's sexual preferences; if she did, she had probably known for some years. Unless she suddenly tried to blackmail him and ruin his career as a writer, bisexuality is a far-fetched motive for murder. If a motive to kill was not supported by this evidence (and that of the "male escort") the prejudicial risk was substantial.

Another factor which rubs against the grain of fairness is the conduct of the prosecutor in his closing argument with respect to the credibility of his witnesses. There is a long-standing cardinal rule that a lawyer trying a case will never give his own personal opinion of the credibility of a witness; if he wishes to do so, he must withdraw from the trial, be sworn in as a witness, and subject himself to cross-examination. Even if all those steps are taken, offering opinions by one witness as to whether another witness has told the truth is clearly a dicey matter. Credibility questions are ordinarily the exclusive province of the jury.

Scott Peterson

Charged with murdering his wife and unborn child on December 23 or 24, 2002

THE DISAPPEARANCE

Laci Peterson, twenty-seven years old and eight months pregnant, disappeared from her La Loma, California, home on Christmas Eve, sparking a media frenzy that swept across the country. The case would fill newspapers, televisions, and radios with speculation of infidelity and Satanic cults. And it would spawn a half-dozen books and no less than two made-for-TV movies.

Scott Peterson told police late Christmas Eve that he last saw his wife at about 9:30 that morning as he left for the Berkeley Marina while she prepared to take their dog for a walk at East La Loma Park. He provided a time-stamped receipt from the marina's boat launch ramp as an alibi.

At the beginning of the case, the families of Laci and Scott were united. They worked together to post missing-person notices for Laci, and attended news conferences. However, when news of Peterson's affair with massage therapist Amber Frey surfaced, Laci's family distanced themselves. Things became increasingly tense when Peterson sold Laci's Land Rover and purchased a new truck.

Peterson, a fertilizer salesman, told the news media that Laci was aware of his affair with Frey and that the two had patched things up. In one interview in February 2003, Peterson said he desperately missed his wife and the child they were going to have. He said he was so consumed with worry and grief that it was difficult to function—to sleep, eat, or work.

Peterson's family accused the police of looking only at him as the suspect, and missing the opportunity to pursue the real killer. Peterson's mother, Jackie, was certain that Laci had been kidnapped by someone who wanted a baby. She was adamant her son would do no harm to his wife.

THE INVESTIGATION

Two bodies, Laci and her child, were discovered in mid-April, about four months after Laci was reported missing. People walking along the shore found them, roughly a mile apart—one body in south Richmond, and the other at Point Isabel.

The Modesto Police Department suspected Peterson early on, but initially lacked evidence.

Through the course of the investigation, the police seized the boat Peterson said he fished in the day of Laci's disappearance, as well as his pickup truck and almost one hundred items from the Peterson home. Police used wiretaps on Peterson's phone and radio transponders on his vehicles, so they could keep track of him, especially when he went to San Diego, where his parents lived. Suspicion grew when Peterson sold his wife's Land Rover prior to her body being discovered, and when news surfaced of his affair with massage therapist Amber Frey.

Throughout the investigation, the police declined to discuss a motive in the murders; and when the bodies were recovered, they would not discuss a possible cause of death. Various sources speculated whether Laci had given birth before she was killed or after. (One report suggested baby Conner was delivered via "coffin birth," which happens when gas builds up in a decomposing body's abdomen and expels the baby through the birth canal.)

LACI DENISE ROCHA

Laci was born May 4, 1975, at Doctors Medical Center in Modesto. The family lived on a large dairy farm in Escalon. Laci's parents divorced when she was two years old, and her mother took her to Modesto. Her older brother, Brent, stayed with their father on the farm. Laci's father, Dennis Rocha, remarried four years later and had another child, Amy, with his new wife. Laci would visit her father on the farm on weekends and ride horses. Laci's mother, Sharon, also remarried, and her new husband, Ronald Grantski, helped raise Laci.

When Laci entered high school, she took fewer trips to her father's farm. She was a cheerleader at Downy High School in Modesto, and she graduated in 1993. Laci's first steady boyfriend was Kent Gain, whom she moved in with after high school. They rented a house in Morro Bay, close to California Polytechnic State University, where she had been accepted. Their relationship lasted about three years. In 1999, Gain would be sentenced to fifteen years for shooting his girlfriend at that time.

Laci met Peterson while she was in college. Her neighbor worked at Pacific Café in Morro Bay, where Scott also worked, and Laci occasionally went there. Their first date was deep-sea fishing.

They married two years later on August 9, 1997, at a resort in San Luis Obispo. The Petersons operated a small restaurant in the town, The Shack, until 2000, when they moved back to Modesto.

According to friends and relatives, Laci loved to cook and garden and watch *Martha Stewart* on television. The country learned all of Laci's hobbies and idiosyncrasies as her murder case progressed.

She worked as a substitute teacher for Modesto schools. In early December, she stopped teaching and began preparing for the baby, whom she and Peterson had decided to name Conner.

SCOTT LEE PETERSON

Peterson was born October 24, 1972, in San Diego, California. His father worked for a trucking company but later purchased and operated a packaging business. Peterson's mother owned the Put On, a small boutique in Modesto.

Peterson attended the University of San Diego High School, was a member of the school's golf team, and caddied at a nearby golf course.

After selling the restaurant he and Laci operated, Peterson worked as an agriculture chemical salesman.

AMBER FREY

Born February 10, 1975, in Los Angeles, Amber alternated living with her parents, who divorced when she was five years old. Her freshman and sophomore years were at Sierra High School in Fresno County; her junior year was at Hoover High School, also in Fresno; and she graduated from Clovis High School in 1993.

She met Peterson on a blind date in November 2002. They dined at a Japanese restaurant, and Peterson told her he frequently traveled around the world for business. He claimed to be single, living in Sacramento and owning a condo in San Diego. Frey reported that she spent that first night with him at his motel, and that she was smitten.

On their second date, she gave him a key to her home.

Later, however, she said he told her he'd been married in the past, and she had a friend of hers in the Fresno Police Department look into his background. When the friend called Frey on December 29 to tell her that her new boyfriend was probably the Scott Peterson whose wife had been missing since Christmas Eve, Frey said she called the Modesto Police Department, and allowed them to put a wiretap on her phone.

One of the calls recorded was one of the most damaging to Peterson. About the time a candlelight vigil was starting on New Year's Eve for Laci, Peterson called her and said he was in Paris on business.

Scott: Amber, it's New Year's here. Are you there?
Amber: Yeah. Are you having a good time?

Scott: I'm near the Eiffel Tower. The New Year's celebration is unreal. The crowd is huge.

PETERSON'S ARREST

Peterson was arrested a week after the bodies suspected of being Laci and Conner were pulled from the shore of the bay. (He had dyed his hair, was carrying his brother's ID on him, and had $15,000 in cash.)

Several hours after the arrest, the California Attorney General's Office reported that DNA tests on the bodies had identified them as Laci and Conner. A police spokesman said they were afraid Peterson would flee to Mexico, and as a result he was arrested before the announcement. The police had wiretaps on Peterson's phones and had been tracking his vehicles with devices they'd attached. Too, they had been watching him, and noticed he was in San Diego, near the Mexican border.

After the arrest, Peterson was taken to the Stanislaus County Jail. (That was shortly before midnight, and the street had been blocked off and extra police were on duty to watch a crowd of a few hundred that had gathered. Many in the crowd cheered when the police drove by with Peterson.)

Because Peterson was charged with two counts of murder, it became a capital case, thus allowing the district attorney to seek the death penalty. Peterson maintained he had nothing to do with Laci's disappearance and said he had gone alone fishing the morning of her disappearance.

THE AUTOPSY REPORTS

Forensic experts could not agree on whether Laci was mutilated before she was dumped in the bay. Santa Clara county coroner Dr. Gregory Schmunk said the body could have been torn apart by boat propellers, feeding fish, and the tides. However, Dr. Michael Baden, a New York forensic pathologist involved with the O. J. Simpson murder case, suggested that the body was dismembered before it was dumped. Baden reported that limbs have been known to separate from torsos in the water, but not in only four months' time. That could take years, he said.

Judge Al Girolami denied the prosecutors' request to unseal the autopsy reports. Prosecutors had argued that the reports should be open because some of the information had been leaked to the press, and that the leaked information was beneficial for the defense. In addition, an attorney representing a group of newspapers requested that the reports be made public, contending most such reports were available to the press. Though Girolami would not reverse his ruling, he did give permission to the coroner's office to issue death certificates, which were public documents.

Laci's certificate listed her death as "homicide," and the cause as unknown. Conner's certificate did not list a cause of death.

WIRETAPS AND GAG ORDERS

Judge Girolami ruled that the lead wiretap investigator had to give the defense all of the documents and recordings related to the wiretaps on Peterson's phones, excluding information on calls made between Peterson and various journalists. In addition, the prosecution would get copies of documents and recordings, except those involving journalists and those between Peterson and his attorneys.

Defense attorney Mark Geragos requested the transcripts from the conferences involving the wiretaps. Unfortunately, no court reporter was present during those conferences, which capital cases require.

Judge Girolami also ruled that a gag order was in place to prevent attorneys, investigators, police officers, judicial officers, court employees, and potential witnesses in the Peterson case from talking to the media.

Girolami said the gag order would help ensure that Peterson received a fair trial.

NO GRAND JURY

Prosecutors decided to begin their case against Peterson with a public preliminary hearing to seek an indictment, avoiding the customary and secret grand jury. The district attorney's evidence presented to a grand jury would be kept quiet until the trial began, which might not be for two more years.

District attorney James Brazelton said the preliminary hearing would be a faster route and would prevent more stories from circulating. Prosecutors would present some of their evidence in an effort to convince a judge that a trial is warranted. Their case was largely circumstantial, as a cause of death could not be proven, and there was a lack of evidence that the murder had taken place at the Peterson home. Too, there were no witnesses and no murder weapon.

THE PROSECUTION'S CASE

On June 1, 2004, the opening day of Peterson's murder trial, DA Rick Distaso played phone calls Peterson made to Amber Frey. "You're just an amazing woman," Peterson said during his January 1, 2003, call. That call was recorded on Frey's line by police. Peterson went on to say: "Our psyches are, you know, kind of relaxed and you are focused on relationships as opposed to getting up in the morning and doing things or, you know, going to pick up dry cleaning, things like that. Our relationship will grow, and know how beautiful you are. Okay, sweetie?"

Distaso told the jurors in another conversation, that Peterson announced to Frey he did not want to have children and was thinking about having a vasectomy. In a separate conversation, Peterson told Frey he was calling her from Paris. A little later that same night, he attended a candlelight service for Laci.

Peterson's whereabouts the day Laci disappeared were the topic of testimony. Distaso said Peterson had told Harvey Temple, Laci's uncle, and two neighbors, that he had golfed all day December 24. However, he later told police and Laci's mother that he had fished alone in Berkeley. Peterson was terse with Laci's relatives, and he did not tell police what kind of fish he was trying to catch, Distaso said.

The DA repeatedly pointed out problems with the time line Peterson gave police. Peterson said to four different police officers that he went to the Berkeley Marina at 9:30 A.M., and that

Laci was watching the *Martha Stewart* television show when he left. However, Distaso said cell phone records prove that Peterson was still in the neighborhood more than a half hour later.

Distaso told the jurors that Laci's missing persons report, which Peterson filled out, said she was wearing diamond earrings, a diamond necklace, and a diamond ring. The ring, however, was in a jewelry shop being repaired, and the necklace was found in the Peterson house.

Throughout the first nineteen weeks of Peterson's trial, beginning in June 2004, district attorneys called more than 150 witnesses. Among them: Laci's sister, Amy Rocha; Laci's mother, Sharon Rocha; Laci's stepfather, Ron Grantski; Laci's brother and sister-in-law Brent and Rose Rocha; several of Laci's neighbors and friends; Laci's mailman; Laci's obstetrician; many officers, evidence technicians, and detectives from the Modesto Police Department; deputies from the Contra Costa County Sheriff's Department; Richmond police officers; jewelers; pawnbrokers; criminalists; Amber Frey; Shawn Sibley, who introduced Scott to Frey; Michael Looby, the walker who discovered Conner's body; Elena M. Gonzalez, the walker who discovered Laci's body; Berkeley Marina employees; technicians from the state DNA laboratory; computer experts; friends of Peterson; telephone company employees; Department of Justice agents; Stanislaus County Drug Enforcement Unit officers and agents; Roger Content, the car dealer who worked with Peterson when he traded in Laci's Land Rover; FBI lab technicians and evidence experts; Peterson's father; Dr. Brian Peterson, the forensic pathologist who performed the autopsies on Laci and Conner; Dr. Ralph Cheng, U.S. Geological Society hydrologist; Mario Ruvalcaba, the owner of a car Peterson considered purchasing; Michael Griffin, who sold a Mercedes to Peterson; and Michael Richardson, a friend of Peterson and best man at his wedding.

WITNESSES FOR THE PROSECUTION

Alison Galloway, a forensic anthropologist who testified for the prosecution, said that Laci's remains had been in the water for three to six months, based on its condition. Laci's body had washed ashore about four months after her disappearance. Galloway told the jurors she put the age of the baby between thirty-three and thirty-eight weeks old. An obstetrician who had testified placed the baby at thirty-three weeks. Galloway said the condition of the baby made it difficult to set the exact age.

Prosecutors showed the jury pictures of Laci's and Conner's remains. The bodies were in a state of decomposition and water-logged, and viewing the pictures caused one juror to cry and others to look visibly shaken. Laci's body was missing the head, forearms, and part of the left leg.

Forensic pathologist Brian Peterson (no relation to Laci's husband) performed the autopsy on Laci. Peterson testified that it was impossible to say if the injuries to Laci's ribs were caused before or after her death. He asserted that the autopsy was difficult because the only organ remaining was her uterus. Peterson added that the remains were in such poor condition he could not determine a cause of death; however, he believed that the baby's body was ejected from Laci's after being in the water, suggesting that the baby was not born live. He said there were no signs of a Caesarean section, and because the baby's body was in better condition, it had likely been expelled after Laci was underwater a few weeks.

(However, when defense attorney Mark Geragos questioned the forensic pathologist, he admitted that he could not rule out a live birth.)

One of the prosecution's first witnesses was Margarita Nava, the Petersons' housekeeper. She testified that when she finished cleaning on December 23, she left a mop outside. Police collected two mops. Nava said Laci seemed tired that day.

Investigators and other witnesses recounted Laci's activities. On the morning of December 23 she went to Trader Joe's and bought almost $100 worth of groceries. At noon, she went to the Sweet Serenity Day Spa for a waxing treatment. In the evening, she and Peterson went to Salon Salon, where Peterson got his hair cut.

Laci's mother, Sharon Rocha, testified that her daughter would not have walked her dog, McKenzie, on December 24, feeling as tired as she was and being that far along in her pregnancy. She also testified that Peterson's behavior turned unusual after Laci's disappearance. Scott did not acknowledge her when they were in the park the night Laci was reported missing, and later that same night at his house, he walked away from her when she tried to approach him. Rocha told the jurors: "It seemed to take Scott a long time to show up in the park." She added that, later, "I was walking over to him to give him a hug, but he kept angling away from me."

Rocha said Peterson had planned on spending that night at their house, but he did not show up or call. She also told the jurors that on the night of a candlelight vigil, with more than a thousand people in attendance, Peterson did not get up on the stage to address the crowd. Finally, when police contacted her to report that bodies were found, and that they might be Laci and Conner, she called Peterson and left a message asking him to call. He never did, she testified.

Rocha told the jurors she tried to get Peterson to talk to her about Laci's disappearance. She said she wanted to know what happened in the hours before her daughter went missing. Rocha said Peterson never gave her many details, and their conversations were never long. However, she said Peterson told her he and Laci watched a movie on the evening of December 23, and that Laci got up about 7:00 A.M. the next day. He told her Laci had planned to go to the store, bake gingerbread, and walk the dog.

Rocha testified that Peterson told her Laci was fixing her hair before he left for his Christmas Eve fishing trip.

When Geragos cross-examined Rocha, he said of Laci: "She was wearing jewelry every day. Stunning pieces, eye catching?" Rocha answered yes. Money could have been a motive in Laci's disappearance, Geragos continued.

Rocha also testified that she became suspicious of Peterson when "he didn't show the concern that I felt he should be showing for Laci being missing." She maintained that they would schedule times to get together and meet, and Peterson always canceled them.

Other witnesses for the prosecution confirmed that Peterson seemed distant and unemotional regarding Laci's disappearance.

One witness testified that on many occasions he had asked Peterson to go fishing with him, and only once did Peterson take him up on that offer. He said Peterson's fishing rod was left behind in his garage, and that it was still there.

Police officers testified that neighbors and friends of Laci's riddled them with questions.

Byron Duerfeldt, a Modesto police sergeant, told the jurors that he was at the Peterson house the night Laci was reported missing. Duerfeldt said he kept neighbors and friends out of the house while other police were inside. He said the yard was chaotic and that relatives were visibly upset. Duerfeldt said Peterson never spoke with him or approached him that night.

Other witnesses testified to various aspects of the case:

Amber Frey, the massage therapist who dated Peterson, spent days testifying. Frey told the jurors that after she spoke at a press conference, Peterson called her to congratulate her on her bravery and said that he was proud of her. She told the jurors that when he considered having his own press conference, she asked him to refer to their time together as a "romantic relationship" rather than an affair. Frey said she did not consider it an affair, since at the time she did not know that Peterson was married. She recounted that Peterson posed as a man who had recently lost his wife—weeks before Laci actually was missing. When defense attorney Geragos cross-examined Frey, she admitted that Peterson never said he loved her. Geragos also got her to admit that Peterson never incriminated himself to her regarding Laci's disappearance. Frey agreed that he'd always said he had nothing to do with Laci's murder. She said most of their conversations were about the media harassing them.

Brent Rocha, Laci's brother, told the jurors that when he heard about Amber Frey, he confronted Peterson. At first Peterson denied the affair, though later he admitted it, Brent said, adding Peterson was adamant that Frey was not involved in Laci's disappearance. Brent testified he pressed Peterson on that.

"Scott, how did you know she had nothing to do with it?" Brent said Peterson answered: "There was no way she could have had anything to do with it. She didn't even know Laci existed."

Ron Grantski, Laci's stepfather, testified that he asked Peterson shortly after Laci disappeared if he had a girlfriend, and Peterson said no. Grantski admitted that he supported Peterson at first. He told the jurors that he also went fishing the afternoon of December 24, but at a different location.

Sandy Rickard, Sharon Rocha's best friend, testified that on the evening of December 24, she approached Peterson. Without prompting, she testified that he told her: "I wouldn't be surprised if they find blood on my truck because I cut my hands all the time because I'm an outdoorsman, a fisherman." Rickard told the jurors that at the time she was puzzled by his comment.

Rose Rocha, Laci's sister-in-law, testified that she once asked Peterson if he was ready to be a father. She told the jurors that Peterson said: "I was kind of hoping for infertility." She added that he did not laugh or smile. She testified: "I didn't know how to read him at that point."

Amie Krigbaum and **Terra Venable,** Peterson's neighbors, testified that he told them he had been golfing during the day that Laci disappeared. Susan Aquino, Laci's aunt, and Harvey Kemple testified that Peterson told them the same thing.

Kemple, married to Sharon Rocha's cousin, testified that he was suspicious of Peterson from the night Laci went missing. He said he followed Peterson on a few occasions. Kemple said once Peterson went in the wrong direction when they were going to post missing person fliers, and that Peterson sat in his pickup for more than forty minutes in the parking lot of a mall. On another occasion, Kemple said Peterson went to Del Rio Country Club. Kemple told the jurors he talked to employees there who told him Peterson had been golfing there on several days since Laci's disappearance.

Karen Servas, Peterson's next-door neighbor, told the jurors that she found McKenzie, Laci's golden retriever, shortly after 10:00 A.M. on December 24. The dog's leash was damp and dirty and had leaves and grass clippings on it. Servas testified that the Peterson's front gate was locked, but a side gate was open. She said she did not see anyone around the house or the yard, so she put McKenzie in the backyard and went home.

THE DEFENSE'S CASE

Defense attorney Geragos, in his opening statement to the jury, said there was no evidence that Peterson killed Laci. Geragos called his client a cad and said that his behavior was boorish, but he asserted that Peterson was not a murderer.

He said evidence would show that Conner's umbilical cord was cut and that he lived a few weeks, dying between late January and late February. Peterson's girlfriend, Frey, was not a motive in the murder. Peterson had only two dates with Frey before Laci was reported missing, Geragos noted.

Geragos told the jurors that police focused on his client, rather than look at other leads. He said that it was possible vagrants in the park where Laci sometimes walked her dog might have taken her. She was known to confront the vagrants, and one resident warned her to be careful with them, Geragos reported.

In addition, Geragos said a witness reported a suspicious van in the Peterson's neighborhood the morning Laci disappeared. He said another person claimed to have seen Laci forced into a dark van days after December 24.

Geragos said Peterson's behavior in the months after Laci's disappearance was easily explained. When Peterson was arrested, he had his brother's ID on him so he could obtain a "resident discount" at Torrey Pines, Geragos said. And he had changed his appearance so news reporters, who had been hounding him, might not recognize him.

Peterson's attorneys began calling witnesses October 18, 2004, the beginning of the twentieth week of the trial. They called fourteen witnesses—less than a tenth of the number the prosecution did. Their witnesses included: Modesto Police Department detectives, a private investigator, a judge who lived near Peterson's house, and Peterson's mother and father, Jackie and Lee Peterson.

THE PENALTY PHASE

After the jury had found Peterson guilty on two counts—first-degree murder in the case of Laci, and second-degree murder for Conner, a penalty phase began to determine Peterson's sentence.

During the penalty phase, prosecutors told the jury that Peterson deserved the "ultimate punishment" for murdering his wife and unborn son. In an opening statement, prosecutor David Harris said, through the course of the trial, they would feel the worry and grief of Laci's family.

Harris said: "When the defendant dumped the bodies of his wife and unborn son into the bay, those ripples spread out and they touched many, many lives." Laci's relatives suffered, he said.

Geragos, Peterson's lead defense attorney, told the jury that his client was "stone-cold innocent." One of Peterson's attorneys said they would introduce Peterson's friends, former teachers, a golf coach, former employers, and relatives who would testify to Peterson's character and would demonstrate that his life was worth saving.

Geragos told the jurors that four days before Laci disappeared she had seen the boat Peterson purchased. A hair collected on pliers in the boat could have gotten there on that day, he said.

The evidence was "flimsy" and circumstantial, Geragos said to the jurors. The child the Petersons had intended to call Conner was born alive, the attorney contended, proving that his client could not have killed Laci.

PETERSON'S SENTENCING

Before the jurors voted on the death penalty, it was reported that they passed around the last picture that had been taken of Laci. She was seated at a Christmas party in Modesto. They also passed around pictures of Laci's and Conner's bodies.

The jurors, six men and six women, voted to give Peterson the death penalty. Some of the jurors later told the media that Peterson seemed callous and sometimes emotionless in the trial, as if the deaths of his wife and child did not bother him. They said that behavior contributed to the sentence.

When the verdict was read, Laci's mother, seated in the front row, cried. Peterson stared and said nothing. A few hundred people gathered outside the courthouse to hear the verdict.

After the verdict, the jurors attended a news conference and explained the process of reaching the verdict. Initially, the jurors were divided on the death penalty issue. However, after the photos of Laci were passed around, they reached a unanimous decision.

One juror said that Peterson should have protected his wife and child, not killed them. Too, the jurors said the killings had to have been planned, not a quick, heated act.

Another juror said that, at the beginning of the trial, he thought Peterson was innocent, perhaps framed, and that police had mishandled the investigation; however, his opinion changed as prosecutors slowly presented their case.

The jurors said one of the factors that contributed to their finding Peterson guilty included that Laci's and Conner's bodies washed up within a mile of where Peterson had been fishing on Christmas Eve. The bodies were near where Peterson had admitted to being. One of the witnesses for the prosecution, who was an expert with currents and tides, had testified that if Peterson had dumped the bodies where he claimed he was fishing, the currents would have carried the bodies to where they were found.

Another piece of evidence that convinced the jurors was that shortly before a candlelight vigil for Laci, records showed that Peterson was on the phone to Frey. (The conversation in which Peterson told Frey he was at the Eiffel Tower.)

One juror told reporters that it was odd that Peterson was seen driving to the Berkeley Marina in rented cars, saying he was checking on the investigation, yet he never talked to anyone working there.

Because Peterson was sentenced to death, his case immediately went into an appeal process.

LACI'S INSURANCE

Sharon Rocha, Laci's mother, was awarded the benefits from Laci's life insurance policy. Rocha had battled Peterson through the courts to get the proceeds from the $250,000 policy. Rocha had initially been awarded the money earlier; however, Peterson's attorneys argued they needed more time to present their case.

One of Peterson's attorneys, Pat Harris, stated that the insurance money should not be decided while Peterson's death penalty case was being appealed.

According to California law, individuals who kill their spouses are denied inheritance rights. Although death penalty cases are automatically reviewed by the Supreme Court of California, that process can take decades, and Rocha's attorney argued that Rocha should not have to wait that long.

THE WRONGFUL DEATH SUIT

Following Peterson's conviction, Rocha filed a wrongful death suit against him. Her ex-husband joined the suit, in which they are seeking $25 million. Rocha's attorney reported that the trial would center on damages for the loss of Laci, rather than on whether Peterson was guilty. There is a civil suit pending. The Peterson and Rocha families also had to contend with splitting the profits from the sale of the house Laci and Peterson lived in. The house sold for about $400,000.

CASE HIGHLIGHTS

DECEMBER 23. at 8:30 P.M., Laci spoke to her mother on the telephone. This was the last time someone other than Peterson confirmed she was still alive.

DECEMBER 24. Laci was reported missing at 5:00 P.M.

DECEMBER 25. News programs broadcasted Laci's disappearance.

DECEMBER 31. Police investigators stated they suspected foul play in Laci's disappearance.

JANUARY 2 AND 8. Divers searched Berkeley Marina for Laci's body.

JANUARY 17. Modesto police showed Laci's family pictures of Scott with another woman.

JANUARY 19. Peterson's relatives coordinated 240 volunteers to distributed fliers about Laci.

JANUARY 25. Amber Frey, Peterson's girlfriend, talked to Modesto police.

JANUARY 28. Peterson admitted in a television interview that he had an affair with Frey.

FEBRUARY 10. Laci was expected to deliver her baby this day.

FEBRUARY 18–20. Modesto police searched Peterson's home.

MARCH 6. Police formally called the case a homicide.

APRIL 13. A full-term fetus was found near the shore.

APRIL 14. An unidentified female body was found near the same location.

APRIL 18. Modesto police arrested Peterson and reported that the bodies were identified as Laci and her son, Conner.

APRIL 21. Peterson pleaded not guilty to the murders of Laci and Conner.

APRIL 25. Stanislaus County district attorney James Brazelton announced that he would seek the death penalty against Peterson.

MAY 2. Mark Geragos, a high-profile attorney, took Peterson's case.

MAY 4. A memorial for Laci was held at the First Baptist Church in Modesto.

MAY 9. Court papers containing evidence police used to arrest Peterson were sealed.

MAY 15. Laci's autopsy report was sealed.

JUNE 12. The judge imposed a gag order on participants, and called the order necessary to guarantee Peterson a right to a fair trial.

JUNE 26. More than 150 tapes from wiretaps of Peterson's telephone were handed over to the defense.

AUGUST 6. Defense attorneys claimed Peterson was offered a plea bargain, and that he was threatened with the death penalty three months before he was actually charged.

AUGUST 12. Forensic experts and Peterson's attorneys examined Laci's and Conner's remains. They said they wanted to find evidence to clear Peterson.

AUGUST 30. Laci and Conner were buried, more than eight months after Laci's disappearance.

SEPTEMBER 26. Laci's mother filed a suit against Peterson that would prevent him from earning money from books or movie projects about the murders.

OCTOBER 29. Peterson's preliminary hearing started. Testimony focused on DNA tests on a hair found on Peterson's pliers.

NOVEMBER 6. A police officer testified that Peterson told his mistress he was a widower on the same day he bought a fishing boat. It was the boat he would take fishing the day Laci disappeared.

NOVEMBER 13. Defense attorney Geragos argued that detectives focused on Peterson when they should have explored other possibilities.

NOVEMBER 14. Detectives testified that Laci's remains were dressed in tan pants, while Peterson said she was wearing black pants when he left to go fishing.

NOVEMBER 17. Prosecutors were allowed to use DNA evidence from a hair found in Peterson's boat.

NOVEMBER 18. Peterson's preliminary trial ended and he was ordered to stand trial for two counts of first-degree murder. Peterson's trial was set to begin in January.

DECEMBER 12. Geragos sought a change of venue, claiming Peterson could not get a fair trial in Modesto.

JANUARY 8, 2004. The judge ruled the trial would move to San Mateo County.

JANUARY 21. Judge Richard Arnason was appointed to preside over Peterson's trial. Arnason, eighty-two, was a retired judge.

JANUARY 22. Peterson's attorneys had Arnason removed, claiming he was biased against them and their client.

JANUARY 27. Judge Alfred Delucchi was named to preside over Peterson's trial.

FEBRUARY 2. Peterson's double-murder trial began. Delucchi ruled against cameras in the courtroom.

FEBRUARY 5. The woman who told police she saw Laci walking her dog on Christmas Eve died. The death was ruled due to natural causes.

FEBRUARY 11. The civil lawsuit filed by Laci's family against Peterson began.

FEBRUARY 24. Witnesses testified that Peterson had at least two extramarital relationships.

FEBRUARY 26. The judge ruled that the jurors would not be sequestered during the trial.

MARCH 3. Wiretap specialists testified behind closed doors. Debates swirled about whether recordings from Peterson's phone would be allowed in evidence.

MARCH 4–5. Jury selection began. About two hundred prospective jurors were given questionnaires to determine if they were suitable for the trial.

MARCH 23. The judge ruled Peterson's comments to the news media about what he did the day Laci disappeared would be allowed as evidence.

APRIL 16. Geragos requested a change of venue, citing prospective jurors who lied in an effort to get on the jury and "get" Peterson.

MAY 27. The jury was seated in the case. There were six men, six women, and six alternates.

JUNE 1: The trial began.

AUGUST 10. Frey testified that Peterson told her he was a widower, and lied about where he lived. The jurors heard tape recordings of her and Peterson's conversations. The recordings were made after Frey went to police.

OCTOBER 5. The prosecution rested its case.

OCTOBER 26. The defense rested its case.

NOVEMBER 1–2. Closing arguments were made.

NOVEMBER 3. The jury began deliberations.

NOVEMBER 12. The jury found Peterson guilty on both counts.

DECEMBER 13. Peterson was sentenced to death.

COMMENTARY: Scott Peterson

An interesting approach to the inner workings of Scott Peterson as a personality involves ignoring the fact that his wife and fetus turned up dead four months after they "disappeared." Assume that she is still missing and examine Peterson's conduct, looking for the sort of cold, cruel tendencies that are the hallmark of a classic sociopath; for certainly it would take a sociopathic personality to cause such a disappearance.

It will be useful to digress for a moment, for most readers do not—thankfully—have to deal on a regular basis with sociopaths. On the other hand, few people reach adulthood without having confronted one or more of these people. Simply put, sociopaths—formerly known as psychopaths—are lacking in what Sigmund Freud called the "superego." In lay terms, they are devoid of what we would call a conscience, a sense of social responsibility. Like wild animals, they take what they want without regard to the hurt done to others. This is not to suggest, however, that they can be recognized by their bare fangs; sociopaths frequently have a smooth exterior, with charming, sometimes gallant ways. This is particularly true of the lower echelon of confidence men, those who would steal the last penny from an elderly, frail widow. (The classier con men go after only the rich, because as famed bank robber Willie Sutton is reputed to have said, "That's where the money is.")

Psychiatrists, psychologists, and sociologists have argued for years as to whether sociopathic qualities are hereditary or are induced by a cruel environment. After fifty years of dealing with these creatures—including the most colorful example, the Boston Strangler—this writer must vote thumpingly for the latter. There are fascinating fictional accounts of sociopaths who were "born that way," such as the little girl in The Bad Seed *and the little boy in* The Omen, *but folk such as these seldom if ever emerge in the real world of criminal conduct.*

If the Strangler, Albert DeSalvo, is a fair example, the cruelty of his childhood is mind-boggling. His father was an intensely perverted and cruel jackal of a man who delighted in tormenting his wife and sons. He also taught young Albert to break and enter, to steal, to seal animals in orange crates and then shoot them with his bow and arrow, and to take sex roughly at every opportunity. There was nothing to suggest that he emerged from the womb with any of these traits.

What clues, therefore, did Scott Peterson leave lying around? More than enough, it would seem, for the jury gave him the ultimate punishment.

First, one must ask: "How would the average person respond to the disappearance of his pregnant wife?" He would probably be frenetically hounding everyone within miles to help locate his beloved. Peterson, it seems, exuded the sort of chilly, calm attitude one might expect from a man who knew there was no reason to get excited; the missing person would stay missing. Selling his wife's motor vehicle is not the sort of thing one would be expected to do if the wife might return and be outraged. Then, too, the ridiculous charade Peterson perpetrated by calling his lover from his wife's candlelight service and claiming he was at the Eiffel Tower in Paris is especially typical of a sociopath bereft of any real concern for either the truth or his lost wife.

While Peterson might have hoped that his wife's corpse would never be found, the four months during which she was missing offered a strong chance to chronicle his day-to-day conduct, which showed that he acted as though he knew Laci would not be returning. Law enforcement seemed to have done at best a mediocre job of exploiting this opportunity.

The investigation had other serious shortcomings that—had they not occurred—might have strengthened the case against Scott. When he said he had been fishing, detectives should have immediately asked that he reenact his day, using the actual fishing tackle, boat, and spot where he anchored, to later measure against emerging evidence. The police should also have asked for a consensual and comprehensive search of Peterson's house almost immediately, not eight weeks later when he had had ample time to tidy up. And it would have been more than useful to ask him to submit to a polygraph test; obviously, he would have been diagnosed as deceptive, and would have probably made other disingenuous statements that could be used against him. It is more than plausible that a truly capable polygraph examiner might have been able to get damaging admissions from him, or even a confession.

Peterson's account of his wife having been adorned with expensive diamonds, when in fact she could not have been wearing what was in the shop for repair, was a transparent effort to entice others to believe that Laci had been waylaid by some robber who decided not to leave any witnesses. Lies of this sort help a jury to conclude that a homicide was premeditated.

For those who followed this trial, it is easy to recall that at one point Mark Geragos—an experienced and highly capable lawyer—assured the court, jury, and public that the defense would present evidence showing that someone other than Scott committed the murders. This bold step was doubtless taken in reliance of something said convincingly by Peterson himself, something that turned out not to be true. When this promise did not come to fruition, it must have called attention to the fact that far from solving the case, Peterson did not even offer his story for the jury to consider. Although the rule says that a criminal defendant's failure to testify should never be weighed against him, the defense's claim must have made their case even more difficult than usual.

The circumstantial case against Peterson was considerable, and perhaps strong enough to support a finding of guilt beyond reasonable doubt. Certainly the discovery of Laci's hair on Scott's pliers was a devastating blow to the defense, despite Geragos's valiant attempt to explain it; his assertion that Laci had been at the boat hardly established a probability that her hair somehow wafted over to his pliers like Tinkerbell alighting from a gentle breeze. But this claim remains a possibility. Further, Peterson's remarks that he admired infertility and was less than thrilled about having children no doubt clobbered him on the issue of premeditation. His grandiose statements to Amber Frey—resurrected as if live in the courtroom by virtue of the wiretap tapes—inspire one to hate this creature who oozes squishy romantic overtures even as his wife and fetus are dead in the water. Clearly he had not the semblance of a conscience, nor remorse, nor regret for what had occurred. And no lawyer, no matter how dazzling and magical as he deploys his courtroom skills, has yet the ability to master the cross-examination of a tape recording.

One must question, however, whether the death penalty is a suitable risk in this case. If a fly on the wall might have seen an argument, a fight with provocation that caused Peterson to kill his wife, the fact that he covered up the killing would not elevate that conduct to capital murder. Amber Frey seems to be the only available motive, since she was a recent acquaintance Scott was clearly trying to "wow," but would he kill a pregnant wife because of this relationship, or simply to prevent the birth of a child? The questions are haunting, and were not answered in a comforting way. Conscientious folks, like the Magi of old in William Butler Yeats's classic poem, must be "all unsatisfied."

If capital punishment is really a useful social tool in our society, it is also one with a bothersome history. Finding thirteen men in Illinois alone, scheduled for execution, who were shown to be totally innocent by DNA evidence—as recently occurred—should have been a humbling event, causing us to demand that death penalty cases be proven "beyond any doubt." No such movement has taken place. Perhaps the fact that most of these thirteen, like their counterparts in other states, were minorities, poor, and poorly defended on a skimpy budget has attenuated what should have been horror at this awful example of a flawed system. We truck on, and if Scott Peterson did not commit cold, premeditated murder—but something less—his sentence, if not changed on appeal, will rub luster once more from American justice.

Mark Hacking

Charged with murdering his wife on July 19, 2004

In the summer of 2004, Lori Hacking believed she would soon be moving to North Carolina. Her husband, Mark, had told her he'd been accepted at the University of North Carolina Medical School in Chapel Hill.

But she would soon discover that not only had he not been accepted at the school, he hadn't even graduated from the University of Utah.

On July 19, Mark Hacking called 911 shortly before 11:00 A.M. and reported Lori missing. He told the emergency dispatcher that Lori left for her regular early-morning jog but had not returned home, nor was she at work. He told police that she usually jogged in the northeast of downtown Salt Lake in the Memory Grove and City Creek Canyon area. Before calling police, Hacking had called some of Lori's friends to find out if they'd heard from her. He told police he went three miles each way along her regular jogging route and could not find her. However, he said her car was at the entrance to the park.

The night of Lori's disappearance, Hacking was found running on the streets, wearing only a pair of sandals. He was admitted to a local hospital for supervision and psychiatric evaluation.

LORI KAY SOARES HACKING

Lori, twenty-seven, and Hacking, twenty-eight, met at Lake Powell, Utah, in 1994. Lori worked as a trading assistant at the Wells Fargo in Salt Lake City.

A memorial service for Lori was held August 14 at the Windsor Stake Center in Orem, Utah. More than six hundred attended, including members of Lori's and Hacking's families. Hacking's father gave the opening prayer, and Lori's mother and other relatives also spoke.

Lori's family believes she was five or six weeks pregnant.

THE POLICE INVESTIGATION

Police searched Hacking's apartment and immediately suspected foul play. They collected several items from the apartment and nearby, including pieces of carpet and clothes, a bloody knife from the bedroom, the mattress box spring, a trash bin from outside the apartment, a sliced-up mattress found in a trash bin near a hospital where Hacking worked as an orderly, and a surveillance videotape from a convenience store. The videotape reportedly showed Hacking buying cigarettes, looking at his hands, and driving away in Lori's car around the time police believed she was killed. Laboratory tests confirmed that the blood found in Lori's car, on the carpet, on the knife, and on the headboard and mattress matched hers.

Police determined that prior to Hacking calling 911 he had purchased a new mattress. (It was during the time he alleged he was searching for her in the park.) Lori's car, at the entrance to the park, had the seat adjusted to fit someone approximately six feet tall. Lori was five foot four. The keys to the car were found at the apartment. Police believed if she'd driven the car to the park to go jogging, then she would have kept the keys with her.

Police learned that Hacking had been telling lies to friends and family for years. He'd managed to keep secret from some of his friends for almost three years that he'd stopped attending college. His mother discovered that deception when she attempted to pay his tuition, and the college told her he wasn't enrolled. Relatives told police that when Lori confronted Hacking with that news, he drove away and stayed at a motel for the night. He later told her he'd forgotten to register, and she and others believed he returned to college.

Hacking reportedly told Lori and their friends and family that he had graduated with honors with a degree in psychology from the University of Utah; however, Hacking's father, Dr. Douglas Hacking, was aware his son had not graduated.

One of Lori's relatives told police that Hacking once pretended to fly to Manhattan to interview for medical school. In reality, during that time, he stayed with a cousin.

Some of Hacking's relatives believe he lied because he wanted his family to think he was doing well for himself.

One of Hacking's friends, Brian Hamilton, said he received an e-mail from Lori on July 15, listing the address they would be moving to in North Carolina.

The following day at work, Lori received a return phone call from the University of North Carolina Medical School, allegedly saying that her husband was not enrolled in the school and that they had never heard of him. Lori left work in tears.

The last time Lori was seen alive was July 18, when she and Hacking went to a convenience store. Early on the following morning, at 1:00 A.M., Hacking returned to the convenience store alone.

On July 25, six days after Lori's disappearance, Scott and Lance Hacking contacted police and said their brother had confessed to them the day before that he'd killed Lori. They said he'd told Lori that he'd been accepted to the University of North Carolina, and that he'd found a rifle when he was packing boxes. They said he told them he shot her around 1:00 A.M., wrapped her body in garbage bags, cut the bloody top off the mattress, and put her body in a Dumpster an hour later.

The gun, which Hacking allegedly threw in another Dumpster, was never recovered.

HACKING'S ARREST

On August 2, Hacking was arrested on a charge of aggravated murder, even though Lori's body had not yet been recovered. Police believe he shot her with a rifle while she slept and dumped her body in a trash bin. On August 9, he was charged with first-degree murder. He was also charged with three counts of obstruction of justice, a second-degree felony, because he lied to police and tried to hide evidence.

Police had collected evidence to support their theory, having found Lori's blood at several locations in Hacking's apartment, including on the headboard of the bed, in Lori's car, and on a knife they found in a bedroom drawer. Further, Hacking's brothers said he confessed to them that he murdered Lori.

Even without Lori's body, prosecutors believed they had a strong case, and they intended to call Hacking's brothers as witnesses in the upcoming trial.

On October 29, Hacking pleaded innocent to the first-degree murder charge, though in the spring of 2005 he would change his mind and plead guilty.

Hacking's bail was originally posted at $500,000, but was soon doubled.

THE SEARCH FOR LORI

On July 20, Lori's family held a press conference urging anyone with information on her disappearance to come forward. Missing persons fliers were put up around the city, and more than one thousand volunteers helped in the search.

Authorities initially thought the landfill search, given its size, could take a month. However, the thousands of tons of compacted garbage were more than thirty feet deep in places. Cadaver dogs were brought in to assist. Searchers raked through trash with pitchforks and their hands.

On the morning of October 1 at the Salt Lake City landfill, searchers found human remains. Sergeant J. R. Nelson of the Salt Lake Police Department was sifting through garbage and found a clump of hair and a jawbone. The section where Nelson was working was cordoned off, and investigators focused their efforts there. It took hours to collect the remains and bits of evidence that could be used at Hacking's trial. By the afternoon, police announced the remains had been identified as Lori's, based on dental records.

Because Lori's body was so badly decomposed, the coroner could not tell if she'd been pregnant, so prosecutors could not also charge Hacking with killing a fetus. Furthermore, the coroner could not rule on a cause of death. The remains were in too many pieces, and a bullet hole could not be found.

HACKING PLEADS GUILTY

In a ten-minute court appearance on April 15, 2005, Hacking pleaded guilty to first-degree murder. In exchange for the plea, the obstruction charges were dropped. He told the judge: "I intentionally shot Lori Hacking in the head with a .22 rifle."

Prosecutors contended that Hacking shot her while she slept, then put her body in a trash bin. Prosecutors intended to push for a life sentence. In Utah, the sentence for a murder conviction ranged from six years to life.

At his sentencing hearing on June 6, Judge Denise Lindberg said she would recommend to the state parole board that Hacking be imprisoned for a long time.

According to reports of the hearing, Hacking said: "She didn't do nothing but love me unconditionally, even when I didn't deserve it. She was the greatest thing that ever happened to me, but I killed her, and took the life of my unborn child and put them in the garbage and I can't explain why I did it. I put them in the garbage, and they rotted out at the landfill. I'm tormented every waking minute by what I did."

In July, Hacking was notified by the state Board of Pardons and Parole that he would spend twenty-nine years in a Utah prison before being granted a parole hearing. That hearing date is August 1, 2034.

COMMENTARY: Mark Hacking

Mark Hacking's case is a sordid little slice of life, obviously involving a sociopathic personality, and probably a severe mental illness. His attempts to be seen as much more than he actually was reveal a fragile ego and probably self-loathing. One suspects a severe mental illness, but in view of Hacking's present and future situation, medical experts will likely never make that determination.

Hacking could not have constructed a much stronger case against himself had he videotaped the moments leading up to the homicide and the murder itself. The victim's blood in all the wrong places, the bloody mattress and the clumsy effort to hide it, the keys to Lori's car being found at home, and the confession to not one but two brothers provided a strong enough case to convict a king. The plea of guilty seems to have been inevitable.

The question remains: Could anything be salvaged from this sorrowful event?

Perhaps.

Perhaps someday people will wake up to the fact that while killings of this type remain unabated over the years, we throw away most opportunities to attempt to sort out the personalities who destroyed human life, whether a single victim is involved or many. Everything we could learn about Mark Hacking and his ilk should be discovered and documented by competent scientists and sent to a central database labeled "Crazies Who Kill People." Although no single study is likely to provide solutions, as with scientific efforts to deal with cancer and other diseases, the data over time might cough up something very useful: How we can learn to recognize these uncontrollably violent people before they kill, so that we can confine them on civil process for society's protection, and their own.

John Mason

Suspected in the disappearance of his fiancée on April 26, 2005

Jennifer Wilbanks disappeared from her Duluth, Georgia, home on April 26. Police immediately suspected foul play, and looked to her fiancé, John Mason. A nationwide search began for Wilbanks. Newspapers and television stations across the country carried updates on the search. Fliers with Wilbanks's picture were plastered on telephone polls and the windows of shops throughout Duluth, a suburb north of Atlanta.

THE PURPORTED KIDNAPPING

Wilbanks and Mason, both thirty-two, were to be married April 30 in a lavish ceremony with a reported near-$50,000 price tag. Wilbanks called Mason on the twenty-ninth, telling him she was in Albuquerque, New Mexico, and that she'd been kidnapped and sexually assaulted. Wilbanks told the 911 dispatcher that her kidnappers had cut her hair. She also gave a description of the kidnappers and their van, and said that they were armed with a small handgun.

However, police quickly learned that this story was a lie, and that she'd run away to avoid the wedding. (Six hundred people had been invited to the wedding, and there were to be twenty-eight attendants.) Wilbanks had left on the spur of the moment, leaving behind her wallet. She cut her hair so she wouldn't be recognized, and when she ran out of money in Albuquerque, she fabricated the story and called her fiancé.

Duluth mayor Shirley Lasseter said it had cost the community more than $40,000 to search for her.

JENNIFER CAROL WILBANKS AND
JOHN MASON

Born August 25, 1973, Wilbanks worked as a nurse. An avid runner dating back to her high school days when she ran in track events, she once competed in the Boston Marathon. Wilbanks's aunt introduced her to Mason, also a runner.

Mason, an office manager for his uncle's medical practice, Mason Medical, proposed to her in August 2004, ten months after they met. Mason was a Sunday school teacher and a church youth basketball coach at Peachtree Corners Baptist Church. Wilbanks and Mason were Baptists, and Mason was known to be mulling over becoming a pastor.

MASON WAS THE SUSPECT

During the search, police seized three computers from the house Wilbanks and Mason shared. Mason was never charged relating to her disappearance, but police and the media severely scrutinized him.

Mason had told police that she had left the house around 8:30 P.M. on the twenty-sixth, saying she was going for a jog and would be back in about forty minutes. Mason reported that, after an hour, he went out looking for her. He said he called local hospitals, and then he called police. He told police she left without her cell phone, wallet, keys, and her diamond ring. He said it wouldn't be like her to simply leave.

Mason hired an attorney when attention turned to him. He took, and passed, an independently administered lie detector test.

On April 28, the day before Wilbanks called Mason, Major Donald Woodruff, of the Duluth Police Department, spoke at a news conference about the case. Woodruff said: "There's been a lot of speculation from that perspective that it could have been a case of premarital jitters. But again, according to all of her friends that have been interviewed, all of her family, that's simply not the case."

Chief of police Randy Belcher said the "cold feet" theory had basically been ruled out. He said the longer the investigation continued, and the longer that she was missing, the less the likelihood that she had gone away on her own.

Police used dogs to search the area she jogged in. Divers from the Department of Natural Resources searched the nearby Chattahoochee River.

RUNAWAY BRIDE TIME LINE

APRIL 26. Mason called police and told them that Wilbanks had been missing for two hours, having not coming back from an evening jog.

APRIL 27. More than one hundred police officers and several hundred volunteers, including many who were invited to the wedding, searched for Wilbanks. Some police officers speculated she might have fled, having prewedding jitters. Police collected evidence, such as clumps of brown hair, near where Wilbanks might have jogged. The evidence proved to be false leads.

APRIL 28. The FBI and the Georgia Bureau of Investigation became involved in the missing persons case. Major Donald Woodruff of the Duluth Police Department announced Wilbanks's disappearance was now being treated as a criminal investigation.

APRIL 29. Wilbanks's relatives posted a $100,000 reward for her return. Also that day, Wilbanks called 911 from a pay phone in Albuquerque, putting on a frantic voice and claiming she had been kidnapped and sexually assaulted and that she had just been released. She then called Mason and told him the same story. Wilbanks told police that a Hispanic man and a white woman, both in their forties, kidnapped her in a blue van in Georgia and drove her west.

MAY 25. Duluth police charged Wilbanks with making false statements.

MAY 31. Wilbanks agreed to pay Duluth more than $13,000 to cover some of the costs incurred in the search.

WILBANKS'S FABRICATED STORY

Police traced Wilbanks's 911 call to a pay phone at a 7-Eleven in Albuquerque. Police had asked her where she was, but she told them she had "no idea." Neither could she tell them which direction her kidnappers drove off in. However, she provided a description of her kidnappers. Later, during questioning by police and FBI agents, Wilbanks admitted that she had not been kidnapped, but disappeared because she felt pressured by her upcoming wedding. Wilbanks said she came up with the sexual assault story because she knew people would be asking how she was.

Albuquerque police and FBI agents said that Wilbanks's story kept changing and lacked information that someone would have after being held by individuals for three or four days.

Wilbanks explained to police that before going jogging on the evening of the twenty-sixth, she called a taxi, which took her to a bus terminal. She started out with $150, took a bus to Dallas, Las Vegas, and then to Albuquerque, where she ran out of money. Although she told them it was a spur-of-the-moment decision, she'd purchased a bus ticket a week in advance.

Wilbanks said she was suicidal before the wedding, and that if she hadn't taken the bus, she might have taken a bottle of pills.

She told police she wasn't aware so many people were looking for her. She said she hadn't watched television or listened to the radio. Too, she said she didn't believe she'd truly done anything wrong, that she just needed some time alone.

Police reports showed that Wilbanks had broken off an engagement earlier to another man, and that she kept "I love you" text messages from 2003 from a man she had dated.

Once she returned to Duluth, the media began to focus on other aspects of the Wilbanks case, including other reports of runaway brides, the racism she exhibited by fabricating a Hispanic kidnapper, and editorializing on what should be done to individuals who falsify reports and tie up community resources.

Family members told the media they were pleased and relieved Wilbanks was safe, though some admitted to being embarrassed. Some of Wilbanks's friends expressed anger at her faked kidnapping and said they felt betrayed. One of the volunteers who had helped with the search called her "selfish and self-centered."

Wilbanks was escorted to Atlanta by her stepfather and an uncle. On the tarmac, she was picked up by a police car and taken to Duluth.

Mason, Wilbanks's fiancé, told reporters he held no hostility toward her.

WILBANKS'S APOLOGY

A statement issued by Wilbanks read:

> *At this time, I cannot explain fully what happened to me last week. I had a host of compelling issues which seemed out of control—issues for which I was unable to address or confine. Please, may I assure you that my running away had nothing to do with "cold feet," nor was it ever about leaving John.*
>
> *Those who know me know how excited I've been, and how excited I was about the spectacular wedding we planned, and how I could not wait to be Mrs. John Mason. In my mind, it was never about the timing, however unfortunate. I was simply running from myself and from certain fears controlling my life. Each day I am understanding more about who I am and the issues that influenced me to respond inappropriately. Therefore, I have started professional treatment voluntarily.*
>
> *I am truly sorry for the troubles I caused, and I offer my deep and sincere apology. I ask for John's forgiveness and that of his family. I also ask for forgiveness of my family, our friends, our respective churches, our communities, and any others I may have offended unintentionally. I am deeply grateful and appreciative to everyone who responded on my behalf. I thank you for every expression of support and effort. Your sacrifices of time and personal inconvenience touched me deeply, and I hope your spirit of care is not lessened. I understand that many people wanted to hear from me personally today, and I wanted to be here. However, I look forward to days ahead when I am strong enough to speak for myself. As John said on countless occasions recently, may we*

follow the teaching of Scripture, in being kind to one another, tender-hearted, forgiving, just as God in Christ forgives us. Thank you.

WILBANKS CHARGED

A Duluth County grand jury indicted Wilbanks for filing a false report. Because she told authorities that she'd been abducted and raped by a Hispanic man and a white woman, she was formally charged with one count of making false statements, a felony that could have carried a five-year prison term, and one count of making a false report of a crime, a misdemeanor punishable by up to a year in jail.

She pleaded "no contest"on June 5, and was sentenced to two years' probation and more than one hundred hours of community service. In addition, Wilbanks was ordered to pay more than $13,000 in restitution to the Gwinnett County Sheriff's Department and the City of Duluth to cover overtime hours of the employees who searched for her. And she was ordered to continue counseling. A charge of filing a false police report was dropped.

In court, Wilbanks said: "I'm truly sorry for my actions and I just want to thank Gwinnett County and the city of Duluth."

COMMENTARY: John Mason

John Mason's place in this book is very similar to that of Michael Schiavo's; neither man was guilty one iota of wrongdoing, and yet each was accused (albeit sub silentio) *of some far-fetched involvement of the plight of a spouse, or in Mason's case, betrothed. Concluding with this chapter underscores what this book is all about: When the husband (including ex-husbands and boyfriends) is the suspect is—always. If the suspect didn't kill his female significant other, he comes to the top of the list like oil rising to the surface of water. As this collection of homicide (or suspected homicide) cases is intended to establish, the male squeeze is always handy, and almost always can be thought to have a motive. He is an easy mark and a quick and tidy solution to an unsolved homicide. And statistically, he is more often than not the culprit, even though it may take law enforcement many years to pin him with a conviction.*

But suspected husbands and lovers also represent a higher percentage of innocent people accused of crime than does any other group. Like those who are guilty, they often make mistakes that sink them deeper in the quicksand of the criminal justice system.

If any evil reader is combing these pages, looking for helpful hints in plotting the successful demise of his now persona non grata woman, beware! You can't learn to fly a modern jet fighter by reading reports of those who crashed, or those who climbed out of a critical situation and survived by the skin of their teeth. Unless we have attracted some professional assassins to our readership group, those contemplating mayhem will fail for lack of training, experience, and discipline, the very gremlins that kill pilots. Divorce, messy and infuriating though it may be, is always the better way.

To those poor souls whose wives are murdered by someone else, but who initially give false alibis because in fact they were at the time at the No Tell Motel with a favorite secretary, woe has caught up with you. Do not try to fix things by belatedly telling the truth to the nice detective; he is not your friend. Get a lawyer, and a good one! Do not let your friends persuade you to hire the local practitioner in order to avoid the appearance of needing a hotshot criminal defense lawyer who is suspected of "beating the rap" for unsavory defendants. You need the best, right now. If his or her skill and experience can ward off an indictment, you will save a lot of grief, embarrassment, and money. If you do get charged, go to trial, and are acquitted, a large segment of the population will always think you got away with something. The "damnation of an acquittal" is to be avoided whenever possible. With proper guidance, an innocent person may well be able to show that he should not be formally accused.

If by virtue of the examples of the cases chronicled herein one innocent suspect is spared the agonies of facing the press and a jury, this book will be entitled to be called useful. After all, innocent people are the ones the justice system most often ignores.

345.7302 Bailey, F. Lee
BAI   (Francis Lee),
           1933-

           When the husband is
           the suspect.